Messiah's Future Triumph as Earth's New Administrator
A Commentary on Revelation

Concise Studies in the Scriptures
Volume Eight

Raymond C. Faircloth

This is the revelation from Jesus the Messiah. God gave this to him to show his bond-servants the things which must speedily take place

Revelation 1:1

Contents

——— ❑ ———

Dedication

This book is dedicated to my loving wife Cherie, who continually supports me in my endeavours to understand and promote the truths of God's written word—the holy Bible.

——— ❑ ———

Bible Translations Referenced

Amp	The Amplified Bible
Barclay	The New Testament by William Barclay
CEB	Common English Bible
ERV	Easy-to-Read version
ESV	English Standard Version
GWT	God's Word Translation
HCSB	Holman Christian Standard Bible
ISV	International Standard Version
KJV	King James Version
KNT	Kingdom New Testament by N.T. Wright
LXX	The Septuagint (Greek Version of the Old Testament)
LEB	Lexham English Bible
MEV	Modern English Version
NAB	New American Bible
NASB	New American Standard Bible
NCV	New Century version
NET	New English Translation
NKJV	New King James Version
NJB	New Jerusalem Bible
NIV	New International Version
NLT	New Living Translation
NRSV	New Revised Standard Version
MOFF	The Moffat Translation of the Bible
REB	Revised English Bible
ROTH.	The Emphasized Bible by J.B Rotherham
S&G	Smith and Goodspeed – An American Translation
UBS	United Bible Societies Interlinear
UVNT	The Unvarnished New Testament – Andy Gaus
Williams	The New Testament by Charles B. Williams
YLT	Young's Literal Translation

J.N Darby—A New Translation
R.F. Weymouth's New Testament

For New Testament quotations I have referenced my own version on occasion: *The Kingdom of God Version–The New Testament (KGV)*.

——— ❑ ———

Preface

As with most Christians I have often been fascinated by the Book of Revelation with its many strange symbols and strange events, and so I have read widely the many commentaries and other works and approaches to this Bible book in my endeavour to grasp the overall themes and purpose of the Revelation and so to try to grasp the finer details of it. For this reason the following commentaries and theological works were all referenced for the research for this commentary and have proved to be most helpful in this endeavour. These were:

The Word Biblical Commentary on Revelation .... David Aune
Revelation (Baker Exegetical Commentary) .... Grant Osborne
The Expositors Bible Commentary (Revelation) .... Alan F. Johnson
The Climax of Prophecy .... Richard Bauckham
The Theology of the Book of Revelation .... Richard Bauckham
The Revelation of Jesus Christ .... George H. Lang
Commentary on the Revelation of John .... George Eldon Ladd
Breaking the Code .... Bruce Metzger
The Fourth Gentile Kingdom .... Charles Ozanne
Empires of the End Time .... Charles Ozanne
                                      (both from the Open Bible Trust)
The Apocalypse .... Joseph Seiss
The Approaching Advent of Christ .... Alexander Reese
Future Babylon .... Charles Dyer
First the Antichrist .... Robert Gundry

However, although all the above commentaries were referenced none of them conveys a majority of points of agreement with this author because some take a Preterist view and others combine Preterism with Futurism in contrast to my taking of a purely Futurist view and so making this commentary quite unique.

Although this is Volume Eight in the series *Concise Studies in the Scriptures* it is the second volume dealing with end-time prophecy. The first volume on end-time prophecy is entitled *Prophecies Related to the Return of Jesus* and explains why only a post-tribulation Futurist view of end-time prophecy does justice to all of the biblical data. It also goes into great detail concerning the five major prophecies in the Book of Daniel, the identification of Gog of Magog in Ezekiel, the Olivet discourse given by Jesus, Paul's teachings on end-time prophecy, and many other details that help toward getting a clear and accurate picture of what Christians should expect as the time arrives for the return of Jesus. So clearly the two books go together so that any reader would benefit from reading this first book on prophecy along with this Commentary on Revelation.

The title of this current book, namely *Messiah's Future Triumph as Earth's New Administrator,* in no way detracts from the fact that Jesus has already triumphed over all wicked forces by his death on the cross to deal with the issue of sin. Nevertheless, there is also a future triumph for him involving his literal and physical return to establish God's Kingdom on the earth and to administer all of earth's affairs. So the Book of Revelation has a very great amount to say on this future triumphant return and administrative work on behalf of mankind.

This current book is a verse-by-verse commentary on the Revelation using the grammatical-historical method of interpretation to explain it, but noting that large sections of the Book concern as yet unfulfilled prophecy as per the Futurist approach taken here.

However, before embarking on commenting on each of the verses, it is necessary to explain the composition of the Book of Revelation, its structure, and the way it uses numbers. It is also important to understand, early on in the book, how the details of the Revelation fit with the biblical schedule of Daniel seventy "sevens," as well seeing the pattern of the seals, trumpets, and bowls of wrath. So these aspects and details are to be found in the early chapters of this book.

Because this book is one of the series *Concise Studies in the Scriptures* the comments are necessarily short and to the point compared with those in many other commentaries on Revelation. Nevertheless, this commentary should bridge the gap between those commentaries which do not give verse by verse comments and those which are long-winded or filled with less significant background information.

However, a considerable amount of comment has been made where there are controversial issues such as explanations of the identity of the seven spirits, of the 144,000, of the small scroll, of the two witnesses, and of Babylon the great.

So in this very basic coverage of interpretive points given in this book there are some areas of uncertainty which are therefore subject to change as further study continues. In other words, any attempts to understand the meaning of prophecy, especially from the Book of Revelation, will always involve some degree of refinement over time. Nevertheless, I hope that this book will be enlightening to the open minded reader and will be thought provoking for discussion concerning the many details and symbolisms given in the Book of Revelation.

———— ❑ ————

Introduction

There is no absolute certainty about who the writer of Revelation was because he is simply named John. However, the style of writing shows him to be someone with a Hebrew background and with considerable knowledge of the Hebrew Scriptures (the Old Testament). It is also clear that he was a particularly well-known John and so has been understood to be the Apostle John by most commentators. This identification was accepted by the early Church fathers Justin Martyr (150 C.E) and Irenaeus (180 C.E) and most other commentators through time.

Although commentators with a Preterist approach propose that the Revelation was written around 65 C.E, and therefore before the destruction of Jerusalem in 70 C.E, there is clear evidence, both external and internal, that the Revelation was written in the mid 90s C.E (please see my book, *Prophecies Related to the Return of Jesus* pp. 35-36) and therefore some twenty five years after Jerusalem was destroyed. Indeed, the Revelation reflects the conditions which prevailed during these latter years of Emperor Domitian (81-96 C.E).

The word "revelation" in its original Greek of *apokalypsis* means "an unveiling" and is indeed the unveiling, by Jesus, of God's plan and purpose for mankind on this earth. In fact, Revelation 1:3 tells us that the entire book is a prophecy. However, similar to the book of Daniel, Revelation uses the ancient Jewish genre of apocalyptic as the vehicle for prophecy, and therefore we may call Revelation an apocalyptic prophecy. As with other apocalyptic works this means that there is a foreshortening of the prophetic horizon i.e. the making of distant events appear to be about to happen. However, unlike the book of Daniel and other apocalypses, the Revelation is highly unusual in its exceptional number of visual images; in other words a great amount of its message is conveyed in symbols which often either convey their own meaning or are interpreted by an angel or can be understood in the light of the symbolisms used in the Hebrew Scriptures. Nevertheless, we must also note that, as with all language, there is an interweaving of the figurative and symbolic with the literal, and that such extreme usage of symbolism makes Revelation a book of the imagination, and less so of the intellect or of the emotions that are found in most other books of the Bible. It is, in fact, the most challenging book in the entire Bible.

Although in the Revelation there are no direct quotations from the Hebrew Scriptures there is an abundance of deliberate allusions to the prophecies of the prophets of ancient times such as Isaiah, Jeremiah, Daniel, Ezekiel, Zechariah and others—all of whose writings are presented in the Hebrew Scriptures. Indeed, of the 404 verses of Revelation there are 278 verses containing allusions to the Hebrew Scriptures. So John's writing is the climax of prophetic revelation by the gathering up of the meaning of those passages from the Hebrew Scriptures and so to show how they are to be fulfilled in the end-times. Furthermore, in addition to the allusions to the Hebrew Scriptures, John alludes to certain of Jesus' parables. For example, in the Olivet Discourse Jesus speaks of the alert servants who are to be aware of any possible thief (Matt. 24:42-44; Luke 12:35-40), and in the parable of the household manager (Luke 12:42-48) Jesus highlights this manager's trustworthiness. Indeed, these qualities of alertness and trustworthiness are focused upon respectively in Revelation 3:3, 20 and 16:15.

In one sense the Revelation is a single vision. However, it is broken down into four major parts and so may be seen as four visions presented to John on four different occasions. In each of these John is transported into God's future for this world. So although the presentation is other-worldly with John being taken mentally in a trance to heaven and seeing God's throne room, it is not particularly about heaven, but about the future of mankind on earth.

Revelation 1:19 gives us one of the keys to understanding the book when John is told to, "write down the things you saw, the things which are, and the things which are about to happen afterward." So "the things that you saw" concern the vision in chapter one. "The things which are" concern the condition of the seven Christian communities in John's time as detailed in chapters two and three. And finally, "the things which are about to happen afterward" concern the visions and details of the future which are described from chapter four to the end of the book. Indeed, this final section primarily focuses on the breaking of seven seals of a scroll which reveals end-time events in the blasting of seven trumpets and with the pouring out of seven bowls of God's punishment on the unrepentant wicked of this world who are led by the Antichrist. At this time Jesus has returned to destroy those unrepentant ones and to establish God's Kingdom on earth for one thousand years, after which a final judgment occurs leading to a perfect world.

———— ❑ ————

Chapter 1

The Composition of the Book of Revelation

The Book of Revelation is an exceptionally complex piece of literature, yet it is a unified work. It is a *prophecy* (1:3) which uses apocalyptic symbolism and is given in four visions and sent in the form of a single circular letter (epistle) to each of the seven communities of believers in Asia Minor, rather than seven separate letters. In fact, the intention was for it to be read aloud in each of those communities. So, with the passage of time it would also have reached most of the Christian communities everywhere.

The Kind of Language Used

THE DEGREE OF LITERALNESS

Much of Revelation is to be taken literally, but not literalistically. Just as the prophecies that applied to Jesus in the first century were literally fulfilled, so too for his second coming. Therefore the miraculous aspects are as literal as were the plagues upon ancient Egypt, even though the descriptions may have metaphorical or symbolic language within them.

THE DEGREE OF HYPERBOLE AND SYMBOLISM

As with the hyperbole that was evident in numerous parables and sayings of Jesus in the gospels, so too in Revelation where there is much that is hyperbolic. This means that a literal interpretation of certain things would result in moral or metaphysical absurdity.

There is also much in Revelation which is metaphorical and symbolic. For instance, where the word *mystery* occurs there would be a symbolic presentation and of the approximately forty mysteries one half are explained within the text. Clearly such items as the manna, the white stone, white garments, a pillar in the temple and such identities as the various riders and their horses, the woman, the dragon, the beast from the earth etc. are all symbols.

However, the fact that Revelation 1:1 says: "he [Jesus] *signified* it by his angel" does not mean that the entire prophecy was given in symbols, but as modern translations state that Jesus *"communicated it"* or *"made it known."* The Greek word for signified is used elsewhere in the Scriptures with no thought of symbolism e.g. John 12:32, 33; 18:32 and 21:19.

1

The Highly Characteristic Literary Techniques

GEZERAH SHAVAH

John has used this Jewish literary technique to interpret the Hebrew Scripture prophecies. This means that one has to observe the verbal coincidences between the scriptural texts i.e. the same words and phrases in one text are used to interpret another text. It is really a network of internal cross-referencing.

FORMULAE

Within the book of Revelation there is repetition of phrases which allude to each other, but are not precisely the same e.g. Rev. 5:9 uses the phrase, "Every tribe and language and people and nation." In various forms this is also to be found in 7:9; 10:11; 11:9; 13:7; 14:6; 17:15.

These techniques run through the entire book.

General Factors in the Composition

There is much overlapping and interweaving throughout the visions. The story of God's people in conflict with Satan through Antichrist which began in Rev.12:1 converges in 15:5 with the narrative begun in 5:1 where the Lamb receives the scroll. Also all of the scenes in heaven are simply to give the heavenly perspective of the Christians' situation i.e. their deaths in faithfulness are actually victories in God's eyes. However, after 19:11 all the scenes are on earth.

ORDER OF EVENTS

The phrase *"After these things..."* occurs ten times in Revelation. Six times it is followed by a verb of perception (*"I saw..."* or *"I heard..."* These occurrences are not indicative of the chronological fulfilment; but of the order in which John sees the visions. The other four times do indicate the chronological fulfilment.

THE PARALLEL SECTIONS

In 17:1-19:10 Babylon is parallel with New Jerusalem (21:9-22:9) and in 4:1 "a door is opened" is parallel with "heaven opened" (19:11).

THE INTERCALATIONS

The term intercalation used by scholars analyzing the book of Revelation means the insertion of a passage into the sequence of the main passages and may be looked upon as an interlude. For example:

2

1.   The intercalation in chapter 7 shows an interval which is for the purpose of protecting God's people from the coming judgments.

2.   The intercalation of Chapters 10 to 11:14 is for the purpose of the giving of a witness. Here the opened scroll is the same as the main seven-sealed scroll. This is seen from the fact that it is modelled on the second part of the description in Ezekiel 3:1, 2; whereas the seven-sealed scroll is modelled on the first part.

The Universal Aspect of the Revelation

The book of Revelation contains much universal language and so indicating how these earlier prophecies expand to encompass Antichrist's kingdom and often times the whole world. For instance:

- *"The hour of trial coming upon the whole world"*(3:10).
- Death and Hades are granted authority *"over a fourth of the earth"* (6:8).
- In the sixth seal *"the kings of the earth...hid themselves in the caves"*(6:15).
- The letting loose of the locusts of the fifth trumpet whose stinging is of all those *"who do not have the seal of God..."* (9:4) and so referring to everyone on earth except true Christians.
- For John, now equipped with the little scroll, he is told *"You must prophesy again concerning many peoples and nations and tongues and kings"*(10:11).
- When the two witnesses are killed *"those from the peoples and tribes and tongues and nations will look at their dead bodies..."*(11:9).
- When the seventh trumpet is blown we learn that *"the nations were enraged"*(11:18).
- The eternal gospel is preached *"to every nation tribe and tongue and people"*(14:6).
- Babylon the great *"made all the nations drink of the wine of the passion of her immorality"*(14:8).
- During the pouring out of the seventh bowl *"the cities of the nations fell"*(16:19).
- The waters *"where the harlot sits are peoples and multitudes and nations and tongues"*(17:16).
- The woman (Babylon the great) *"reigns over the kings of the earth"* (17:18).

3

- After the millennium Satan will *"deceive the nations which are in the four corners of the earth, Gog and Magog"* (20:8).

Clearly, in Revelation there are also some localized events relating to the Middle-East such as the literal city of Babylon the great (Rev. 17 & 18) and possibly Jerusalem if the description *"the great city where their lord was also crucified"* (Rev. 11:8) is referring to Jerusalem!

Three Realms of People in Revelation

In the Book of Revelation there are three realms or classes of people. Because there is symbolism concerning Satan as the red Dragon we are led to a realization that others who are key players in these chapters are also presented symbolically. Some of these are:

1. "Those dwelling (Gk. *skynontes*) **in heaven**"
   This is symbolic of the Christian Holy Ones. They are those who have their citizenship in heaven (Phil. 3:20), and are "born from above" (John 3:3; 1 John 5:18). They see things from a heavenly perspective. Also Ephesians 2:6 shows Christians as seated "in the heavenly places incorporated into" Jesus. Heaven is associated physically with Mount Zion because of the worship of God there.
   It is sometimes assumed that the phrase *"those who dwell in heaven"* is a reference to angelic beings. However, all derivatives of the Greek verb *skynoo*, which means "to dwell" or "to tabernacle," are used in the Scriptures with reference only to humans and to God rather than to angels. This fits with the fact that in Daniel 8 "the holy ones" on earth are called *"the host of heaven."* Hence the phrase is symbolic of Christian Holy Ones who, although literally on earth, are spiritually in heaven and are actually viewed as God's dwelling.

2. "Those dwelling **on earth**" or "earth-dwellers *(Gk katoikountes)*."
   This is symbolic of the followers and worshippers of Antichrist. They see things from an earthly perspective. This phrase is used thirteen times (three are variations) in the Book of Revelation. It is similar to *"kosmos"* in John's gospel as referring to the inhabitants of the world alienated from God. This does not mean absolutely all of mankind, but fits well with the description of these worshippers of Antichrist. So Grant Osborne explains that:

4

The term "earth dwellers" is important in the book and always refers to the unbelievers, the enemies of God who not only worship and follow the beast but also persecute the believers.
Revelation-Baker Exegetical Commentary p.193.

In the Book of Revelation the phrase "earth-dwellers" can be found in 6:10; 8:13; 11:10; 13:8, 12, 14; 17:2, 8.

3. "Those dwelling **in the sea**" (which is associated physically with the Mediterranean and also is the same as the abyss).

    This is very similar to the "earth-dwellers" inasmuch as it is symbolic of the domain of evil i.e. wicked mankind and Antichrist. In fact, Isaiah shows that, "'the wicked are like the tossing sea; for it cannot be quiet, and its waters toss up mire and dirt. 'There is no peace,' says my God, 'for the wicked'" (Isa. 57:20, 21). Please note that in Revelation 13 one beast—the Antichrist—emerges from the sea; whereas the second beast—the false prophet—emerges from the earth (the land). However, all these wicked individuals form what is turbulent compared to the earth-dwellers and so "sea-dwellers" also must include Satan and the demons who are involved with the abyss (another term for the very deep sea).

These factors concerning these three categories of people noted throughout Revelation will help us in our identifying of the events which happen in the various stages of the Revelation.

"Stars" as Angels and as Humans

The International Standard Bible Encyclopedia states that "Stars can stand for exalted creatures (no doubt because of their brilliance and glory) either foes of God or His servants." Therefore, angelic beings are described as stars as in Revelation 1:20: "the seven stars are the seven angels of the seven communities." Indeed, the human Messiah is described in Numbers 24:17 as, "a star shall come forth from Jacob." Furthermore, Christians are described as "like stars" in Daniel 12:3 and Daniel 8:10 applies the term "stars" to Christians when the Antichrist causes "some of the stars to fall to earth and it trampled them down."

§

Chapter 2

The Four Linguistic Markers and the Structure of the Visions

After the prologue of 1:1-8 the first vision begins with the phrase *"in the spirit."* This means *"in a prophetic trance"* as rendered below by professor of theology David Aune in the *Word Biblical Commentary.* The markers for the beginning of each of the four visions are: 1:10, 11; 4:2; 17:3; 21:9, 10.

THE FIRST VISION

1:10, 11: "I fell <u>into a prophetic trance</u> **on the Lord's day** and heard a loud sound behind me (like that of a trumpet), saying. "Write what you see in a roll and send it to the seven churches, to Ephesus…" *This vision finishes with the last comment to the community of believers in Laodicea* (3:22).

THE SECOND VISION

4:2: "Immediately I was <u>in a prophetic trance,</u> and behold **a throne was situated in heaven,** and someone was seated upon the throne." *This vision finishes with* "It is done!" (16:17).

THE THIRD VISION

17:3: "He then carried me to **the desert** <u>in a prophetic trance.</u> I saw **a woman** sitting on a scarlet beast covered with blasphemous names, with seven heads and ten horns." *This vision also finishes with* "It is done!" (21:6).

THE FOURTH VISION

21:9, 10: "Then came one of the seven angels with the seven libation bowls full of the seven last plagues and spoke to me, saying, "Come, I will show you the bride, the wife of the Lamb." [10]He then transported me <u>in a prophetic trance</u> to **a great and high mountain** and showed me **the holy city Jerusalem** descending from heaven from God." *This vision finishes at the end of the book.*

Structure of the Visions

THE FIRST VISION 1:9 to 3:22

After the prologue showing John as located on the island of Patmos and describing the vision as prophecy (1:3) with the theme of Jesus' coming with the clouds, John then begins to describe his visionary experience:

1. John is experiencing these visions on "the Lord's day" (probably resurrection day i.e. Sunday) with the voice of Jesus telling him to write to the seven communities. John then has a glorious vision of Jesus who gives him a number of reassurances, after which he is told what to write to the seven churches. 1:9-20.

2. John writes to the seven communities of believers. 2:1-3:22

THE SECOND VISION 4:2 to 16:17

1. A heavenly scene showing God's throne and the praise given to God by the four living creatures (seraphs) and the 24 elders (heavenly beings). 4:1-11.

2. The investiture *of the lion of the tribe of Judah* and his receiving of the seven-sealed scroll. 5:1-14

3. The Seven Seals
   a) The first six seals are broken by Jesus. 6:1-17.
   b) *Interlude:* The Two Multitudes:
      - The 144,000 to be sealed. 7:1-8.
      - The Vast Crowd come out of the great tribulation. 7:9-17

4. The Seventh Seal is broken for the Seven Trumpet blasts. 8:1-14:20.
   a) Preparation for the first six trumpets to be blown 8:2-6.
   b) The blowing of the first six trumpets 8:7-9:21
   c) *Interlude:* 10:1-11:13.
      - The angel and the little scroll. 10:1-11.
      - The measuring of the temple. 11:1-2.
      - The Two Witnesses 11:3-14

   d) The Seventh Trumpet blast. 11:14-19
   e) *Interlude:* 12:1-14:20
      - The Dragon, the Woman, and the Male-child. 12:1-17
      - The Two beasts. 13:1-18
      - 144,000 are now on Mount Zion. 14:1-5.

   f) The three angels declaring: 1) the Good News, 2) the fall of Babylon of great, 3) God's wrath upon those with the mark of the Beast. 14:6-13.
   g) The angelic Reapers of the Earth-harvest and the Grape-harvest. 14:14-20.

h) The Seven Bowls of Wrath. 15:1-16:21
- Preparation for the seven bowls to be poured out 15:1-8.
- The pouring out of all seven bowls 16:1-21

THE THIRD VISION 17:1 to 21:8
1. Babylon the great. 17:1-19:5
   a) Babylon the great. The city as a harlot 17:1-18
      - She sits on the Scarlet Beast as the mother of harlots. 17:1-6
      - The Beast (the Antichrist) was, is not, and is about to come from the abyss. 17:7-8.
      - Seven kings. The Beast is an eighth. The Ten Horns in alliance with Antichrist for one hour.17:9-13.
      - Victory of the Lamb. 17:14-18.

   b) More on the destruction of Babylon the great. 18:1-19:5
      - Angelic announcement of Babylon's fall. 18:1-3.
      - Call for God's people to come out of her. 18:4-5.
      - Cry for Vengeance so she will be burned with Fire. 18:6-8.
      - The mourning over her by the kings, the merchants, and the ships captains. 18:9-19.
      - Rejoicing over her demise. 18:20.
      - The destruction of Babylon. 18:21-24.
      - The vast crowd and the 24 elders praise God over her judgment. 19:1-5.

2. The Final Triumph over the Enemies. 19:6-21:8
   a) The Marriage of the Lamb 19:6-10.
   b) Messiah's Arrival. 19:11-16.
   c) Messiah defeats the Beast and the kings and their armies. 19:17-21
   d) The Binding of Satan. 20:1-3.
   e) The Resurrection of Christians to reign for a thousand years. 20:4-6.
   f) The final destruction of Satan and of death. 20:7-15.
   g) The New Creation 21:1-8.

THE FOURTH VISION 21:9 to 22:9
   1. The New Jerusalem.

§

Chapter 3

How Numbers Are Used in Revelation

In the book of Revelation all numbers have some spiritual significance. However, if one takes all the numbers in the Revelation to be only symbolic then one has moved into the interpretive realms of the failed systems of Amillennialism and Historicism. (Please see my book *Prophecies Related to the Return of Jesus* Volume 7 of *Concise Studies in the Scriptures* to understand why these systems do not fit the biblical data.)

The Spiritual Significance of Numbers

2 = the number of witness, contrast, difference, division, opposition.
3 = divine completeness.
4 = foursquare and all encompassing. Comprehensive extent of things relating to the earth.
5 = life, a short period of time
6 = the hall-mark of human works, generally in defiance of God.
7 = the hall-mark of God's work, spiritual completeness.
8 = a new beginning, regeneration, resurrection.
10 = ordinal completion regarding law, order, or government.
12 = Israel/spiritual Israel—divine organization or government.
24 = organizational or governmental completeness in heaven "thrones, authorities."
1,000 = Ordinal completion to the power of 3, as often a reference to an army in marching order.

Throughout Revelation there are many details that are listed a certain number of times:
- Four times: The seven Christian communities are mentioned indicating all the Christian communities in the world.
- Seven times: The Lord God Almighty;" "the One who sits on the throne;" "Christ;" "Every tribe and language and people and nation."
- Fourteen times: "Jesus."
- Twenty eight times: "the Lamb."

Literal Numbers

A) *Literal Time Periods,* but with a Spiritual Significance:
"Time, times and half a time" [a literal 1,260 days/42 months] = one half of the seven years in God's end-time timetable (Dan. 9:24-27). Also note the seven years of plenty/seven years of famine in Joseph's time.

9

The 1,000 years in 20:1-7 is a literally ordinal complete time, but with spiritual significance.

B) *Literal Fractions for Populations.* These are approximations (rounded up/down), but with spiritual significance *e.g.* one tenth, one quarter, and one third.

Numbers of Exaggeration - Hyperbolic

POPULATIONS: 200 million.

MEASUREMENTS OF LENGTH:
The symbolic New Jerusalem: 144 cubits = 210 ft thick wall; 12,000 stadia = 1,380-1,500 mile long wall (21:16);
Blood from the symbolic winepress: flowing for 1,600 stadia = 180-200 miles (14:20).

SHORT PERIODS OF TIME:
2:10: "and for **ten days** you will have tribulation." This refers to a complete but relatively short period of intense persecution of Christians.

3:10: "I will keep *(protect)* you from **the hour** of trial...." This refers to the relatively short period of time of God's expressing His wrath upon wicked mankind—a time when Christians will be protected.

11:9, 11 "**Three and a half days**" as symbolic of the "times, time and half a time" and so showing the relative shortness of this period of persecution and other events.

17:12: "Ten kings receive authority as kings for **one hour**." This time period is the same as "the hour of trial" and so refers to the period of "the great tribulation" in which these ten kings will persecute Christians.
There is no reason to suppose that because figurative terminology has been used in these instances that other periods are not literal. So these three verses refer to the literal approximately 3½ years of great tribulation.

Symbolic Numbers with No Literal Element
e.g. 12,000, 144,000, 7,000, and 666.

§

10

Chapter 4

The Time Periods Connecting Daniel to Revelation

The prophecies in both the Book of Daniel and the Book of Revelation give connected and very significant time periods for understanding when certain major events will take place. Indeed, there is every reason to understand these timings as being quite literal. For instance, because "a time, times and half a time" equals three and a half years and is also noted as equal to 1,260 days and to 42 months it would be difficult to see these as being symbolic timings.

Furthermore, these timings are connected to events described in Jesus' Olivet discourse. In fact, Jesus directed Christians to note the details of the Book of Daniel (Matt. 24:15) and he was also the one who presented the Revelation to John via his angel. However, the earliest and foundational statements regarding these timings are found in Daniel chapters 8, 9, and 12—the most important of which concern the prophecy of the seventy periods of "seven" in Daniel 9.

The Seventy Periods of "Seven"

❖ "Seventy 'sevens' (490 years) are decreed for your people and your holy city 1) to finish transgression, 2) to put an end to sin, 3) to atone for wickedness, 4) to bring in everlasting righteousness, 5) to seal up vision and prophecy and 6) to anoint the Most Holy Place"

(Dan. 9:24 NIV).

As shown in my book *Prophecies Related to the Return of Jesus* this period of 490 years began in 444 B.C., with the order from Persian King Artaxerxes to restore Jerusalem. The period was interrupted at the end of the 69th "seven" (after 483 years) in 33 C.E with the ride of Jesus into Jerusalem at which point he was acclaimed as King. This leaves one "seven" of years unaccounted for and so yet to commence. This will take place when, "he *[the Antichrist—the prince who is to come]* shall make a strong covenant for one "seven." i.e. the 70th "seven." This period of one "seven" amounts to 2,520 days. However, a major event will occur at the half way point during this last period of "seven," because "he *[the Antichrist]* will confirm a covenant with many *[Jews]* for one 'seven.' In the middle of the 'seven' he will put an end to sacrifice and offering. And at the temple "he will set up a sacrilegious object that causes desolation, until the fate decreed for this defiler is finally poured out on him" *(Dan. 9:27 NLT).*

11

The Particular Events in the 70th "Seven"

Time, times and half a time:
Dan. 7:25: Little horn persecutes God's people i.e. the great tribulation
Dan. 12:7: The shattering of the holy ones i.e. the great tribulation.
Rev. 12:14: The woman escapes to the wilderness to be nourished.

NOTE: A 'time' is a prophetic year of 360 days. This is based on the ancient calendar as used in Genesis 7 and 8 where 5 months = 150 days and thereby indicating the use of a 30 day month x 12 = 360 days.

1260 days:
Rev 11:3: The prophesying of Two Witnesses.
Rev 12:6: The woman escapes to the wilderness to be nourished

42 months:
Rev. 11:2: The Gentiles tread down the holy city.
Rev. 13:5: Antichrist's rule

These three equal periods of time, namely, "time, times and half a time," 1260 days, and 42 months—all equalling 3½ years—do not all refer to the same events in the same period of time. While most commentators put their full focus on the last half of the seventy "sevens," it is evident that at least one of these timings refers to an event in the first half of Daniel's seventieth "seven."

3½ days:
Rev. 11:9, 11 gives an allusion to the "time, times and half a time." i.e. three and a half years noted in both Daniel and Revelation in its different forms and as symbolic of that period to show the relative shortness of it. (See Aune in the *Word Biblical Commentary Vol. 52b p.609*).

FIRST HALF EVENT – *"the beginning of the birth pains"* – *Matt. 24:4-8*
Rev 11:3: The prophesying of the Two Witnesses, after which Satan wars with them i.e. the great tribulation.

SECOND HALF EVENTS – *The great tribulation* – *Matt. 24:9-22*
Dan. 7:25: Little horn persecutes God's people.
Dan. 12:7: The shattering of the holy ones.
Rev. 11:2: The Gentiles tread down the holy city.
Rev. 11:7: The warring against and killing of the Two Witnesses.
Rev. 12:6, 14: The woman flees to the wilderness and is nourished there.

Rev. 13:5: The rule of Antichrist after he "puts an end to sacrifice and offering." Indeed, in the sanctuary he will have set up a "sacrilege which causes desolation" at the beginning of the 3½ year great tribulation.

Parallels of Daniel's and Jesus' Words Concerning the Breaking of the Seals in Revelation

The breaking of the seals seems to parallel Jesus' Olivet discourse, as recorded in Matthew 24. Indeed there are literary and structural arguments for taking Matthew 24:4-28 as a single time period and as the answer to the disciples question of, "what will be the sign that you are coming as king" and when is "the end of the age" (vs. 3)? Furthermore, Matthew 24 has the prophecies of the book of Daniel as its background (vs. 15). In particular these are the time frame and details of Daniel 9:24-27 and the events of Daniel 11 concerning the end-time warring activities of the King of the North—the Antichrist.

After detailing, in verse 2, the destruction of a future temple (Hag. 2:3), it appears that Jesus speaks in Matthew 24:4-8 of the events to occur in the first half of the seven year period (Gk *heptad)* and in verses 9 to 22 of the events to occur in the second half of the seven year period that complete the seventy "sevens" of Daniel 9. These first half future events concern Antichrist's dispatching of false messiah's and with Jesus' warning for Christians not to be deceived by them or to be deceived when they hear of and see the Middle East wars of Antichrist taking place (Dan. 11). Neither should they be deceived by the results of these wars in causing local food-shortages. These along with earthquakes in the area are only, "the beginning of the 'birth pains'" (vs. 8).

However, from verse 9 Jesus moves into the situation of the great tribulation (persecution) which occurs during the second three and a half years of the final "seven" and is triggered by "the sacrilege which causes desolation (Antichrist)...standing in the holy place" (vs. 15)—a yet to be built Jewish sanctuary in Jerusalem.

Jesus' comment that, "if those days **had not been cut short** no one would be saved" *(Matt. 24:22)* is often taken to mean that the 1260 days of the last half of Daniel's seventieth "seven" will be shortened. In Mark's version he presents a different verb tense: "And if the LORD **hadn't cut** those days short, no one would be saved. But because of the chosen ones whom He chose, He **has cut** them short" (Mark 13:20).

13

So, it seems that Jesus was not particularly referencing the 1260 days, but rather he has the entire period of the end-times in mind. Furthermore, the 1260 day period is the period of Antichrist's rule which is never shown in Scripture to be shortened.

Other Connected Periods in Daniel

1,290 and 1335 days

❖ "How long will it be until these shocking events are over?" ...[7]"It will go on for a <u>time, times, and half a time</u>. When the shattering of the holy people has finally come to an end, all these things will have happened."... [11]"From the time the daily sacrifice is stopped and the sacrilegious object that causes desecration is set up to be worshiped, there will be 1,290 days. And blessed are those who wait and remain until the end of the 1,335 days!" *(Dan. 12:6-7, 11-12 NLT)*

The 1,290 days and the 1,335 days also seem to start when "the sacrilege that causes desolation" is set up in the sanctuary and so bringing an end to the offering of sacrifices. So these give an extra 30 days and a further 45 days after the 70th "seven" is completed.

Certainly, there is a distinction between "the sacrilege that causes desolation" and "the desolator" himself as the personification of "the sacrilege" (Dan. 9:27). So because there is a gap in time of 30 days concerning when these two aspects come to an end, perhaps it will be the effect of "the sacrilege" which lingers on for this extra 30 days and so making a total of 1,290 days; whereas the actual removal of this "sacrilege" from the sanctuary occurs at the 1,260 days point. Indeed, "the desolator" will have been ejected from Jerusalem at the 1,260 days point, but he is still alive to fight against Messiah in the vicinity of Jerusalem, at which point he gets killed i.e. after the 1,290 days.

The 2,300 evenings and mornings

❖ "Another holy one said to the speaker, "How long will the events of this vision last—the daily sacrifice, the rebellion that makes desolate, and the giving over of the sanctuary and of the host to be trampled?" He said to me, "For 2,300 evenings and mornings; then the sanctuary will be restored." *(Dan 8: 13, 14 HCSB)*

This period of the 2,300 evenings/mornings also runs **from** when the sacrifices are terminated by the desolator and the sanctuary is trodden down **until** it is **restored**. *This seems to indicate a period 2,300 actual days.* However, unless the 2,300 evenings/mornings represent each sacrifice and therefore last only 1,150 actual days this detail would seem to contradict the details of Daniel 9:24 which show that the sanctuary must be restored by the end of the 70th "seven." If they are to be 2,300 actual days this would make them extend several years into the Millennium for the restoration of the sanctuary, and therefore, beyond the boundary of the 70th week. Nevertheless, on page 229 of *The New American Commentary on Daniel* convincing proof from Keil and S. J. Schwantes is given "that the 2,300 evenings and mornings [do] represent a total of 2,300 days." (please see my book *Prophecies Related to the Return of Jesus.* p.158).

The Five months of Locust Attack

This period is shown in Revelation 9:5 when the fifth trumpet is blown. It concerns locusts as picturing a demonic attack upon the followers of Antichrist. These locusts are to inflict severe pain upon these people for five months, but not to kill them (see Job 2:6). Although some commentators feel that this is a literal five month period, such a period does not fit with the usual pattern of timing details of the end-times. Indeed, the *Word Biblical Commentary* explains this "five months" as symbolic because such a time "reflects the life-cycle of a locust." Also the number "5" is often used in the Scriptures to mean "a few" or a limited time. Additionally the *Baker Exegetical Commentary* on Revelation by Grant Osborne says that: "the main point is that God had placed a strict limit on the torture, possibly to give people time to repent." So in trying to understand the pattern of end-time days we need not attempt to incorporate a literal five month period into the scheme of things.

....

With all of this information we can soon examine how the seals, trumpets, and bowls in Revelation fit into a form of time-line.

§

Chapter 5

The Prologue to Revelation
Revelation 1:1-8

THE TEXT

The revelation from Jesus the Messiah! God gave this to him to show his bond-servants the things which must speedily take place. He communicated it by sending his angel to his bond-servant John, **2**who, by reporting everything that he saw, testified to God's message and the testimony of Jesus the Messiah. **3**Blessed is the one reading the words of this prophecy aloud, and blessed are those hearing and obeying the things written in it, because the time is near!

4John: To the seven communities of believers that are in the province of Asia:

Gracious favour and peace to you from "the One who is and who was and who is coming," and from the seven spirits in front of His throne, **5**and from Jesus the Messiah, the faithful witness, the firstborn from the dead, and the ruler of the kings of the earth.

To the one who loves us and has released us from our sins by shedding his own blood, **6**and has made us a kingdom, priests to his God and Father—glory and the dominion be to him forever. Amen. **7**Take note: he is coming with the clouds, and every eye will see him; even those who pierced him. And all the tribes of the earth will lament in remorse because of him. Yes! Amen.

8"I am the Alpha and the Omega," says the LORD God—the One who is and who was and who is coming—the All-Powerful.

TRANSLATION POINTS

1:1a: "The revelation <u>from</u> Jesus the Messiah." Several commentators, including Grant Osborne in his commentary on Revelation, show that, although originating with God, both the grammar and the context here indicate that this is not a revelation "about" Jesus, but comes from him via his angel and via John to the communities of believers.

1:1b: "Speedily take place." In the book of Revelation the Greek words in the *taxos* group are usually rendered, "soon" or "shortly." However, *taxos* (the root noun from which we get the noun *taxei)* is defined in *Bauer's Greek/English Lexicon* as: a very brief period of time, with focus on speed of activity or event, speed, quickness, swiftness, and haste. Also *taxu* (neut. of the adj. *taxus*) adv., is defined as: quickly, speedily, (without delay). *The United Bible Society 4th edition, Nestle-Aland 26th edition Interlinear* gives the following translations in all cases:

taxu = "quickly" in Rev. 2:16; 3:11; 11:14 and 22: 7, 12, 20.

en taxei = "with speed" in Rev. 1:1 and quickly in 22:6.

The preposition *en* is coupled with *taxei* making it an adverbial phrase. So both *taxu* and *en taxei* function adverbially.

In their renderings of Revelation Young's Literal and Rotherham's translation consistently translate as above i.e. with speed, speedily, quickly. NASB, NKJ and KJV mostly do the same.

There are adverbs of manner, place, time, or correlative adverbs. In today's most authoritative Greek grammar by Blass, Debrunner, and Funk, no example of the *tachos* family of Greek words is listed under "adverbs of time," but rather the *tachos* family comes under the classification of "**adverbs of manner.**"

Furthermore, renowned Greek scholar Nigel Turner supports the adverb of manner sense for *taxu* as meaning "quickly."

Lexicons generally demonstrate that all of the occurrences in Revelation are adverbs of manner i.e. the way or manner in which something is done. Hence, *taxu* and *en taxei* indicate the rapidity of execution of an event, rather than when it is to be executed.

Examples outside of Revelation are:

❖ "…he said to him, 'Take your bill, and sit down quickly *(taxeos)* and write fifty'" *(Luke 16:6 NKJV).*

❖ "…he will give justice to them speedily *(en taxei)" (Luke 18:8 ESV).*

❖ "Get up quickly *(en taxei)" (Acts 12:7b NAB)* or "with quickness" *(UBS).*

❖ "…get out of Jerusalem quickly *(en taxei)" (Acts 22:18 NRSV)* i.e. with speed or in haste.

❖ "Do not lay hands on anyone hastily *(taxeos)" (1 Tim. 5:22 NKJV).*

According to the above information it is inappropriate to translate these Greek terms as "soon" or "shortly" i.e. adverbs of time because the actual Greek words are adverbs of manner. These statements in Revelation seem also to fit well with Jesus' earlier statements concerning the suddenness or unexpectedness of his return for those who are not watchfully waiting for him.

So with the rendering "must speedily take place" we see that when Jesus returns all of the actions he takes will happen very quickly.

1:1c: "Communicated." The Greek word *esemanen* is often rendered "signified." However, it is misguided to try to turn this word into "sign-i-fied" as if it means 'given in signs' or symbols, so that everything in the Book of Revelation is given in symbols. The word simply means "made it known," as in most modern translations.

17

Comment on the Prologue

1:1: "**The revelation from Jesus the Messiah! God gave this to him to show his bond-servants the things which must speedily take place. He communicated it by sending his angel to his bond-servant John**" As with John's gospel the message of revelation originates with God, is given to his prime agent Jesus (John 5:20) as the one who reveals it and is the mediator of it, and who uses his angel to convey it to John for the benefit of Christians. So there are four individuals who are involved in the expressing of this message in a four stage process. Throughout the Revelation God and Jesus function together as shown in 1:1, but please note the distinction between God and Jesus and so showing that Jesus is not God Almighty. (Please see my book *God, Jesus, and the Holy Spirit).*

This revelation focuses on the events leading to the coming Kingdom of God when Jesus returns. It includes factors about what life will be like in that Kingdom.

1:2: "**Who by reporting everything that he** *[John]* **saw, testified to God's message and the testimony of Jesus the Messiah.**" Again the emphasis is that this message originates with God and that Jesus has mediated it as the testimony given by him, rather than it being a testimony "about" him. Here John testifies to the truthfulness of this message.

1:3: "**Blessed is the one reading the words of this prophecy aloud, and blessed are those hearing and obeying the things written in it, because the time is near!**" This apocalyptic prophecy is meant for public reading by a lay reader at Christian meetings and so blessing the audience. But, clearly today it is also meant for private reading for the blessing of the individual.

The "time is near" language of imminence, presented here, is an example of foreshortening of the prophetic horizon i.e. the making of distant events appear to be about to happen. This works toward giving the reader a sense of expectation and so focusing their minds on the need to be obedient to the message. It is a call to live for God right now.

1:4a: "**John: To the seven communities of believers that are in the province of Asia: Gracious favour and peace to you from "the One who is and who was and who is coming."**" These are seven literal Christian communities in the Asian part of modern-day Turkey.

Contextually, "the One who is and who was and who is coming" is

18

proven to be God Himself because the phrase is contrasted in verse 5 by the phrase: "and from Jesus the Messiah." The phrase "the One who is" etc., seems to be a paraphrase of "I will be what I will be" in Exodus 3:14 (Moff, Amp, CJB, and footnotes in REB and ESV) or "I will become whatsoever I please" (Ro). This refers to the divine name "Yahweh" in Exodus 3:15 and shows God's decisive intervention in history and so focusing on His future intervention in human affairs.

1:4b: "**And from the seven spirits which are in front of His throne** " (also 3:1; 4:5; 5:6). Although it is popular to interpret this phrase as referring to "the holy spirit" it more likely refers to the seven principle angels (Heb. 1:1, 14 and Rev. 8:2: *"the seven angels who stood before the throne"*). Mounce understands the seven spirits to be the <u>seven principle angels</u> as does Aune who in *the Word Biblical Commentary* states:

> A second important view, in my opinion certainly the correct one, understands the seven spirits as the seven principal angels of God. In early Jewish literature the term "spirits" was used only rarely as a synonym for "angels" (*Jub.* 1:25; 2:2; 15:31–32; *1 Enoch* 61:12, "spirit of light"), or of various types of heavenly beings (*1 Enoch* 75:5, "the spirit of the dew"; see *2 Enoch* 12:2 [J], "flying spirits"; 16:7, "the heavenly winds, and spirits and elements and flying angels"); see *TDNT* 6:375–76. …However, angels are designated "spirits" in the Qumran literature (Sekki, *RUAH* 145–71). In 1QM 12:8–9 the phrase…"host of angels," is used as a parallel to…"host of his spirits" … The unique phrase "Lord of Spirits" occurs *104 times* in the Parables of Enoch, i.e. *1 Enoch* 37–71, and only there in *1 Enoch* (see Black, *Enoch*, 189–92). Elsewhere the phrase is rare and occurs in 2 Macc 3:24; LXX Num 16:22; 27:16; *1 Clem* 64:1; two Jewish grave inscriptions from Delos, dating from the second or first century B.C. (Deissmann, *Light*, 423–35). The phrase may have an exegetical origin in the phrase "God of the spirits of all flesh," which occurs in Num 16:22; 27:16. The closest parallel is 2 Macc 3:24, "the Sovereign of spirits and of all authority" (NRSV). Ps 104:4 reads "who makest the winds thy messengers, fire and flame thy ministers," an important passage in view of the association with the seven spirits of God with seven torches of fire in 4:5. In an explanatory gloss in 4:5, the seven torches of fire burning before the throne are interpreted by John as the seven spirits of God. Again in 5:6 the seven eyes of the Lamb are interpreted as "the seven spirits

of God sent out into all the earth." Though commentators formerly noted the absence of the phrase from the OT and early Jewish literature (Beckwith, 424), that situation has changed with the publication of the Dead Sea Scrolls, for "spirits"... is a common designation for angels at Qumran...In the NT, only in Heb 1:14 are angels called spirits. The "seven spirits" of Rev 1:4 are equivalent to "the seven spirits of God" of 3:1, 4:5; 5:6 and must be identified with "the seven angels who stand before God" in 8:2. Thus the view that the seven spirits are the seven archangels *(TWNT 6:450)* seems correct.

1:5a: "**From Jesus the Messiah, the faithful witness, the firstborn from the dead, and the ruler of the kings of the earth.**" It is likely that these three phrases focus on different stages of Jesus' ministry, namely, his life on earth as God's witness (3:14), his resurrection, and finally in the future kingdom as the exalted ruler of Earth.

The term "firstborn" (Gk *prototokos*) does not only mean the first one born into a family, but is often used figuratively and so highlights such a person's prestige, status, and succession in that family i.e. as being next in charge after the father and having a double inheritance (Deut 21:15-17). So, although Jesus is the first to be raised to immortality, the term "firstborn" focuses on his primacy and priority in God's purpose (Ps.89:28). Nevertheless, by his "resurrection from the dead" (Acts 26:23) Jesus does provide the precedent for the subsequent resurrection of all believers who have died.

These "kings of the earth" are originally enemies of God and Jesus, but they do finally submit to Jesus' rulership (Rev. 21:24).

1:5b: "**To the one who loves us and has released us from our sins by shedding his own blood.**" This is the earliest praising (doxology) of Jesus alone, rather than of God. Indeed, Jesus' voluntary sacrifice for mankind's sins was a supreme act of love for each individual human (Gal. 2:20; Eph. 5:2). Certainly, he has acted as our substitute i.e. dying the death that each one of us would otherwise deserve because of sin. This act is proof of his continuing love for each person and means that each person who seeks forgiveness is released from their sins and ransomed to God by that shed blood of Jesus.

1:6a: "**And has made us a kingdom, priests to his God and Father.**" This is not a kingdom of priests, but is showing the two distinct privileges of priesthood and kingship for Christians in the concrete Kingdom, the latter being a reign on earth (5:10). This thought is taken from Exodus 19:6 and also shows that "the body of Christ" is the true Israel of God (Gal. 6:16; 1 Pet. 2:9). The concept of these ones as being kings and priests reflects the Order of Melchizedek in Hebrews 7.

Furthermore, the phrase "his God and Father" shows that Jesus has a God and therefore cannot be the Almighty God. Along with many other Scriptures which show that Jesus was and is always subordinate to his Father, this means that there can be no doctrine of the trinity i.e. a co-equal and co-eternal Father and Son.

1:6b: "**Glory and the dominion be to him forever. Amen.**" This continues the doxology in praise of Jesus for offering himself in sacrifice to rescue mankind from sin. These two terms of "glory and dominion" concern the Kingdom where "glory" equals "kingdom" (compare Mark 10:37, "glory" with Matthew 20:21, "kingdom") and "dominion" refers to rulership in that Kingdom.

1:7a: "**He is coming with the clouds.**" This is an allusion to Daniel 7:13, which shows the Messiah as coming to establish the Kingdom i.e. the transfer of sovereignty from the nations under Satan to Jesus. In all of the passages which speak of the return of Jesus, the *clouds* literally refer to earth's atmosphere, but with spiritual significance as indicating God's presence. Figuratively clouds can indicate the presence of God, as with God's leading of the Israelites through the wilderness, and a cloud hovering over the tabernacle, as well as a cloud being at Solomon's dedication of the temple. So here, in 1:7 such presence of God is because Jesus is His prime representative.

1:7b: "**And every eye will see him.**" This is part of the conflation of Daniel 7:13 with Zechariah 12:10 which says, "they will look to me, the one they have pierced. They will lament for him as one laments for an only son, and there will be a bitter cry for him like the bitter cry for a firstborn." It is a literal seeing of Jesus. Indeed, Jesus was "seen" being received into a physical cloud when he departed and he will return "in the same way" (Acts 1:9-11). This is as he also stated that: "the Son of Man's coming as king will be just as when lightning comes from the east and flashes to the west." Furthermore, Christians will physically rise up into the literal clouds "in the air" to meet Jesus at his return (1 Thess. 4:17).

But how will "every eye" see Jesus? Certainly, he will be visible as shown above. Nevertheless, it would seem to be that only by a circumnavigation of the earth in the atmosphere will every eye see him.

1:7c: "**Even those who pierced him.**" This "seeing of Jesus" by those "who pierced him" cannot refer to those who actually literally killed him, namely the ancient Romans who are long dead. However, the Jewish religious leadership of the time concocted the false charges against Jesus and called for his execution and so making them culpable of "piercing him," but they, too, are long dead. Nevertheless, God looks at things so that there is community responsibility, so that the entire Jewish nation and Gentile world, right up to Jesus' return, must take responsibility for the killing of their Messiah.

1:7d: "**All the tribes of the earth will lament in remorse because of him. Yes! Amen.** " This is also part of the reference to Zechariah 12:10. So here in 1:7 it refers to the total repentance of Israel and the Gentile world in all its "tribes of the earth." i.e. penitential grief over what their ancestors did in murdering Jesus.

1:8: "**I am the Alpha and the Omega,**" **says the LORD God—the One who is and who was and who is coming—the All-Powerful.**" This is the first occurrence of this title *"Alpha and Omega"* which appears only in Revelation 1:8, 21:6 and 22:13. In 1:8 it clearly applies to *"the LORD God...the Almighty"* and not to Jesus. In 21:6 it clearly applies to *"He who sits on the throne"* (verse 5) and not to the Lamb. However, please see the notes on the application of the phrase in 22:13.

Alpha and omega are the first and last letters of the Greek alphabet and to the Jews the term simply meant "the whole extent of a thing i.e. something in its entirety—a totality," or 'that which contains everything else.' In the context of the statements in Revelation it gives complete assurance that God is "all in all" and that he has the total power and control to bring about His complete purpose for the world.

§

Chapter 6

The Vision of the Resurrected Jesus
Revelation 1:9-20 ... The beginning of Vision One

TEXT

⁹I, John, am your brother and partner in the suffering, Kingdom, and patient endurance in following Jesus. I was on the island called Patmos for proclaiming God's message and the testimony of Jesus. ¹⁰I was in a prophetic trance on the Lord's day when I heard a loud voice behind me like a trumpet, ¹¹saying: "Write on a scroll what you see and send it to the seven communities of believers—to Ephesus, Smyrna, Pergamum, Thyatira, Sardis, Philadelphia, and Laodicea."

¹²I turned to see the voice that was speaking with me. As I turned, I saw seven golden lampstands, ¹³and in the middle of the lampstands one like a son of man, dressed in a robe reaching down to his feet and with a wide golden sash wrapped around his chest. ¹⁴His head and hair were as white as wool—white like snow, and his eyes were like flames of fire. ¹⁵His feet were like burnished bronze refined in a furnace, and his voice was like the sound of torrents of waters. ¹⁶He held seven stars in his right hand, and a sharp two-edged sword came out from his mouth. His face was like the sun shining at its maximum.

¹⁷When I saw him, I fell down at his feet as though dead; but he placed his right hand on me and said: "Stop being afraid! I am the first and the last, ¹⁸and the living one! I was dead, but look—I am alive forever and ever and I hold the keys of Death and Hades! ¹⁹So write down the things you saw, the things which are, and the things which are about to happen afterward. ²⁰The divine secret of the seven stars that you saw in my right hand and the seven golden lampstands is this: the seven stars are the angels of the seven communities and the seven lampstands are the seven communities."

TRANSLATION POINT

1:10: "In a prophetic trance." This phrase was chosen by David Aune in the *Word Biblical Commentary* as a paraphrase of the literal term "in the spirit." It very well clarifies the meaning of the Greek and is similar to Paul's experience of being "caught up to the third heaven" (2 Cor. 12:2) i.e. in a trance. Furthermore Peter's experience of falling into a "trance-like state" (Acts 10:10), is also expressed as, "I was in a trance and I saw a vision (Acts 11:5).

Comment on the Vision of the Resurrected Jesus

1:9a: "I, John, am your brother and partner in the suffering, Kingdom, and patient endurance in following Jesus." These three terms form a conceptual unity which is the shared experience of true Christians. Nevertheless, the central term is "kingdom," with its current in-breaking rule in the lives of Christians, but which will only be consummated with the second coming of Jesus. In fact, Jesus had warned his followers that, "in the world you will have persecution, but I have conquered the world" *(John 16:33)*. Paul had also warned, "We must suffer many hardships on our way into the Kingdom of God" *(Acts 14:22)*. Such sufferings may include: imprisonment, social ostracism, slander, poverty, economic exploitation, violence, or various threats. However, no Christian should feel alone in this because, as with John, we are all partners and participants in such suffering. So John is showing his social equality with his fellow Christians. Furthermore, the Apostle Peter said that, "these trials make you partners with the Messiah in his suffering. Therefore, keep on celebrating, so that you may be overjoyed at the revelation of his glory" *(1 Pet. 4:13)*. All of this concludes with the suffering that will ensue in the great tribulation—this term referring to the final sharp burst of intense persecution in the end-times. Indeed, such persecution is what each true Christian must patiently endure or persevere through in imitation of the patient endurance of Messiah Jesus. In fact, Paul showed that "suffering produces endurance" *(Rom. 5:3)*.

1:9b: "**I was on the island called Patmos for proclaiming God's message and the testimony of Jesus**." This rocky, volcanic, but inhabited and civilized island in the Aegean Sea is situated some thirty seven miles from Miletus and about fifty miles from Ephesus and is about thirty miles in circumference. There is some agreement that John was temporarily banished to Patmos by Emperor Domitian in the year 95 C.E., but released in 96 C.E., after Domitian's death. It seems likely that John had the freedom of the island, unlike Paul's house arrest (Acts 28:16, 30).

1:10: "**I was in a prophetic trance on the Lord's day when I heard a loud voice behind me like a trumpet**." This begins the first vision and runs all the way to 3:22. The specific timing of the phrase "the Lord's day" is difficult to determine. Does it mean "the day of the Lord" i.e. "the day of God's wrath"? Or, does it mean "resurrection day" as being the Sunday to celebrate the occasion when Jesus was raised from the dead. In fact, because it is mentioned only in regard to Vision One which does not speak of "the day of God's wrath" and because the grammar does not favour that application, it seems that the reference is to "resurrection day" i.e. a Sunday.

This is the voice of Jesus as shown by the statement in verses 12 and 13.

24

1:11: "Saying, 'Write on a scroll what you see and send it to the seven communities of believers—to Ephesus, Smyrna, Pergamum, Thyatira, Sardis, Philadelphia, and Laodicea.'" This command of "write what you see" is mentioned twelve times in the Revelation and is a commissioning of John to convey this inspired message.

All of these cities were in the Roman province of Asia and their order forms a circular route for a letter carrier. These seven communities formed an organizational and distributive centre for the whole of the province so that the other cities, namely, Troas, Colossae, Magnesia, and Tralles would also finally receive the message of the Revelation.

1:12: "I turned to see the voice that was speaking with me. As I turned, I saw seven golden lampstands." One cannot see a voice, so this term is a metonymy for the speaker, which, in this case, is Jesus as the same voice noted in verse 10.

The concept of seven golden lampstands is based upon the vision in Zechariah 4:1-14. Indeed, Revelation 1:20 identifies these lampstands as the seven communities of believers and they give a temple setting with the purpose of showing the light that God's people shine upon the nations.

1:13: "And in the middle of the lampstands One like a son of man, dressed in a robe reaching down to his feet and with a wide golden sash." The phrase "One like a son of man," is originally taken from Daniel 7:13-15, and shows Jesus as being not a mere man, but a perfect man during his life on Earth, and even a supernatural man since his exaltation. Nevertheless, this phrase "son of man" always refers to his 100% humanity and shows that he cannot illogically be 100% man and 100% God as in the blasphemous teaching of Trinitarianism.

Some think that this description is of Jesus as a High Priest. However, it seems more likely that it focuses on Jesus as an exalted king who brings about divine judgment rather than any priestly work. This is shown by his use of the sharp two-edged sword in verse 16.

1:14: "His head and hair were as white as wool—white like snow. His eyes were like flames of fire." This is similar to the description of God as "the ancient of days" in Daniel 7:9 and shows Jesus' position now in his eternal existence just as the Father has immortality. It also shows Jesus' dignity and accumulated wisdom.

"Eyes like flames of fire" pictures his penetrating insight and seems

25

to indicate Jesus' ability to search into any matter i.e. to analyse the very motives of individuals. Please see 2:23.

1:15: **"His feet were like burnished bronze refined in a furnace, and his voice was like the sound of torrents of waters."** This shows Jesus' power and stability. Because his feet have been "refined in a fire" the very purity of Jesus is indicated and therefore his judgments against what is sinful will be of perfect justice.

In being "like the sound of torrents of waters" Jesus' voice is shown to be majestic and awe-inspiring (Ezek. 43:2).

1:16: **"He held seven stars in his right hand, and a sharp two-edged sword** (Gk *romphaia)* **came out from his mouth. His face was like the sun shining at its maximum)."** This sword is a symbol of "the sword of the spirit" (Eph. 6:17; Heb. 4:12) as a sword of judgment; and so whatever Jesus speaks simply happens, as when God spoke in Genesis 1:3 etc, and it was done. Jesus uses this metaphorical sword to destroy the wicked nations (Rev.19:15). It is also described as "the breath of his mouth" with which he destroys the Antichrist (2 Thess. 2:8).

In being "like the sun" Jesus' face reflects the very glory of his Father as will Christians in the Kingdom (Matt.13:43).

1:17: **"When I saw him, I fell down at his feet as though dead; but he placed his right hand on me and said: "Stop being afraid! I am the first and the last."** The phrase "the first and the last" carries the same thought as does "the alpha and the omega" and so means "the whole extent of a thing." Again this is a term that is applied to God in the Scriptures, but can equally well be applied to Jesus as God's representative. Therefore, in its context, when Jesus applies this phrase to himself he simply means that he is the whole extent of things concerning the resurrection because he "was dead, but look...(he is) alive forever and ever." He is "the one who pioneered the faith and brought it to completion" (Heb. 12:2). In fact, he has been granted the total power and control to bring about God's complete purpose for the world. So by saying this to John, Jesus is giving him the full assurance that all of God's promises are certain of fulfillment.

1:18: **"And the living one! I was dead, but look—I am alive forever and ever and I hold the keys of Death and Hades."** Keys are a symbol of authority. Indeed, since Jesus' resurrection, he holds the keys of Death and Hades i.e. the common grave and so has been granted the privilege of being the one to bring the Christian dead back to life (John 5:27-29). Other keys in Revelation are: "the key of David" (3:7), "the key to the shaft of the abyss (9:1), and "the key to the abyss" (20:1), these last two being the same metaphorical key, and which includes authority over the spirit realm.

1:19: "**So write down the things you saw, the things which are, and the things which are about to happen afterward.**" This is a common apocalyptic formula, likely taken from the Hellenistic world. "The things you saw" concern the vision of the glorified Jesus. "The things which are" concern the condition of the seven Christian communities. "The things which are about to happen afterward" concern the visions of the end-times and the coming Kingdom, all of this begins with the breaking of the seven seals. However, throughout the Revelation there is an interweaving of the past, present and future.

1:20a: "**The divine secret of the seven stars that you saw in my right hand and the seven golden lampstands is this: the seven stars are the angels of the seven communities and the seven lampstands are the seven communities.**" Because "One like a son of man" is "in the midst of the lampstands" it shows that Messiah Jesus is always working in the lives of the communities of believers.

1:20b: "**The seven stars are the angels of the seven churches.**" There is no biblical reason to interpret this as meaning overseers or bodies of overseers. A symbol is only a symbol of one literal thing. In both Job 38:7 and Isaiah 14:13 stars represent angels. The fact that the seven letters were addressed to the angels has the same meaning as when all of Paul's letters were addressed to the Christian "holy ones" rather than to the body of elders because the angels are corporately identified with these communities of believers.

NOTE: The Scriptures also speak of guardian angels (Ps. 34:7; 91:11; Matt. 18:10; Acts 12:15; Heb. 1:14).

§

Chapter 7

Letters to the Seven Christian Communities
Revelation 2 and 3

Chapters two and three of Revelation concern letters that were written to seven literal Christian communities located in the cities of Ephesus, Smyrna, Pergamum, Thyatira, Sardis, Philadelphia, and Laodicea and all located in ancient Asia Minor which is now the Western Asian area of modern-day Turkey. However, these are not letters in the manner which Paul wrote letters to Christian communities, but rather these are prophetic letters, that is, divine messages in a stereotyped pattern as a memory aid for those who couldn't read (it is estimated that only about 15% of people could read in the first century Roman world).

TEXT   **1. Ephesus**

"To the angel of the Christian community in Ephesus write: 'This is the message from him who holds the seven stars in his right hand, and who is walking about among the seven golden lampstands. ²I know your activities, your hard work, and your resolute endurance. I know that you cannot tolerate wicked people, but you've tested those claiming to be apostles but are not, and you've discovered that they are liars. ³Indeed you have endurance and have persevered resolutely for the sake of my name, yet you haven't grown weary. ⁴But I have this against you: you've abandoned the love you had at first. ⁵So remember from where you have fallen and turn back to it, and do the activities you did at first. If not, I will come to you and remove your lampstand from its place—that is, if you don't turn back. ⁶Yet in your favour: you hate the practices of the Nicolaitans, which I also hate. ⁷Anyone who has ears ought to listen to what the spirit is saying to the communities. To anyone who overcomes I will grant for them to eat of the tree of the perfect life, which is in the paradise of God.'"

Comment on Ephesus

2:1: "**To the angel of the Christian community in Ephesus write: 'This is the message from him who holds the seven stars in his right hand, and who is walking about among the seven golden lampstands.**" As shown earlier these are literal angels, and not simply human messengers. They are symbolized by stars as in others biblical texts. However, because the message is written <u>to</u> "the angel" he is best understood as being the guardian angel of this Christian community in Ephesus, as well each angel being so for each of the Christian communities.

28

2:2: "I know your activities, your hard work, and your resolute endurance. I know that you cannot tolerate wicked people, but you've tested those claiming to be apostles but are not, and you've discovered that they are liars." Rather than the false teaching of once-saved-always-saved with no need for any Christian activities, Christians must be productive if they want to have Jesus' favour and blessing.

This action of testing of the teachings of some by the Ephesians complies with the admonition of the Apostle Paul, namely, to "test everything and hold on to what is good" (1 Thess. 5:21), as well as John's own admonition in 1 John 4:1-3 for Christians to:

❖ "stop believing every spiritual statement, but keep testing them to see whether they are from God. Indeed, many false prophets have gone out into the world. This is the test for recognizing the spirit of God: every spiritual statement confessing Jesus the Messiah, who came as a human, is from God. Every spiritual statement that doesn't confess the specific Jesus we speak of isn't from God."

2:3: "Indeed you have endurance and have persevered resolutely for the sake of my name, yet you haven't grown weary." Endurance and perseverance are essential qualities for those who are loyal to Messiah Jesus; especially so when the great tribulation begins. Certainly, the development of these qualities is required before that tribulation begins.

Along with enduring various kinds of suffering caused by the world these loyal Christians in Ephesus had to persevere through the ongoing problem of false teaching by some amongst them (Eph. 4:14).

Because "name" is a metonymy for the person, this means that they were enduring and persevering "because of me" i.e. Jesus himself.

2:4: "But I have this against you: you've abandoned the love you had a first" Because of their struggle with false teachers and their hatred of heretical teaching their hearts had hardened into harsh attitudes toward one another. Doctrinal purity and loyalty can never be a substitute for love. Indeed, the activities here are *works of love* and their failure to love one another would result in the disbanding of their community.

2:5: "So remember from where you have fallen and turn back to it, and do the activities you did at first. If not, I will come to you and remove your lampstand from its place—that is, if you don't turn back." It is vital for Christians to recall their early enthusiasm for Christian activities, especially their works of love for each other and for outsiders, and then to have a change of mindset so that they recover that early enthusiasm.

29

2:6: "**Yet in your favour: you hate the practices of the Nicolaitans, which I also hate**" There is great uncertainty concerning who the people of this cult were, except that they were false teachers. Irenaeus claims that they were connected with Nicolaus who first taught that one's body must be beaten into submission. His later followers reversed this view and decided that the body had no effect on the spirit, and so they began to live an immoral lifestyle while compromising with the world.

2:7: "**Anyone who has ears ought to listen to what the spirit is saying to the communities. To eat of the tree of life, which is in the paradise of God.**" It is the "spirit of Jesus" (Acts 16:7; Rom. 8:9) which is giving this warning that shows that each Christian must open his heart and mind to Kingdom truths.

To eat of the tree of life concerns the promise of the immortal life of the age to come in the consummated kingdom on earth.

▲

TEXT ## 2. Smyrna

[8]"And to the angel of the Christian community in Smyrna write: 'This is the message from the first and the last, the one who was dead, but came to life. [9] I know your sufferings and your poverty (but really you are rich). I know the slander against you by those who claim that they are Jews, but really they are not; they are a synagogue belonging to the Satan. [10]Stop being afraid of the things you are about to suffer. Take note: the Devil is about to throw some of you into prison, so that you may be tested, and you will suffer oppression for ten days. Remain faithful even in the face of death, and I will give you the crown of the perfect life. [11]Anyone who has ears ought to listen to what the spirit is saying to the communities. Anyone who overcomes will never be harmed by the second death.'"

Comment on Smyrna

2:8: "**Write: 'This is the message from the first and the last, the one who was dead, but came to life.**" As in 1:17 this means "the whole extent of a thing." So Jesus is giving John the full assurance that all of God's promises are certain of fulfillment.

2:9: "**I know your sufferings and your poverty (but really you are rich). I know the slander against you by those who claim that they are Jews, but really they are not; they are a synagogue belonging to the Satan.**" The real Jew is one on the inside—a spiritual Jew (Rom. 2:29). In contrast these natural Jews who rejected the Messiah also opposed the true Jews—the Christians, and were really doing the Satan's bidding.

2:10a: "Stop being afraid of the things you are about to suffer. Take note: the Devil is about to throw some of you into prison, so that you may be tested, and you will suffer oppression for ten days." Because, "God is our refuge and strength" (Ps. 46:1) Christians should be fearless. This is seen in Jesus' words when he said, "Stop being afraid of those who kill the body, but cannot kill the soul. Instead, fear the One who is able to destroy both soul and body in the Gehenna fire" (Matt. 10:28).

The term "devil" is synonymous with the term "Satan" whose purpose is to destroy the faith of the Christian. However, by the use of the grammatical divine passive such testing is allowed by God who wishes to see how strong the faith is of each Christian; but such local persecution will probably last a relatively short period of time as indicated by its being only for "ten days."

2:10b "Remain faithful even in the face of death, and I will give you the crown of the perfect life." This symbol of "the crown of life" is borrowed from the festivities of the athletic games (1 Cor. 9:25). It means that faithful Christians will be given the immortal life of the age to come (Jas. 1:12).

▲

TEXT   **3. Pergamum**

¹²"And to the angel of the Christian community in Pergamum write: 'This is the message from him who has the sharp two-edged sword. ¹³I know where you live—where the Satan's throne is. Yet you continue to be committed to everything that I stand for, and you didn't renounce my faith even in the days of Antipas my faithful witness, who was killed there among you, where the Satan lives. ¹⁴But I do have a few things against you: you have some people there who are committed to the teaching of Balaam, who instructed Balak to lay a trap for the children of Israel, so that they would eat food sacrificed to idols and commit sexual immorality. ¹⁵You also have some who are committed to the teaching of the Nicolaitans. ¹⁶Turn away from these things! If not, I will come against you suddenly and make war against those people with the sword of my mouth. ¹⁷Anyone who has ears ought to listen to what the spirit is saying to the communities. To anyone who overcomes I will give some of the hidden manna. I will also give them a white stone with a new name written on it, one that no one is able to understand except the one who receives it.'"

Comment on Pergamum

2:12-13a: "Write: 'This is the message from him who has the sharp two-edged sword. I know where you live—where the Satan's throne is." The

31

city of Pergamum was the centre of pagan worship in Asia Minor (Turkey) of which there were several forms including, the worship of Aesclepius, the serpent-god—a reminder of the serpent in the Garden of Eden, and the worship of Zeus at his altar. Also there was the worship of the Roman emperor—a form of worship prevalent in most cities.

However, in Revelation 13:2 we learn that, concerning "the beast...the Dragon gave him his power, <u>his throne,</u> and total authority." Also, the references to Gog (Antichrist) in Ezekiel 38, 39 link him with Asian Turkey. So could it be that some part of Antichrist's rule will be from Satan's throne in Pergamum in Asia Minor?

2:13b: **"Yet you continue to be committed to everything that I stand for, and you didn't renounce my faith even in the days of Antipas my faithful witness, who was killed there among you, where the Satan lives."** This brother seems to be the only one to have died for his faith in the previous persecution of Christians; yet he may have been representative of other martyrs in the Christian assembly.

2:14-15: **"But I do have a few things against you: you have some people there who are committed to the teaching of Balaam, who instructed Balak to lay a trap for the children of Israel, so that they would eat food sacrificed to idols and commit sexual immorality. You also have some who are committed to the teaching of the Nicolaitans."** Balaam is the prototype of those who promote compromise with paganism in idolatry and immorality (Num. 22). So this teaching may have been the same as that which was practiced by the Nicolaitans who promoted a sexually immoral lifestyle. Please see *2:6:* for comments on the Nicolaitans.

2:16: **"Turn away from these things! If not, I will come against you suddenly and make war against those people with the sword of my mouth."** This is not the Second Advent but Jesus' visitation that is the on-going judgment of the believing communities (1 Pet. 4:17).

2:17a: **"Anyone who has ears ought to listen to what the spirit is saying to the communities."** As in 2:7 this is a warning that each Christian must open his heart and mind to Kingdom truths and it is the "spirit of Jesus" (Acts 16:7; Rom. 8:9) which is stating it.

2:17b: **"To anyone who overcomes I will give some of the hidden manna."** Manna is "bread from heaven" (Ps. 105:40) as is Jesus himself (John 6:31-33) inasmuch as this bread is his sacrificed flesh (vs.51), so

32

that, "everyone who continues feeding on my flesh and drinking my blood has the life of the age to come, and I will raise them up on the last day" (John 6:54). Therefore this manna spiritually sustains true Christians, but is "hidden" from the unsaved.

2:17c: **"I will also give them a white stone with a new name written on it, one that no one is able to understand except the one who receives it."** The white stone is probably a reference to the semi-precious stone called beryl. In being white it indicates a favourable token of acquittal in a court setting, no doubt, from all sin. This therefore, indicates that those who receive it have been victorious and so may enter the messianic banquet.

The new name is as Jesus said in 3:12, "I will write on them the name of my God and the name of the city of my God, the New Jerusalem, which comes down out of heaven from my God, and my new name." So these rewards are metaphors for the messianic banquet and of admission into it.

▲

TEXT   **4. Thyatira**

[18]"And to the angel of the Christian community in Thyatira write: 'This is the message from the Son of God, who has eyes like a flame of fire, and whose feet are like burnished bronze. [19]I know your activities: your love and faith and service and resolute endurance, and that your later activities exceed the earlier ones. [20]But I have this against you: you are tolerating that woman Jezebel, who claims to be a prophetess. She teaches and deceives my bond-servants to commit sexual immorality and to eat food sacrificed to idols. [21]I gave her time to turn from her sin, but she isn't willing to turn away from her sexual immorality. [22]Take note: I will throw her onto a bed of serious illness, and bring down severe suffering on those who commit adultery with her, unless they turn away from following her activities. [23]I will kill her children with death-dealing disease, and all the communities of believers will know that I am the one who searches thoughts and motives. I will give to each of you whatever your activities deserve. [24]But to the rest of you in Thyatira, who haven't accepted this teaching—who haven't learned 'the deep things of the Satan,' as they call them; to you I say: I won't put any further burden on you. [25]Nevertheless, stay committed to what you have until I come. [26]To anyone who overcomes and who continues in my ways until the end I will give authority over the nations. [27]They will rule them with an iron sceptre, as when earthenware pots are broken in pieces! That is the authority I have received from my Father. [28]Furthermore, I will give them the morning star. [29]Anyone who has ears ought to listen to what the spirit is saying to the communities.'"

Comment on Thyatira

2:18: "Write: 'This is the message from the Son of God, who has eyes like a flame of fire, and whose feet are like burnished bronze.** As in 1:14 Jesus' "eyes" have the ability to search into any matter while also analyzing the very motives of individuals.

His feet show his power and stability as "refined in a fire." So, as in 1:15, the very purity of Jesus is indicated and therefore his judgments will be of perfect justice.

2:19: "I know your activities: your love and faith and service and resolute endurance, and that your later activities exceed the earlier ones."** "Activities" also refer to works and so here we can see some of the major categories of works required of Christians, but with love having the primary place and being the basis for all activities toward others.

2:20: "But I have this against you: you are tolerating that woman Jezebel, who claims to be a prophetess. She teaches and deceives my bond-servants to commit sexual immorality and to eat food sacrificed to idols."** This appears to be a particular woman of whom Jezebel was the prototype (1 Kings 18-21; 2 Kings 9). Rather than prediction, her prophesying would have been in the form of inspired teaching from her claimed revelations. From this she promoted herself as an authority in the Christian assembly.

The danger from this Jezebel was that she was encouraging the brothers and sisters, "to commit sexual immorality and to eat food sacrificed to idols"—a quite different situation to the one Paul wrote about in 1 Corinthians 8:1-8. In Thyatira there were *guild feasts,* which involved meat offered to idols, since the patron gods were always worshipped at the feasts and the feast often led to sexual immorality. This antitype of Jezebel probably misused Paul's words in 1 Corinthians 8 stating that "an idol is nothing" so as to encourage Christians to participate in such pagan feasts; whereas Paul, in writing to the Corinthians was simply speaking of the meat that had been offered to idols and had now been sold through the meat market. Thus Paul was certainly not allowing Christians to participate in any pagan meals.

2:21: "I gave her time to turn from her sin, but she isn't willing to turn away from her sexual immorality."** Evidently this Jezebel had earlier been rebuked, but here we see an example of God's amazing level of patience. Nevertheless, there is always an end-point to that patience as shown in the case of the wicked in Noah's day (2 Pet. 2:5; 3:9-10).

34

Here the refusal to change her ways reflects the refusal to repent by the Jezebel of ancient times (1 King 21:23), but as in all of Revelation the "sexual immorality" is metaphorical for ethical corruption as on a bed of idolatry (Isa. 57:3, 8; Hos. 9:1).

2:22: "**Take note: I will throw her onto a bed of serious illness, and bring down severe suffering on those who commit adultery with her, unless they turn away from following her activities**." This "bed of serious illness," as a punishment, contrasts with her bed of immorality. The bringing of suffering upon these spiritual adulterers appears to have the purpose of leading them toward repentance.

2:23a: "**I will kill her children with death-dealing disease**." These are not the same group as those who have committed adultery with Jezebel. However, these are not her literal children, but rather they are those who have unreservedly committed themselves to the teaching of the false prophetess as if she had birthed them.

2:23b: "**And all the communities of believers will know that I am the one who searches thoughts and motives. I will give to each of you whatever your activities deserve**" Jesus can know the very inner being of those who claim to follow him (Matt. 9:4; 12:25; John 1:47-49; 13:5; Isa. 11:3). He was granted to do what God Himself can do (Jer. 17:10; Heb. 4:12) in knowing how we think and what our deepest motives are. This is why silent prayer can be heard by both God and Jesus.

Once again we can see that the once-saved-always-saved teaching contradicts what Jesus requires of Christians, because we will only be rewarded if we are active Christians.

2:24: "**But to the rest of you in Thyatira, who haven't accepted this teaching—who haven't learned 'the deep things of the Satan,' as they call them; to you I say: I won't put any further burden on you.**'" The Jezebel woman had tried to persuade the assembly that she taught the deep things of God, but the reality was that she taught what was false and damaging to the Christian community. These false things leading to sexual immorality and idolatry were actually "the deep things of the Satan."

The statement of "no further burden" upon them probably refers to there being nothing extra than for them to continue to remain faithful.

2:25: "**Nevertheless, stay committed to what you have until I come.** So, Christians must "hold on to the teachings handed down" (2 Thess. 2:15)

35

i.e. keep a strong grip on the biblical truths of the faith. This contrasts with the later man-made church creeds.

2:26-27: "To anyone who overcomes and who continues in my ways until the end I will give authority over the nations. They will rule them with an iron sceptre." "The end" always refers to the end of the age when Jesus returns. However, at the very beginning of the Millennium the nations who oppose the kingdom will be dealt with by Jesus. In fact, this passage alludes to Psalm 2:9 where Jesus' role in this is described.

Additionally, during the one thousand year period, the body of Christ will rule and even destroy any rebellious ones in the nations. This is confirmed by the further statement that they could be "broken in pieces" by "the iron sceptre." Any who disobey God's arrangements under the Kingdom government will be disciplined as shown in Zechariah 14:16-19. So Christians, as supporters of Jesus, will use strong means to bring them back under their authority.

2:28: "Furthermore, I will give them the morning star." Jesus is called "the bright morning star" (Rev. 22:16) and the messianic prophecy in Numbers 24:17 states that, "a star shall come forth from Jacob." There is a further reference to Daniel 12:3 where Christians will "shine like the stars," the brightest of which is the morning star. So, the giving of the morning star by Jesus is likely to refer to those who conquer as sharing in Jesus' messianic glory with him.

▲

TEXT   **5. Sardis**

"And to the angel of the Christian community in Sardis write: 'This is the message from the one who has the seven spirits of God, namely the seven stars. I know your activities. You have the reputation of being truly alive, but in reality you are dead. [2]Be vigilant! Strengthen the remaining things that were about to die, because I haven't found your activities complete in the sight of my God. [3]So remember how you received and heard the message! Keep it, and turn your thinking and behaviour around. If you are not watchful, I will come like a thief, and you won't know at what time I will come to you. [4]Yet you have a few people in Sardis, who haven't dirtied their clothes, and they will walk with me in white, because they are worthy. [5]Anyone who overcomes will similarly be clothed in white clothing, and I will never erase their name from the book of life. I will confess their name in the presence of my Father and of His angels. [6]Anyone who has ears ought to listen to what the spirit is saying to the communities.'"

36

Comment on Sardis

3:1: "Write: 'This is the message from the one who has the seven spirits of God, namely the seven stars. I know your activities. You have the reputation of being truly alive, but in reality you are dead." Please see 1:4 which shows that these "seven spirits" are seven principle angels i.e. archangels.

The traditional rendering for "reputation" is "name of" which does not refer to any personal name, but rather to the reputation or character or authority of the person, i.e. all that he or she stands for.

3:2: "Be vigilant! Strengthen the remaining things that were about to die, because I haven't found your activities complete in the sight of my God." Having failed to be spiritually vigilant these Christians must prepare much better so that they are ready for Christ's future inspections of them. Here the activities which those in Sardis have partly failed at were their love, faith, service and endurance—all of which Jesus shows to be incomplete.

3:3: "So remember how you received and heard the message! Keep it, and turn your thinking and behaviour around. If you are not watchful, I will come *(Gk hexoo)* like a thief, and you won't know at what time I will come to you." This "coming" of Jesus does not refer to his *parousia*, but his on-going judgment of them. The phrase "like a thief" emphasizes the unexpectedness of this coming.

3:4: "Yet you have a few people in Sardis, who haven't dirtied their clothes, and they will walk with me in white, because they are worthy." These ones were not defiled by sexual immorality or idolatry (usually by eating the meat offerings in the pagan temples). This is a picture of their spiritual and moral purity which will also be seen as the radiance of their glory in the Kingdom.

3:5: "Anyone who overcomes will similarly be clothed in white clothing, and I will never erase their name from the book of life. I will confess their name in the presence of my Father and of His angels." Here, Jesus promises three rewards for those who are "overcomers." These are:

1. Being clothed in white. This means that they, as victors, will participate in Messiah's future triumphal procession.

2. The having of all the benefits of keeping their name in the book of life. This book was first mentioned by Moses when acknowledging his failure with Israel, in his concern that God might not forgive him and so he says "then blot me out of the book you have written." More positively Jesus says to Christians, "continue celebrating the fact that your names have been recorded with Heaven" (Luke 10:20).

3. As with Jesus' statement that, "if anyone declares themselves as united with me in the presence of humans, I will declare myself as united with them in the presence of my Father in heaven" (Matt. 10:32), so too, here we have the same promise as one that gives faithful Christians great encouragement concerning their future. So those in Sardis must stop being ashamed of Jesus because of wishing to be accepted by non-Christians.

3:6: "**Anyone who has ears ought to listen to what the spirit is saying to the communities**." Again this warning is given that each Christian must open his heart and mind to Kingdom truths, this being said by the "spirit of Jesus" (Acts 16:7; Rom. 8:9).

▲

TEXT   **6. Philadelphia**

[7]"And to the angel of the Christian community in Philadelphia write: 'This is the message from the holy one, the authentic one, who has the key of David. When he opens a door, no one can close it, and when he closes it, no one can open it. [8]I know what your activities have been, but take note: I have set in front of you a door which has been opened and no one is able to shut. You have only a limited influence, yet you have kept my message and didn't repudiate the things I stand for. [9]Take note: I am going to make those people of the Satan's synagogue, who declare themselves to be Jews though they aren't, but are lying—take note, I will make them come and kneel in honour at your feet, and they will know that I have loved you. [10]You preserved the message concerning my resolute endurance, so I will preserve you through the time of trial that is about to come upon the whole world, to test those who live on the earth. [11]I am coming quickly! Hold on to what you have so that no one can take your crown. [12]I will make anyone who overcomes a pillar in the sanctuary of my God, and they will not go out of it anymore. I will write on them the name of my God and the name of the city of my God, the New Jerusalem, which comes down out of heaven from my God, and my new name. [13]Anyone who has ears ought to listen to what the spirit is saying to the communities.'"

Comment on Philadelphia

3:7: "Write: This is the message from the holy one, the authentic one, who has the key of David. When he opens a door, no one can close it, and when he closes it, no one can open it." This is the key to David's house—the Messianic kingdom. Because Jesus is the holy one, the authentic one he alone is the one who has absolute authority to give admission into the kingdom of God. Therefore Jesus' decision on this will be final.

3:8: "I know what your activities have been, but take note: I have set in front of you a door which has been opened and no one is able to shut. You have only a limited influence, yet you have kept my message and didn't repudiate the things I stand for." This Christian community in Philadelphia is commended by Jesus for having struggled with certain bad influences.

The most common view of the "door which has been opened" is that it is the door to the Kingdom.

Rather than the literal rendering in many versions of, "thou hast a little strength" which is often misconstrued as a criticism of them, this is not critical of them, but rather, it means that in the wider community they were small in numbers and therefore, limited in influence in that wider community as rendered: "You have only a limited influence."

3:9: "Take note: I am going to make those people of the Satan's synagogue, who declare themselves to be Jews though they aren't, but are lying—take note, I will make them come and kneel in honour at your feet *(Gk. proskyneo),* and they will know that I have loved you." In biblical times a synagogue was the people who assemble in a building, more so than the building itself.

These ethnic Jews reject the Messiah, and so God no longer views them as Jews (Rom. 2:28-29). They are forced, then, to pay homage to the faithful Christians and, in fact, to be in submission to them. Nevertheless, this is not worship of these Christians because worship belongs only to God. All of this brings these Jews to a realization that God's prime love is for those who acknowledge Jesus as Messiah.

3:10: "You preserved the message concerning my resolute endurance, so I will preserve you through the time of trial that is about to come upon the whole world to test those who live on the earth." This time of trial encompasses the whole of the end-times, both the great tribulation and

God's day of wrath—His pouring out of His punishment on a rebellious and wicked world, particularly those who worship the Antichrist. This is seen in the blasting of the symbolic trumpets and the pouring out of the plagues from the symbolic bowls. It occurs after the great tribulation and will affect everyone except Christians. Indeed, the further passages in the Revelation show that the people of the world are given several opportunities to repent.

In the Book of Revelation there are three realms of intelligent creatures described (please see Chapter 1 pages 4 and 5). So these who live on the earth, also known as "the earth-dwellers," are pictorial of God's enemies who follow and worship "the Beast," as well as engaging in the persecuting of Christians.

3:11: "**I am coming quickly! Hold on to what you have so that no one can take your crown.**" This is the fourth time the coming of Messiah is mentioned as the ongoing inspection of Christians.

The things that they "have" concern their walk with Jesus in truth. Here the Calvinistic view of salvation in its "once saved always saved" teaching is shown to be false because failure to "hold on" could mean a Christian's loss of his crown i.e. the crown of life (2:10).

3:12a: "**I will make anyone who overcomes a pillar in the sanctuary of my God, and they will not go out of it anymore.**" Pillars have stability and permanence. So this promise gives the Christian assurance of entry into the Kingdom, their permanence in it, and their total security.

3:12b: "**I will write on them the name of my God and the name of the city of my God, the New Jerusalem which comes down out of heaven from my God, and my new name.**" This shows the falseness of the doctrine of the Trinity. Jesus speaks of "my God" i.e. one whom he worships. This would not be appropriate if Jesus were a co-equal God Almighty.

This is the first mention of the New Jerusalem, although it is also expressed as "the Jerusalem that is above (Gal. 4:26) and "the heavenly Jerusalem" (Heb. 12:22). This is a symbolic way of expressing the citizenship that each one who overcomes will have in the Kingdom.

3:13: "**Anyone who has ears ought to listen to what the spirit is saying to the communities.**" The "spirit of Jesus" (Acts 16:7; Rom. 8:9) is "the spirit" which gives this warning, so that each Christian will open their heart and mind to Kingdom truths.

▲

40

TEXT   **7. Laodicea**

¹⁴"And to the angel of the Christian community in Laodicea write: 'This is the message from the Amen, the faithful and authentic witness, the ruler of God's creation. ¹⁵I know your activities: you are neither cold nor hot. I wish you were either cold or hot! ¹⁶So, because you are lukewarm, neither hot nor cold, I am about to spit you out of my mouth. ¹⁷You are saying, "I am rich and have become wealthy and need nothing," so you don't realize that you are wretched, pitiful, poor, blind, and naked. ¹⁸I strongly advise you: buy gold refined by fire from me so that you may be rich. Buy white clothing so that you may clothe yourself, and the shame of your nakedness may not be seen. Also buy ointment from me to rub on your eyes so that you may see! ¹⁹All those I hold dear, I reprove and discipline. So be constantly zealous and turn away from your indifference! ²⁰Take note: I'm standing at the door and knocking. If anyone hears my voice and opens the door, I will come in to them and we will share a meal together.

²¹To anyone who overcomes I will give permission for them to sit with me on my throne, just as I also overcame and sat down with my Father on His throne. ²²Anyone who has ears ought to listen to what the spirit is saying to the communities of believers.'"

TRANSLATION POINT

3:14: "the ruler (Gk *arche*) of God's creation." The Greek word *arche* is variously rendered: beginning, origin, originator, cause, source, originating source, head, chief, sovereign, or ruler. *Arche* has a double meaning of which head, chief, sovereign, or ruler fit better with the context of the new Creation described in Revelation 3. *Arche* is also rendered "ruler" in the CEB, the CJB, the ERV, the NCV, and the NIV.

Comment on Laodicea

3:14: "**Write: This is the message from the Amen, the faithful and authentic witness, the ruler of God's creation.**" As the Amen Jesus confirms or verifies the solemn truths that are given in these messages to the seven communities. He also confirms his authority to give the necessary judgments because he, as the slaughtered lamb, overcame the world (John 16:33).

Regarding Jesus as "the ruler of God's creation" the context shows that "the creation" noted here began with Christ's death and resurrection so that Jesus became the beginning or ruler of the New Creation, he being the first to be resurrected to immortality and therefore: "...the firstborn (pre-eminent one) of the dead" *(Rev. 1:5, 18)* just as Paul had earlier called Jesus, "...the firstborn from the dead" *(Col. 1:18)*. Indeed,

41

the immediate context of Revelation 3:14 is that of his words to the New Creation in the seven communities, so that they would remain as faithful Christians. To this New Creation Jesus says, "Hold on to what you have so that no one takes your crown" (vs. 11), "I will make them pillars in the temple of my God...I will write on them the name of my God and the name of the city of my God, the New Jerusalem that comes down out of heaven from my God. I will also write on them my own new name" (vs 12), and "I will grant to him to sit with me on my throne" (vs 21).

Also, please note that the context or 3:14 is in the present tense showing that this is not a reference to the time of the original creation. It refers to the creation which came into existence at the time of writing for: "...us to be a certain first fruits of his creatures" or "first fruits of his creation" (*Jas 1:18 REB)*. This is just as the phrase "firstborn of creation" refers to the new creation rather than meaning that Christians were the first ever of creation. For the above reasons the translators of the NLT saw fit to render verse 14 as:

❖ "This is the message from the one who is the Amen—the faithful and true witness, the beginning of God's new creation."

This New Creation, noted in Galatians 6:15 and 2 Corinthians 5:17 will finally involve the ultimate regeneration of believers, rather than the material creation. Sadly, the focus by Justin Martyr in 150 C.E on a pre-existent Christ as creator of the physical creation effectively removed Jesus from his status as the ruler, beginning, the first-born, pre-eminent one, and agent of the new creation.

3:15-16: "I know your activities: you are neither cold nor hot. I wish you were either cold or hot! So, because you are lukewarm, neither hot nor cold, I am about to spit you out of my mouth." The Laodiceans would understand the term "lukewarm" very well because their piped in water from hot springs arrived lukewarm. When applied to them it showed them to be self-satisfied, indifferent, and complacent, even feeling that they were doing very well spiritually. In reality, they were simply Christians in name only. Because of this there were not even any false teachings to be dealt with and whatever works they were doing seem to be "dead works."

The spitting, spewing, or vomiting out of the mouth is a figure of speech meaning "to completely reject someone" and so warning them of the very dangerous spiritual condition that they were in.

3:17: "**You are saying, 'I am rich and have become wealthy and need nothing. So you don't realize that you are wretched, pitiful, poor, blind, and naked.**" This threefold statement to emphasize the material prosperity and self-sufficiency of Laodicea contradicts the proposal by some that Revelation was written in the late 60s C.E. This is because at that time Laodicea had experienced a severe earthquake which had largely destroyed it and so making her no longer prosperous. Nevertheless, by the mid-90s this Christian community incorrectly thought that their relatively new material prosperity was a sign that they had God's favour.

The Laodiceans' self-evaluation was misguided. Spiritually they were literally wretched and pitiful, but the last three terms are metaphorical language used to underline their wretchedness and truly pitiful spiritual condition. They were suffering from spiritual poverty in contrast to their material wealth. Their blindness shows their inability to understand their true spiritual condition, and their nakedness shows them to be in a shameful state in contrast to the pride that they displayed concerning themselves. Nevertheless, the Laodiceans were not completely beyond hope as shown by the following call to repentance.

3:18a: "**I strongly advise you: Buy gold refined by fire.**" If gold is refined then it will not tarnish. This refined gold really illustrates that when a Christian undergoes trials and suffering he/she will become refined in faith which has now grown stronger.

3:18b: "**Buy white clothing so that you may clothe yourself, and the shame of your nakedness may not be seen.**" Being naked was seen as shameful to Jews and so these Christians needed to cover themselves because Jesus describes them as being naked. However, they must have a covering that shows their purity which is what white clothing will do for them and meaning that they will remain "unspotted from the world" (Jas. 1:27).

3:18c: "**Also buy ointment from me to rub on your eyes so that you may see!**" The Laodicean Christians could easily obtain the famous Phrygian eye-salve and so understand that Jesus speaks of figurative eye medication that was for removing spiritual blindness. James 1:23-25 says,

"If anyone is merely a hearer of the message and not one who lives it out, he's like a man observing his face in a mirror. He looks at

43

himself and goes away and immediately forgets what he looked like. But the person who peers into the perfect law—the law of freedom— and continues looking, so that they are not a forgetful hearer but an active doer, will be blessed in their actions."

By such peering into "the law of freedom" they would see themselves as they actually are and be helped to correct their thinking with their newly acquired clear spiritual eyesight.

3:19: "**All those I hold dear, I reprove and discipline. So be constantly zealous and turn away from your indifference!**" The phrase "hold dear" is the Greek word *phileo* as meaning "to have affection for." This shows that reproof and discipline can be acts of love for a person as shown in the Proverbs 3:11-12; 13:24, and in Hebrews 12:5-6. This reproof is given hoping for the right response from the reproved person as shown here concerning their necessary change of mindset. The term "to reprove" can also be rendered "to correct" as pointing out a problem to someone and directing them to do something about it to save them from being on a course that will be detrimental to them.

3:20: "**Take note: I'm standing at the door and knocking. If anyone hears my voice and opens the door, I will come in to them and we will share a meal together.**" In John 14:23 Jesus says, "If anyone loves me they will follow my teaching, and my Father will love them, and we will come to them and make our home with them." It is in this sense that Jesus knocks at the door of each Christian so as to "come in to them and...share a meal together."

3:21: "**To anyone who overcomes I will give permission for them to sit with me on my throne, just as I also overcame and sat down with my Father on His throne.**" Thrones indicate sovereignty and Jesus has been allowed to share God's sovereignty. However, this goes one step further than Jesus' promise that, "when the Son of Man is seated on his glorious throne, you who have followed me will also sit on twelve thrones, justly governing the twelve tribes of Israel" (Matt.19:28), because here Jesus is offering to share his sovereignty with those who are conquerors.

§

Chapter 8

Preparing for Spiritual Preservation

I hope that the following drawing together of the various aspects of the above divine messages to the seven Christian communities will prove helpful to readers. Indeed, because these messages are in a stereotyped pattern what is said to all seven of them can be set under the following headings:

1. Jesus' Description of Himself for All Seven Communities

Ephesus: "him who holds the seven stars in his right hand, and who is walking about among the seven golden lampstands."
Smyrna: "the first and the last, the one who was dead, but came to life"
Pergamum: "him who has the sharp two-edged sword."
Thyatira: "the Son of God, who has eyes like a flame of fire, and whose feet are like burnished bronze...I am the one who searches thoughts and motives"
Sardis: "the one who has the seven spirits of God and the seven stars."
Philadelphia: "the holy one, the authentic one, who has the key of David. When he opens a door, no one can close it, and when he closes it, no one can open it."
Laodicea: "the Amen, the faithful and authentic witness, the ruler of God's creation."

2. The Strengths of the Seven Communities

Ephesus: hard work, resolute endurance, cannot tolerate wicked people, but you've tested those claiming to be apostles but are not,"
Smyrna: "your sufferings and your poverty (but really you are rich)."
Pergamum: "you continue to be committed to everything that I stand for, and you didn't renounce my faith even in the days of Antipas my faithful witness"
Thyatira: "I know your activities: your love and faith and service and resolute endurance, and that your later activities exceed the earlier ones."
Sardis: "you have a few of people⬧in Sardis, who haven't dirtied their clothes,"
Philadelphia: "yet you have kept my message and didn't repudiate the things I stand for."
Laodicea: NONE

3. The Weaknesses of the Seven Communities

Ephesus: "you've abandoned the love you had at first."
Smyrna: NONE
Pergamum: "you have some people there who are committed to the teaching of Balaam, who instructed Balak to lay a trap for the children of Israel, so that they

would eat food sacrificed to idols and commit sexual immorality. **¹⁵**You also have some who are committed to the teaching of the Nicolaitans."

Thyatira: "you are tolerating that woman Jezebel, who claims to be a prophetess. She teaches and deceives my bond-servants to commit sexual immorality and to eat food sacrificed to idols."

Sardis: "I haven't found your activities complete in the sight of my God."

Philadelphia: "You have only a little power,"

Laodicea: "neither cold nor hot...you are wretched, pitiful, poor, blind, and naked."

4. The Counsel Given to the Seven Communities

Ephesus: "remember from where you have fallen and turn back to it, and do the activities you did at first."

Smyrna: "Stop being afraid of the things you are about to suffer. Take note: the Devil is about to throw some of you into prison, so that you may be tested, and you will experience tribulation for ten days. Remain faithful even in the face of death"

Pergamum: "Turn away from these things!"

Thyatira: "stay committed to what you have until I come."

Sardis: "Wake up! Strengthen the remaining things that were about to die...**³**So remember how you received and heard the message! Keep it, and turn your thinking and behaviour around.

Philadelphia: "Hold on to what you have"

Laodicea: "buy gold refined by fire from me so that you may be rich. Buy white clothing so that you may clothe yourself...Also buy ointment from me to rub on your eyes so that you may see!

4. Actions That Jesus Will Take For Failure to Apply the Counsel

Ephesus: "If not, I will come to you and remove your lampstand from its place— that is, if you don't turn back."

Smyrna: NONE

Pergamum: "If not, I will come against you suddenly and make war against those people with the sword of my mouth."

Thyatira: "I will throw her onto a bed of suffering, and bring down severe suffering on those who commit adultery with her, unless they turn away from following her activities. **²³**I will kill her children with death-dealing disease...and all the communities of believers will know that I am the one who searches thoughts and motives... I will give to each of you according to your activities."

Sardis: "If you are not watchful, I will come like a thief, and you won't know at what time I will come to you."

Philadelphia: "I am going to make those people of the Satan's synagogue, who declare themselves to be Jews though they aren't, but are lying—take note, I will make them come and kneel in honour at your feet, and they will know that I have loved you."

Laodicea: "I am about to spit you out of my mouth."

6. The Rewards Offered to Conquerors in the Seven Communities

Ephesus: To "grant for them to eat of the tree of the perfect life, which is in the paradise of God.'"

Smyrna: They "will never be harmed by the second death.'"

Pergamum: "I will give [them] some of the hidden manna. I will also give them a white stone with a new name written on it."

Thyatira: They will be "given authority over the nations, to rule them with an iron sceptre. And I will give them the morning star."

Sardis: They will be "clothed in white clothing." Jesus will "never erase their name from the book of the perfect life." "I will confess their name in the presence of my Father and of His angels."

Philadelphia: Jesus will "make them...a pillar in the sanctuary of my God, and they won't go out of it anymore. I will write on them the name of my God and the name of the city of my God, the New Jerusalem, which comes down out of heaven from my God, and my new name."

Laodicea: "I will give permission for them to sit with me on my throne."

So if Christians individually analyse themselves in relation to all these points that have been made to these seven communities and then, where applicable, apply Jesus' counsel to themselves, they will stand in a much better position before God and Jesus the Messiah and in a good position to stand fast during the great tribulation.

§

Chapter 9

A Picture of God's Throne Room in Heaven
Revelation 4 ... The beginning of Vision Two

TEXT

After these things I looked, and there was an opened door in heaven! The first voice that I had heard speaking to me sounded like a trumpet. It said to me: "Come up here, and I will show you what must happen after these things." [2]Immediately I was in a prophetic trance. A throne was in place in heaven with someone sitting on it! [3]And the One sitting on it was like jasper and carnelian in appearance, and a rainbow with the appearance of emerald encircled the throne. [4]Around the throne were twenty-four other thrones, and sitting on those thrones were twenty-four elders, having been dressed in white robes and with golden crowns on their heads. [5]Flashes of lightning, rumblings, and thunderclaps were coming out from the throne; and seven fiery torches, which are the seven spirits of God, were burning in front of the throne. [6]Also in front of the throne was something like a glassy sea, like crystal.

In the centre, around the throne, were four living creatures full of eyes in front and behind. [7]The first living creature was like a lion, the second creature like a young bull, the third creature had a face like a man's, and the fourth creature looked like a flying eagle. [8]Each one of the four living creatures had six wings, and they were full of eyes all around and inside. Day and night they have no rest as they say: "Holy, holy, holy is the LORD God, the All-Powerful, who was and who is, and who is coming."

[9]And whenever the living creatures give glory, honour, and thanks to the One who was sitting on the throne, who lives forever and ever, [10]the twenty-four elders fall to the ground in front of the One who was sitting on the throne and kneel in worship of the One who lives forever and ever. They throw their crowns in front of His throne, saying:

[11]"Our LORD and God, you are worthy to receive glory and honour and power, because you have created all things, and because of your will they existed and were created."

Comment on the Throne Room Events

4:1a: "**After these things I looked, and there was an opened door in heaven!**" This is simply the door to revelation for John, so that in his trance-like state he has access to heaven right up to the events in 10:1.

4:1b: "**The first voice that I had heard speaking to me sounded like a trumpet. It said to me: "Come up here and I will show you what must happen after these things.""** In being like a trumpet, this voice is one which makes prophetic announcements. However, this is not any kind of

48

literal taking of John into heaven in the first century or even a picture of the future rapture. There is nothing in the Scriptures to indicate that John is representative of the body of Christians. He was, in fact, spiritually in God's presence in the heavenly sanctuary in preparation to receive the visions that he was to record.

4:2-3: "**Immediately I was in a prophetic trance. A throne was in place in heaven with someone sitting on it! ³And One sitting on it was like jasper and carnelian, and a rainbow with the appearance of emerald encircled the throne.**" This trance is the marker for John's second vision and which runs right up to the events in 16:17. Evidently this is God Himself on the throne in the throne room which is the Holy of Holies part of the temple existing in heaven.

The two jewels are symbolic of God's glory and the rainbow is the reminder of God's covenant not to flood the land again (Gen. 9:12-17).

4:4: "**Around the throne were twenty-four other thrones, and sitting on those thrones were twenty-four elders, having been dressed in white robes and with golden crowns on their heads**" These are not Christians, but angelic creatures because:

- They are called *"thrones, powers, or authorities"* (Col. 1:16); therefore sitting on thrones and wearing crowns is appropriate. Angels are often seen wearing white. In fact, the phrase "His elders" in Isaiah 24:23 may refer to angels.
- The context of Rev. 5:8-10 shows that, as the singers of the song about the priests to our God, they are differentiated from Christians.
- In Rev.14:1-5 the elders are mentioned as separate from the company of the "first fruits" of 144,000.
- In Rev.11:16-18 the 24 elders are separate from the holy ones i.e. Christians.
- The 24 elders are not shown to have come from the earth.

It is likely that the twenty-four elders, as well as the four living creatures, are God's divine and royal council (Dan 7:9) and that it was to these that He spoke in the Genesis accounts.

4:5a: "**Flashes of lightning, rumblings, and thunderclaps were coming out from the throne.**" These are conventional ways of expressing the power and majesty of God's judgments. They are mentioned later in 8:5, 11:19, and 16:18 and help to identify the sequence of certain events.

4:5b: "**And seven fiery torches which are the seven spirits of God.**" These "fiery torches" are the seven archangels (see 1:4). As Hebrews 1:7 shows, "He makes his angels winds and his ministers <u>a flame of fire</u> …ministering spirits."

4:6a: "**Also in front of the throne was something like a glassy sea, like crystal.**" This glassy sea is likely a reference to the expanse of waters in Genesis 1:7, or "the shape of an expanse, with a gleam like awe-inspiring crystal" beneath God's throne *(Ezek. 1:22-26)* and is simply to further show the majesty and tranquillity of God's presence.

4:6b: "**In the centre, around the throne, were four living creatures full of eyes in front and behind.**" This description seems primarily to be a description of the *cherubim* with their four wings each (Ezek. 1:5-14; 10:14-15). However, in this verse, these four spirit creatures have six wings (vs. 8) which is a feature of the *seraphim* (Isa. 6:2). So because the description here is mostly the features of the cherubim, David Aune uses the term "cherubim" in his rendering of these passages, although other commentators see these creatures as *seraphim* because of their each having six wings.

However, if these creatures are cherubs then their location seems to be that they are positioned at the four corners of God's throne, but below it (Ezek. 1:22-26).

These ones appear to be the very highest order of heavenly beings. Their functions appear to be: taking the lead in worship, standing guard over the throne, and taking the lead in pouring out God's judgments. Their eyes picture their complete ability to see everything that happens and with ceaseless vigilance (Zech. 4:10).

4:7: "**The first living creature was like a lion, the second creature like a young bull, the third creature had a face like a man's, and the fourth creature looked like a flying eagle.**" This picture is drawn from Ezekiel 1:5-6, 10-11a. The most viable interpretation is that the faces of these four spirit creatures is that they represent the whole of animate creation detailing what is noblest, strongest, wisest, and swiftest in this description combining the features of the *seraphim* and the *cherubim.*

4:8a: "**Each one of the four living creatures had <u>six wings</u>, and they were full of eyes all around and inside.**" Again "the six wings" on each creature strangely focuses on a major feature of the seraphim, even though all other features are those of cherubim.

50

4:8b: "**Day and night they have no rest as they say: "Holy, holy, holy is the LORD God, the All-Powerful, who was and who is, and who is coming**." The phrase of, "who was and who is, and who is coming" seems to be a paraphrase of "I will be what I will be" in Exodus 3:14 (Moffatt Amplified, CJB, and footnotes in REB and ESV) or "I will become whatsoever I please" (Ro). This refers to the divine name "Yahweh" in Exodus 3:15 and it shows His decisive intervention in history as well as His future intervention in human affairs.

4:9: "**And whenever the living creatures give glory, honour, and thanks to the One who was sitting on the throne, who lives forever and ever.**" Even some of the highest ranking creatures in the universe humbly give glory, honour, and thanks to Yahweh God, because He is God.

The four living creatures i.e., the cherubs, praise God because of His essential nature i.e. He is the One "who was and who is, and who is coming" (verse 8b).

4:10: "**The twenty-four elders fall to the ground in front of the One who was sitting on the throne and kneel in worship of the One who lives forever and ever. They throw their crowns in front of His throne.**" The order of the concentric circles around the throne is firstly the four living creatures, then the 24 elders, and finally the myriads of angels in 5:11. All of these join in worship of God Almighty who sits on the throne.

4:11: "**Saying: "Our LORD and God, you are worthy to receive glory and honour and power, because you have created all things, and because of your will they existed and were created.**" When combined with Isaiah 44:24 this verse becomes a proof text showing that Jesus was not the creator of the physical universe. Only Yahweh is the creator of the physical universe and was completely unaided as shown by Isaiah.

The worship given by the 24 elders is for a different reason than that offered by the four living creatures. Here the 24 elders praise God because He is the creator of everything. However, the rather strange statement of "they existed and were created" probably means that the creation existed in God's mind first and then later it was actually created.

§

51

Chapter 10

Jesus Receives the Seven-Sealed Scroll
Revelation 5

TEXT

The Lamb Receives the Scroll

Then I saw a scroll in the right hand of the One who was sitting on the throne. It was written on the inside and on the back, and it was sealed with seven seals. **2**And I saw a powerful angel proclaiming in a loud voice: "Who is worthy to open the scroll by breaking its seals?" **3**But no one in heaven or on earth or under the earth was able to open the scroll or look inside it. **4**So I began crying bitterly because no one was found who was worthy to open the scroll or to look inside it. **5**Then one of the elders said to me, "Stop crying! Take note, the Lion of the tribe of Judah, the root-shoot of David, has conquered; so that he may open the scroll and its seven seals."

6Then I saw, standing between the throne and the four living creatures, and among the elders, a Lamb as though it had been slaughtered. It had seven horns and seven eyes, which are the seven spirits of God sent out into all the earth. **7**Then he came and took the scroll from the right hand of the One who was sitting on the throne. **8**When he had taken the scroll, the four living creatures and the twenty-four elders fell to the ground in front of the Lamb. Each one had a harp and a golden bowl full of incense, which symbolize the prayers of God's holy people. **9**They are singing a new song:

"You are worthy to take the scroll, and to open its seals because you were slaughtered, and with your own blood you have ransomed people for God. These are from every tribe, language, nation, and race. **10**You have made them a kingdom and priests for our God, and they will reign on the earth**."**

11As I looked, I heard the voice of many angels around the throne, the living creatures, and the elders. Their number was ten thousand times ten thousand— thousands times thousands—**12**all of whom were saying with a loud voice:

"Worthy is the slaughtered lamb to receive power, wealth, wisdom, strength, honour, glory, and praise!"

13Then I heard every creature in heaven, on earth, under the earth, in the sea, and everything that is in them saying:

"To the One seated on the throne and to the Lamb be praise, honour, glory, and dominion forever and ever!"

14And the four living creatures were saying "Amen," and the elders fell to the ground and knelt in worship.

TRANSLATION POINTS

5:5: "The root-shoot (Gk *riza*)." Although the word *riza* means "root" it also means, "that which grows from a root," according to *Bauer's Greek-English Lexicon*, hence the rendering "root-shoot" here showing that Jesus is a descendent of David.

5:10: "Made <u>them</u> a kingdom and priests for our God." In verses 8 and 9 the twenty-four elders are shown to be singing a new song. However the KJV rendered verse 10 as "us" and so making it appear that the 24 elders were singing the new song to themselves and that therefore the 24 elders were to be understood as being Christians. However, modern study of the text and translations shows that the rendering should be "they" so that the twenty-four elders are a separate group from the Christians.

Comment on Jesus Receiving the Scroll

5:1: "**Then I saw a scroll in the right hand of the One who was sitting on the throne. It was written on the inside and on the back. It was sealed with seven seals**" This scroll is a symbol of God's promises and affirms the Lamb's right to rule. It is a contract deed containing God's plan of redemption along with end-time prophecies and judgments that lead to the inauguration of the Kingdom.

The scroll is not opened until all seven seals are broken. The number seven simply shows that the scroll is completely and tightly sealed. So after the breaking of the seventh seal the contents of the scroll are revealed—the first half of which concerns the first six trumpets and the second half concerns the seventh trumpet which reveals the seven bowls of plague. This second half is only available to John after he digests this information as described in Revelation 10.

5:2: "**And I saw a powerful angel proclaiming in a loud voice: "Who is worthy to open the scroll by breaking its seals?"**" This powerful angel appears three times in the Revelation (10:1-2; 18:21) and is most likely an archangel acting as a royal herald. Although God Himself is worthy to open the scroll He delegates this task to someone else who is also worthy.

5:3: "**But no one in heaven or on earth or under the earth was able to open the scroll or look inside it.**" Because of the early belief in a three tiered cosmos this phrase, came to mean "no one or nowhere in the entire universe."

53

5:4: "**So I began crying bitterly because no one was found who was worthy to open the scroll or to look inside it.**" The reason that no one was found was because in the entire universe no one except Jesus had made the necessary sacrifice so that sin and all evil might finally be wiped out.

So John's weeping was over the likelihood that all the events concerning the coming Kingdom will not finally be realized and his anticipation of seeing these things revealed in the scroll seemed to be dashed.

5:5: "**Then one of the elders said to me, "Stop crying! Take note, the Lion of the tribe of Judah, the root-shoot of David, has conquered; so that he may open the scroll and its seven seals.**" This is one of the 24 elders i.e. a heavenly being.

"The Lion of the tribe of Judah" is the messianic royal title taken from Genesis 49:9, 10 and applied to Jesus; and "the root-shoot of David" is another messianic royal title and alludes to Isaiah 11:1. The root and the shoot both grow out of the seed (David) of a plant which shows that Jesus originated from David, and therefore he did not exist in any form other than human before David existed.

5:6: "**Then I saw, standing between the throne and the four living creatures, and among the elders a Lamb as though it had been slaughtered. It had seven horns and seven eyes, which are the seven spirits of God sent out into all the earth.**" Please see *4:4* and *4:6b*. Along with the "four living creatures" the twenty-four elders constitute God's heavenly court which bows in honour to the Lamb.

Not only is Jesus viewed as the Lion of the tribe of Judah, but also as the atoning sacrificial Lamb having paid for mankind's sins.

These horns and eyes symbolize complete power and total ability to see everything that happens (Zech. 4:10). The resurrected Jesus now has at his disposal the seven principle angels with their full power and vision. These are also the "*seven torches of fire*" of 4:5. These archangels act as the power and discernment of Jesus. But unlike Jesus as "the spirit" whose sphere is the Christian communities, these seven spirits are sent out into all the earth. This is also the time of the investiture of the Son of man as noted in Daniel 7.

5:7: "**Then he came and took the scroll from the right hand of the One...**" This demonstrates a transfer of authority from God to the Lamb, so that he is now in a position of authority as Lord of all affairs in heaven and on earth.

5:8: "When he had taken the scroll, the four living creatures and the twenty-four elders fell to the ground in front of the Lamb. Each one had a harp and a golden bowl full of incense, which symbolize the prayers of God's holy people." Indeed, none of the Greek words for "worship" are used here. This falling to the ground is simply in honour of the Lamb who has now been charged and entrusted with bringing about God's purpose for the earth, including that of judgment.

These harps were not like the Welsh harp, but more like a lyre with ten or more strings, only with a shallower sounding board. Indeed, these harps are the musical accompaniment to the singing of the new song in the next verse.

Each golden bowl is a reference to temple utensils (1 King 7:50) and the incense symbolizes prayers as also in Psalm 141:2 and Luke 1:10.

5:9: "They are singing a new song: "You are worthy to take the scroll, and to open its seals because you were slaughtered, and with your own blood you have ransomed people for God. These are from every tribe, language, nation, and race. This is a new kind of song sung to the Lamb. It is eschatological and concerns the rejoicing over the redemption of God's people and the future establishment of the Kingdom.

The basis of Jesus' worthiness to break the seals of the scroll is his sacrificial death (Isa, 53:7) which resulted in a victory over Satan and will later result in the conquering of Antichrist. This sacrificial death also ransoms (1 Cor. 6:20) people and so making it a payment to buy people for God to set them free from bondage to sin. It is the basis for reconciling them to God.

5:10: "You have made them a kingdom and priests for our God, and they will reign on the earth." This statement alludes to Exodus 19:6 concerning the promise made to Israel that they will become "a kingdom of priests." In fact, two roles are presented here which can be seen later in the listing of the 144,000 and the description of "the great multitude" (Rev. 7). This concept of kings and priests reflects the Order of Melchizedek in Hebrews 7. So Jesus' sacrificial death also enables Christians to become rulers with him. These ones are corporately a "kingdom" and individually they are priests.

5:11: "As I looked, I heard the voice of many angels around the throne, the living creatures, and the elders. Their number was ten thousand times ten thousand—thousands times thousands." This picture moves the events on to a new section where we have an allusion to Daniel 7:10 with its picture of an infinite number of angels. Here in Revelation the number 10,000 is the highest number that was used in the Greek world. So this, too, is a picture of an infinite number of angels who form the fourth circle around the throne.

5:12: "**All of whom were saying with a loud voice: "Worthy is the slaughtered lamb to receive power, wealth, wisdom, strength, honour, glory, and praise!**" Again Jesus' worthiness is highlighted in the phrase "slaughtered lamb." It focuses on Jesus' sacrifice to deal with human sin and to bring about reconciliation to the Heavenly Father. So these seven attributes of the Lamb leave nothing missing from Jesus' great qualities and so giving faithful ones great confidence in him as earth's future administrator.

5:13: "**To the One seated on the throne and to the Lamb.**" Because authority has been transferred from God to the Lamb for the establishment of the Kingdom the Lamb is also praised. However, he is praised and revered, not only as the sacrificial Lamb, but also as "the lion of the tribe of Judah"—the Messiah (5:5). So he is not praised as if he were God Almighty who is always shown as completely separate from the Lamb.

5:14: "**And the four living creatures were saying 'Amen,' and the elders fell to the ground and knelt in worship.**" Although Jesus certainly should be praised and revered, only God should be worshipped, as seen in 19:10 and 22:8 where John knelt in worship of the angel who corrects him by saying, "Don't do that!...You must worship God!"

§

Chapter 11

The Pattern of the Seven Seals, Trumpets, and Bowls

One's view of the pattern of the seals, trumpets, and bowls of wrath has a significant bearing on where one understands the placement of the various factors and events to be in the sequence of things in Revelation. But before examining that sequence there are some important details to take note of. These are:

SEVEN SEALS (Rev. 6:1-8:2) are laid out as 4 + 1 + 1 then the insertion of Chap. 7 sealing of 144,000 + 1.

The first four are the horse riders, then the fifth seal Christian martyrs, then the sixth seal announcement of the Day of the Lord, then the Chapter 7 insertion concerning the 144,000, and finally the seventh seal which concerns the seven trumpets.

SEVEN TRUMPETS (Rev. 8:2, 6 to 9:21 and 11:15-19) are laid out as 4 + 1 + 1 then the insertion of Chap. 10—opened scroll to Chap. 11—two witnesses + 1.

The first four of the trumpets apply to the four divisions of creation—earth, sea, fresh waters, sky (sun) affecting one third of each aspect of creation. The fifth trumpet is a locust/demon attack which merely causes severe pain to those without the seal of God. The sixth trumpet is that of the four demon angels with their 200 million cavalry/demons which actually kill one third of wicked mankind. The seventh trumpet zooms in closer to the final judgment of the seven bowls of plague. Therefore, it is the same final judgment that is reached in the seventh of each of the three series.

THREE WOES (Rev. 8:13; 9:12; 11:14) indicate sequence and correspond to the blowing of trumpets 5, 6, and 7.

SEVEN BOWLS (Rev. 15:1; 15:5 to 16:21) form a 4 + 3 pattern, but without any interlude. The first four of the bowls also apply to the four divisions of creation—earth, sea, fresh waters, sky (sun) affecting each aspect of creation entirely. The last three bowls are concerned with the judgment of the beast and his city.

Some scholars propose any one of the following patterns:
- Seals, trumpets and bowls as all running in parallel so that Bowl 1 is contained within Trumpet 1 which is contained in Seal 1.

- Seals, trumpets and bowls as running completely sequentially.
- A so-called Semitic style, whereby Trumpet 1 is blown at the time of Seal 4, and so forth; and Bowl 1 is poured out with the blowing of Trumpet 4, and so forth.

However, none of these patterns or adaptations of them seems to fit the details presented in the Revelation.

What the Seventh Seal Encompasses

The following is the pattern that is most accepted by the various scholars, because it seems clear from Revelation 8 that the seven trumpet blasts are contained within the seventh seal. The seventh trumpet blast (11:15-19) speaks of, *"the time to punish"* the nations *"has arrived,"* and that it is *"the time to destroy those who are destroying the earth."* This fits well with the outpouring of the bowls of plague described in Revelation 15 and 16 as being within the time of this seventh trumpet blast. So the pattern for the **seventh seal** is:

$$<\text{--------- } 7^{\text{th}} \text{ S e a l } \text{-------------------------------} >$$

Trumpets: 1 2 3 4 5 6 $<\text{---------} 7^{\text{th}} \text{ Trumpet} \text{------------} >$
Woes: 1 2   3
              Bowls: 1 2 3 4 5 6 7

Here the scroll will only be opened when the seventh seal is broken. So it is the seven trumpets which constitute the seventh seal and the seven bowls which constitute the seventh trumpet. Only the trumpets and bowls are the contents of the scroll and these bowls are not poured out on all of mankind, but only on "the earth-dwellers," that is, the followers of Antichrist.

A further factor indicating that this pattern is correct is the fact that the phrase, *"and there were thunderclaps, rumblings, flashes of lightning, and an earthquake"* is common to the seventh of each of the seals, trumpets, and bowls. This is seen in *8:1-5* (seventh seal); *11:15, 19a* (seventh trumpet); and *16:18* (seventh bowl of plague).

The seventh trumpet (Rev. 11) is also the time when God's servants get their rewards and so indicating that the great tribulation has ended. The Apostle Paul shows that the first resurrection takes place during *"the last trumpet"* (1 Cor. 15:52) when Jesus appears so that: *"he will send* out his angels with a **loud trumpet** call, and they **will gather** His elect from the four winds..." (Matt. 24: 30, 31 ESV). Paul gives us further information on this when he says:

❖ "The Lord himself will descend from heaven...with the voice of an archangel, and with the *sound of the* **trumpet** *of God*...the dead in Christ will rise first. Then, we who are alive, who are left will be caught up *together with them* in clouds to meet (Lit. *"for a meeting with"* Gk. *apantesis*) the Lord in the air" *(1 Thess. 4:16-17 ESV)*.

THE SEVENTH TRUMPET IN RELATION TO THE SEVEN BOWLS

Furthermore, the blasting of the **seventh trumpet** (11:15-19) may either encompass all seven bowl judgments or each bowl runs parallel to each trumpet. The proofs of this connection are:

1) The same event of the use of the incense altar (*8:1-5*—seventh seal) when God's **sanctuary in heaven is opened** and the ark of his covenant is seen within his temple (*11:15, 19a*—seventh trumpet) and when the seven angels bring out the seven bowls of plagues from the sanctuary in *15:5.*
2) The seventh of each series is linked by the flashes of lightning, rumblings and peals of thunder, and **earthquake** (8:5, 11:19, and 16:18). There is a further link back to the throne of God event in Revelation 4, but without mention of the earthquake.
3) The verbal parallels between each trumpet and each bowl give strong reason to understand this pattern as being that of actual parallels between the trumpets and the bowls. For instance the first four of the trumpets and bowls are poured out on the land, the sea, the rivers, and the atmosphere. This makes this the more likely pattern. However, there are no true parallels between seals and trumpets.

The Overall Pattern of End-Time Events

With all of the above factors noted it is now possible to construct a further chart involving the timings given first by Daniel and factors added by Jesus concerning the future events. Indeed, this pattern shows that Christians are never snatched up into the air **to escape** either the great tribulation or the time of God's wrath. However, during this latter time they are fully protected.

1260 days	30 days (end of 1290 day period)
Seals 4, 5 and 6a	Seals 6b and 7 (trumpets/bowls)
Great Tribulation	Celestial Phenomena
	Day of the Lord
	God's Wrath
	Descent of Jesus
	Resurrection (sixth bowl)

A notable proof of the time of the rapture is found in Revelation 16:16 —a text which shows that Christians still have not been given immortality at the time of the gathering of the armies in Armageddon and so are still on earth.

In later chapters we will examine more on how this pattern fits with Daniel's 70th "Seven," other time periods, and the timing of the first resurrection and rapture.

Now we move on to examine the details of the scroll which Jesus has been handed and to note his breaking of its seals.

§

Chapter 12

Breaking of the First Four Seals
Revelation 6:1-8

TEXT

The First Seal

I watched as the Lamb broke open one of the seven seals. Then I heard one of the four living creatures saying as with the sound of thunder, "Come!" **²**So I looked, and there was a white horse! The one riding it had a bow. He was also given a crown, and as a conqueror he rode out in order to conquer.

The Second Seal

³Then when he broke open the second seal, I heard the second living creature saying, "Come!" **⁴**And another horse, fiery red, went out. The one riding it was given permission to take peace from the earth, so that people would kill each other, and he was given a large sword.

The Third Seal

⁵Then when he broke open the third seal, I heard the third living creature saying, "Come!" So I looked, and there was a black horse! The one riding it had a pair of scales in his hand. **⁶**Then I heard something like a voice from among the four living creatures saying, "A quart of wheat for a denarius, and three quarts of barley for a denarius; but don't damage the olive oil and the wine."

The Fourth Seal

⁷Then when he broke open the fourth seal, I heard the voice of the fourth living creature saying, "Come!" **⁸**As I looked, there was a deathly pale horse! The name of the one riding it was Death. Hades followed right behind him. They were given authority over a quarter of the earth, to kill with the sword, and with famine, and with plague, and by means of the ferocious beasts of the earth.

Overview

Clearly the riders and horses in the following scenarios are simply pictures i.e. symbols of certain realities. However, to say, as some do, that all of these riders are simply the concepts of war, famine and plague rather than concerning the known individual who causes these devastations seems to ignore all of the connected Scripture statements about the Antichrist. So in the first four seals each rider and horse likely is a picture of the circumstances and **stages of the career of Antichrist** as he initially imitates Christ, but is soon revealed to be an enemy. This is the view of some including Arthur Pink in his book, *The Antichrist.* So

61

with the background of the Olivet Discourse and Daniel's 70th "seven" we see the rider on the white horse as riding forth in a highly controlled peace which turns into outright war with the fiery-red horse rider and then famine (the black horse) as the result. So these first three seals seem to occur during the first half of the final seven year period.

Then, from the mid-point of the 70th "seven" the fourth horse rider pictures the great tribulation, better expressed as "the great persecution" because it will be Satan's wrath against Christians (Rev. 12:9-12).

Comment on the Breaking of Seals One to Four

SEAL 1

6:1: "**I watched as the Lamb broke open one of the seven seals. Then I heard one of the four living creatures saying as with the sound of thunder, "Come!"** Certainly, a literal lamb could not respond and easily break open a seal. So here John, in vision, sees Jesus as the one breaking open this first seal and therefore showing that the term "Lamb" is simply descriptive of him because he had been the sacrificial "Lamb of God—the one who takes away the sin of the world" (John 1:29, 36).

The command "come" by each of these angelic beings is not directed to Jesus but to each of the riders of the horses.

6:2a: "**So I looked, and there was a white horse! The one riding it had a bow. He was also given a crown.**" This first rider engages in peaceful conquests and appears to be the false and deceptive messiah—the Antichrist; yet, many have taught that this horse rider pictures Christ Jesus. This is because they see a parallel with the picture of him in Revelation 19:11ff. However, this rider on a white horse cannot be Jesus because Jesus is, at this time, in heaven as the one who is opening each of the seven seals (Rev 6:1). Also there are other details which are different between these two white-horse riders. Although the colour white in the Scriptures is symbolic of righteousness and victory, yet with worldly armies it was not always the good leaders or generals who rode white horses. Even the Roman commanders rode white horses in their triumph over enemies. Instead, such white horses often pictured prestige, rather than any moral characteristic. So in the opening of this first seal we see a deception and the rider is actually the Antichrist.

Additionally, unlike Christ in 19:11-16 who has a sword, this white horse rider is like an Assyrian or Persian archer with his bow or even like the most feared archers of the east, namely, the Parthians. In fact, Antichrist is shown in Ezekiel 39:3 as carrying a bow, so that the first readers of Revelation would naturally think of an Oriental rider because the bow was not the weapon of choice of the Romans.

Furthermore, this rider's crown is a (*stephanos*) wreath of victory, not a diadema-royal crown as Christ has in Revelation 19:11ff. This is not to say that Christ could not wear a *stephanos,* but that the picture is different in the two accounts. In fact there are very few similarities or contact points between this description of a horse rider and the one in Revelation 19. Also, the parallels with Jesus' Olivet Discourse strongly indicate a rider who is a picture of the leading "false messiah" i.e. the Antichrist. Indeed, the details of this rider point to an early stage in the career and activities of Antichrist and, as stated above, this ride would seem to begin at the beginning of the final "seven" year period as detailed in Daniel 9.

6:2b: "**And as a conqueror he rode out in order to conquer.**" Compared to Seal Two there is no statement here of any slaughter in the conquering that takes place during this first ride. The fact that the rider on the red horse takes peace from the earth by bloodshed implies that the rider on the white horse first acted during peace time. So this seems to indicate Antichrist's lust for conquest or his bloodless, peaceful conquests. These conquests are effected no doubt by the use of deceptive tactics just as Antichrist appears as a benefactor of mankind in the early stages. This deceptiveness is as described by the prophets (Dan. 8:23, 25; 11:23) and by the Apostle Paul (2Thess. 2:9-11). Indeed, Antichrist's true colours are shown with the opening of the second seal.

....

SEAL 2

6:3-6:4a: "**Then when he broke open the second seal, I heard the second living creature saying, "Come! And another horse, fiery red, went out."** If one acknowledges that the rider of the first horse is a person, but that the other three horse-riders picture devastations without noting the particular rider as the one who causes these things, then there seems to be a mismatch. As Arthur Pink shows it appears that all four horse riders picture the Antichrist, but at various stages of his career as "the King of the North" described in Daniel 11 and during the first half of the final "seven" year period explained in Daniel 9.

Furthermore, the description of the horse as being coloured fiery-red matches the description of Satan as a "fiery-red dragon" (12:3). Also this colour shows the war-like nature of both Satan and his agent, the Antichrist—the prime enemies of God and His people.

6:4b: "**The one riding it was given permission to take peace from the earth. So that people would kill each other and he was given a large sword.**" In this second seal we see Antichrist engaging in warfare and shedding the blood of his enemies, including the holy ones. This seems to indicate that Antichrist's warfare involves the causing of civil war.

The fact that the great sword used here is the *makaira,* as used by the Romans, hints that this is activity within the western section of Antichrist's empire that is in view. Just as Christ is seen as a warrior defeating evil with a sword projecting from his mouth in Revelation 19, so too, Antichrist imitates him with his sword, but this time causing innocent bloodshed (red horse). This ride likely begins part way through the first half of Daniel's 70th "seven."

....

SEAL 3

6:5a: "**Then when he broke open the third seal, I heard the third living creature saying, "Come!" So I looked, and there was a black horse!**" This rider follows on closely behind the rider on the red horse during the first half of the seventieth "seven" (Dan. 9:27).

The colour black signifies the sorrow and mourning that will be caused by the following conditions.

6:5b-6a: "**The one riding it had a pair of scales in his hand. °Then I heard something like a voice from among the four living creatures saying, 'A quart of wheat for a denarius, and three quarts of barley for a denarius.'**" The act of weighing items on scales pictures the food-shortages caused by Antichrist's wars. Indeed, wheat was a main staple and barley was the food of the poorer people. A quart of wheat was the average daily amount consumed by a working man and a denarius was his average daily pay. So these factors indicate the exorbitant prices and great scarcity of food, which would cause great difficulty for people.

6:6b: "**Don't damage the olive oil and the wine**." This refers to olive trees or vines producing oil and wine. These products were not the items of the rich only, but were also seen as vital staples for everyone. So this would limit the extent of the food scarcity so that it would not result in total famine.

SEAL 4

6:7-8a: "Then when he broke open the fourth seal, I heard the voice of the fourth living creature saying, 'Come!' ⁸As I looked, there was a deathly pale horse! The name of the one riding it was Death. Hades followed right behind him." The colour of this horse is the pallor of death from starvation and pestilence. Again this rider is the Antichrist and his ride pictures the great tribulation as Satan's wrath against God's people is poured out (Rev. 12:12b) by means of the Antichrist.

The Jews had made *"a covenant with Death and Sheol"* (Isa. 28:15)—sheol being the equivalent of "hades." Shortly after this at the midpoint of the seventieth "seven" (Dan. 9:27) Antichrist breaks this covenant. He turns on God's people bringing about the great persecution (tribulation). The terms "Death" and "Hades" are personifications of malignant cosmic forces, and the "following right behind him" is as if Hades (the common grave) is walking behind Death to gather up the corpses of those who have been killed.

"The Dragon"—Satan, is "the one who has the power of death" (Heb. 2:14b); yet the causing of death is seen primarily through his representative, the Antichrist (Rev. 13:2).

6:8b: "They were given authority over a quarter of the earth to kill with the sword, with famine, with plague, and by means of the ferocious beasts of the earth."" This ride seems to summarize the results of Seals Two and Three, inasmuch as war pictured by "the sword," and "famine" both result in pestilence and death.

Approximately one quarter of earth's population claim to be Christian along with believing Jews. So Satan is granted authority over them to test their loyalty to God and Jesus, firstly by the long bladed Oriental sword *(Gk romphaia)* indicating Antichrist's eastern origin. However, please note that it does not say that these two actually kill "a quarter of the earth," but only that they have authority to do so.

The Greek word here is correctly rendered as "famine" rather than "food-shortages. In fact, Revelation 13:17 shows that during Antichrist's persecution of God's people, "...no one will be able to buy or sell, except the one who has the mark of the Beast." This, therefore, excludes loyal Christians who would refuse to take the mark of the Beast. Unlike the food-shortages as a result of Antichrist's wars against "the King of the South," under the third seal these Christians suffer real famine.

Even more so than food shortages, famine results in a great amount of disease. However, it seems that here Antichrist, with Satan's miraculous power is able to directly introduce plague into the lives of God's people.

Regarding "the ferocious beasts" the Greek here does not mean "by" as in most versions, but "by means of" as in the NAB and N.T. Wright's New Testament. So these beasts do not appear to refer to ordinary animals, but rather they may be beasts in the prophetic sense of the term in being the emissaries of "Death" and "Hades" namely, the Antichrist, the second beast (the enforcer) of Revelation 13:11-17, and possibly the enlivened image of the beast (Rev.13:14-15).

Chapter 13

Breaking of Seals Five and Six
Revelation 6:9-17

Fifth Seal

⁹When he broke open the fifth seal, I saw under the altar those who had been violently killed because of God's message and the testimony they had given. ¹⁰They cried out with a loud voice, "How long, holy and true Sovereign Master, will you refrain from judging and avenging our blood on those who live on the earth?" ¹¹Each of them was given a white robe, and they were told to rest for a little while longer, until the completed number of their fellow servants, namely their brothers and sisters, were killed just as they had been.

Comment on the Breaking of the Fifth Seal

SEAL 5

6:9: "**When he broke open the fifth seal, I saw under the altar—those [souls] who had been violently killed because of God's message and the testimony they had given.**" This pictures the altar of burnt offering on which sacrifices were made. This is because these Christians have sacrificed their lives in loyalty to God and to Jesus and therefore they are martyrs. In fact, the term "souls" or "lives" really pictures their shed blood which has been poured out at the base of the altar (Lev. 4:7).

So this scene pictures the results of Satan's wrath by the end of the great tribulation and so showing the deaths of many faithful Christians, including "the two witnesses" (Rev. 11:3-14).

6:10: "**They cried out with a loud voice, "How long, holy and true Sovereign Master, will you refrain from judging and avenging our blood on those who live on the earth?"**" This is a call for divine justice. It is similar to when Abel's blood cried out from the ground (Gen. 4:10) and is in harmony with Jesus' rhetorical question of, "Don't you think God will give justice to His chosen ones, when they are crying out to Him day and night? Will He make them wait long? I'm telling you, He will give them justice speedily" *(Luke 18:7-8).*

"Those who live on the earth" i.e. the earth-dwellers are the followers of Antichrist. (Please see Chapter 1 pages 4 and 5).

6:11: "**Each of them was given a white robe** (Gk. *stole*), **and they were told to rest for a little while longer, until the completed number of their fellow servants, namely their brothers and sisters, were killed just as they had been.**" This white robe concerns the martyred holy ones. The *stole* was a robe of rank—a stately robe and was "the best" robe provided for the prodigal son (Luke 15:11-32). Because Christians are shown to be priests, then whenever the white robe is mentioned it indicates their priesthood as with the great multitude in Revelation 7:9.

The phrase "until the completed number of their fellow servants, namely their brothers and sisters, were killed just as they had been" does not mean that God has determined a set number who will die; but rather it does let John know that the end is not immediately to come, because there will be further martyrdom of Christians.

▲

TEXT
The Sixth Seal
   ¹²I watched as he broke open the sixth seal. A powerful earth-quake occurred. The sun became as black as sackcloth made of hair. The full moon became like blood. ¹³The stars in the sky fell to the earth as a fig tree drops its unripe figs when being shaken by a powerful wind. ¹⁴The sky was split apart like a scroll being rolled up, and every high hill and island was jolted out of its place. ¹⁵Then the kings of the earth, the prominent people, the military leaders, the rich, the powerful, and everyone, bond-servant and free person, hid themselves in the caves and among the rocks of the high hills.¹⁶"Fall on us!" they were saying to the hills and rocks. "Hide us from the face of the One who is sitting on the throne, and from the retribution of the Lamb! ¹⁷The great day of their retribution has come, and who is able to withstand it?"

Comment on the Breaking of the Sixth Seal

SEAL 6

6:12: "**I watched as he broke open the sixth seal. A powerful earth-quake occurred. The sun became as black as sackcloth made of hair. The full moon became like blood.**" This darkening is the sign that the end of the age has come (Matt. 24:29). It is a cosmic sign that the whole world will actually see and is followed by the very sign of the Son of Man—possibly some kind of ensign (Matt. 24:30). Finally Jesus physically appears in the darkened sky.

6:13: "**The stars in the sky fell to the earth as a fig tree drops its unripe figs when being shaken by a powerful wind.**" Although the earthquake and darkening of the sun and moon are quite literal there is often a problem in interpreting the "stars" that fall to earth in this verse. Clearly, they cannot be actual stars because these are massive gas giants which run as nuclear powerhouses. Indeed, some have proposed that these "stars" must be shooting stars—meteors—and this is quite feasible. However, it seems more likely that they refer to demons. The reason for this is that angelic beings are called "stars" (Job 38:7; Isa. 24:21, and 14:12-14) as are some humans (Gen. 37:9-10; Rev. 12:4). So these stars may be "the powers of heaven that are shaken" as a reference to corrupt angelic beings as recorded in the Luke 21 version of Jesus' Olivet discourse.

6:14: "**The sky was split apart like a scroll being rolled up and every high hill and island was jolted out of its place.**" This poetic language pictures God's peeling back of the sky so that mankind is now exposed for judgment (Isa. 64:1-3) along with cosmic catastrophes from which wicked mankind cannot hide for long. As God's appointed King it will be Jesus who descends to conduct this judgment process.

6:15: "**Then the kings of the earth, the prominent people, the military leaders, the rich, the powerful, and everyone, bond-servant and free person.**" These rulers and all the other classes of people with them make up the army and supporters of the Antichrist as seen in Rev. 16 and 17.

6:15b-17: "**Hid themselves in the caves and among the rocks of the high hills.**" Fall on us!" they were saying to the hills and rocks. "**Hide us from the face of the One who is sitting on the throne, and from the retribution of the Lamb! The great day of their retribution has come, and who is able to withstand it?**" This picture is based on Isaiah 2:19. These ones have decided to hide in what will soon disappear (vs.14), leaving them to face God and His coming retribution.

Here we have another example of God as a separate being from Jesus, so that Jesus is not the Lord God Almighty, but rather he is His primary representative who also pours out God's punishment on the wicked.

The breaking of this sixth seal brings us to the threshold of "the end" immediately after the tribulation (Matt 24:29). However, it is the breaking of the seventh seal which allows the scroll to be opened to allow for the carrying out of the retribution from God and of the Lamb. But before that we see the interlude which serves to seal God's people for protection from the coming retribution of God and of the Lamb.

§

Chapter 14

Different Views on Identifying the 144,000
Revelation 7

TEXT

After this I saw four angels, standing at the four corners of the earth, holding back the four winds of the earth, so that no wind could blow on the land, on the sea, or on any tree. **²**Then I saw another angel coming from the sun-rising, having the seal of the living God. He shouted out with a loud voice to the four angels who had been given the authority to damage the earth and the sea: **³**"Don't start damaging the land, or the sea, or the trees until we have put a seal on the foreheads of the bond-servants of our God." **⁴**Then I heard the number of those who were sealed: 144,000, sealed from all the tribes of the children of Israel:

⁵From the tribe of Judah, 12,000 were sealed, from the tribe of Reuben, 12,000, from the tribe of Gad, 12,000,**⁶**from the tribe of Asher, 12,000, from the tribe of Naphtali, 12,000, from the tribe of Manasseh, 12,000, **⁷**from the tribe of Simeon, 12,000, from the tribe of Levi, 12,000, from the tribe of Issachar, 12,000, **⁸**from the tribe of Zebulun, 12,000, from the tribe of Joseph, 12,000, from the tribe of Benjamin, 12,000 were sealed.

⁹After these things I looked, and there was a vast crowd that no one was able to count, made up from every race, tribe, nation, and language. They were standing in front of the throne, and in front of the Lamb, dressed in white robes, and with palm branches in their hands. **¹⁰**They were shouting out in a loud voice, "Salvation belongs to our God, who sits on the throne, and to the Lamb!" **¹¹**And all the angels who were standing around the throne and the elders and the four living creatures, fell down with their faces to the ground in front of the throne and knelt in worship of God, **¹²**saying,

"Amen! Blessing and glory, and wisdom and thanksgiving, and honour and power and strength be to our God for ever and ever! Amen!"

¹³Then one of the elders asked me, "Who are these people dressed in white robes, and where have they come from?"

¹⁴"My lord," I replied, "you know the answer!"

So he said to me, "These are the ones who have come out of the great tribulation. They have washed their robes and made them white in the blood of the Lamb. **¹⁵**For this reason they are in front of God's throne, devotedly serving Him day and night in His sanctuary. The One seated on the throne will spread His tent over them. **¹⁶**They will hunger no more, and thirst no more, and the sun won't beat down on them, or any scorching heat, **¹⁷**because the Lamb in the centre by the throne will caringly guide them and lead them to fountains of living waters, and God will wipe away every tear from their eyes."

The 144,000 Are the Same Group in Both
Revelation 7 and 14

After the description of Jesus' opening of each of the first six seals of the end-time scroll in Revelation 6, we come to an interlude. It is here in chapter 7 verses 3 to 8 that we first read about the group numbered 144,000 with its listing as twelve tribes and given a certain context. Immediately following this passage there is a description of a multi-ethnic "great multitude" in the end-time (Rev. 7:9-17). Whereas it is relatively easy to show that the "great multitude" is a description of multi-ethnic Christians, it is difficult to determine the identity of the 144,000!

Later we find a further description of the 144,000 given in chapter 14 verses 1-5, but here they are shown in quite different circumstances to those described in 7:3-8, so we must ask: are they still the same group?

Presented below are three significant reasons to believe that the 144,000 in Revelation 14 are, in fact, the same group as those in Revelation 7:

1. Because the number 144,000 is <u>mentioned only twice</u> in the entire Bible and because it is mentioned in the same Bible book, it would seem strange if it spoke of two different groups.

2. The <u>close proximity</u> of the two occurrences of the number 144,000 seems to indicate John's intention for the reader to correlate the details of the two passages concerning the one same group.

3. The statement in Revelation 14:1 that the 144,000 <u>have Jesus' "name</u> and the name of his Father written on their foreheads" is the same as their being "sealed" as belonging to God and to Jesus in chapter 7.

So it logically appears that the 144,000 in chapter 7 are shown as being sealed at one particular time, but later, in chapter 14, the same body of people are shown standing on Mount Zion.

NOTE: The 144,000 of Revelation 7 are seen to be <u>on the earth</u> and in a situation of <u>imminent danger</u> because they are being sealed against the devastation about to be launched upon the earth. Then again, the scene in Revelation 14 is also on earth because the voice that John hears is from heaven, hence John is back on earth vision-wise, in addition to the fact that these ones are shown as standing on Mount Zion in Jerusalem and therefore on earth.

There are two primary issues concerning the identity of the 144,000:

- Are they ethnic Jews or multi-ethnic Christians?
- Is the number literal or symbolic?

Apart from these basic questions there are a number of other aspects involved in identifying the 144,000 including the taking into account of what they do and so leading to at least five main different views about them. Yet, some readers may claim that identifying the 144,000 is not so difficult and so arrive at the conclusion that these ones must be Jewish because they are listed as 12,000 each from the twelve tribes of Israel and so they must be 144,000 Jews. In fact, it appears that there is much more to solving this puzzle than one might think from only a surface reading. This deeper reading results in a variety of different views regarding their identity, including those presented by a number of leading theologians who propose that these ones are Christians. So now we will list the various common views:

Five Main Different Views

View 1: A literal number of 144,000 of the entire *age-long* multi-ethnic Christian *"Israel of God"* (spiritual Israel) from the <u>first century</u> onward.

View 2: A symbolic number of 144,000 of the entire *age-long* multi-ethnic Christian *"Israel of God"* (spiritual Israel) from the <u>first century</u> onward. This is a very common view.

View 3: A literal number of 144,000 of an unconverted remnant of ethnic Israelites in the <u>end-time</u> who become Christians by the time of the situation described in Revelation 14. This is mainly a Dispensationalist view.

View 4: A literal number of 144,000 Jewish Christians who form the Messianic army of the Lion of Judah in the <u>end-time.</u> They have been separated out from among *"the great multitude"* of Gentile Christians. This view is also very popular generally, as well as being particularly a Dispensationalist view and so including a future pre-tribulation rapture position.

View 5: A symbolic number of 144,000 of the multi-ethnic group of Christians existing world-wide <u>in the end-time</u>. These have come from

72

all of spiritual Israel i.e. the entire age-long Christian *"Israel of God."* They are presented in their role as the Messianic army of Jesus— *"the Lion of the tribe of Judah;"* whereas they are presented in their priestly role as the *"great multitude."*

▲

From our research it seems that View #5 is the most likely correct basic identification of the 144,000. Both the next chapter and Appendix A at the back of this book give numerous major reasons for the failure of views #1, #2, #3, and #4. However, some have proposed additional factors as involved and so giving variations to View #5. These are:

View 6: A symbolic number of 144,000 Christians selected from the *"great multitude"* for special work. They are protected so that they all survive the great tribulation. This approximates the view of Professor David Aune in the *Word Biblical Commentary*.

View 7: A symbolic number of 144,000 Christians who are the true church and who are taken from the professing church in the end-time.

View 8: A symbolic number of 144,000 of the multi-ethnic group of Christians living in Judea in the end-time. These have come from all of spiritual Israel i.e. the entire age-long Christian *"Israel of God."* They are presented in their role as the Messianic army of the Lion of the tribe of Judah; whereas they are presented in their priestly role as the *"great multitude."*

▲

Chapter 16 explains the details of views #6, #7, and #8. Also Appendix B demonstrates the reasons for the failure of these views regarding the 144,000 in Revelation 7.

So now we shall begin to examine why View #5 fits best with all of the available biblical data, so that the 144,000 is a symbolic number concerning Christians.

§

Chapter 15

The 144,000 Are Christians, but the Number Is Symbolic

When Do the 144,000 Appear on the Scene?

To help in our analysis of who the 144,000 represent there are certain ones of the above views that can be discounted fairly quickly. One important factor concerns the timing of the appearance of the 144,000 in the biblical record. So we start with the last thought from the sixth seal:

❖ "Fall on us!" they were saying to the hills and rocks. "Hide us from the face of the One who is sitting on the throne, and from the retribution of the Lamb! <u>The great day of their retribution</u> has come, and who is able to withstand it?"" (*6:16, 17*)

The answer to this rhetorical question is that it will be those sealed for protection during the great day of God's and Jesus' retribution (wrath). This day is presented to us in 7:1 as the picture of *"the four winds"* to be destructive of the things of the followers of Antichrist. This great day of God's wrath—the day of the Lord—follows on after the great tribulation i.e. Satan's wrath against God's people (Matt 24:29; Joel 2:31). So the first mention in *7:1-8* of the 144,000 states that:

❖ "After this I saw four angels standing at the four corners of the earth holding back <u>the four winds of the earth,</u> so that no wind could blow on the earth or on the sea or against any tree. Then I saw another angel ascending from the rising of the sun, with the seal of the living God. And he called out in a loud voice to the four angels who had been given power to harm the earth and the sea, saying, "Do not harm the earth or the sea or the trees <u>until we have sealed the servants of our God</u> on their foreheads."
    And *I heard* the number of those who were sealed, *one hundred forty-four thousand.*"

So the picture here is of the end-times for the appearance of the 144,000 who are to be sealed as <u>belonging to God</u> for their protection when He pours out His wrath on wicked mankind. There is no biblical reason to imagine that this is a picture of this body of people as existing from the first century onward. This means that we can discount Views #1 and #2 described in the previous chapter.

The Irregularity and the Peculiarity of the List of the Tribes Indicate that Ethnic Israel Is Not in View

1. The list of the tribes in Revelation 7 has some correspondence with the births of the original twelve sons of Jacob from their mothers according to the collating of the details in Genesis 29:32-30:24; 35:16-26. However, this is not an exact correspondence. Also, the Genesis list concerns the sons rather than the tribes.

2. The following details make the list in Revelation 7 very different from the other nineteen lists:

- With the exceptions of the military census lists given in Numbers 2:3, 7:12, and 10:14, Revelation 7 is the only list which positions Judah first instead of Reuben, the first-born of Jacob. This is a Christian Messianic detail because Jesus is *"the lion of the tribe of Judah"* (Rev. 5:5).
- Levi is included. However, as the priestly tribe, it was never included in the other census lists because Levites were redeemed in place of the firstborn of the other tribes (Ex. 13:1, 2, 11-16; Num. 3:14) and therefore were exempt from Israel's warfare. Yet in this list in Revelation the tribe of <u>Levi no longer maintains its special status as a priestly tribe</u> under the old, pre-crucifixion arrangement of the Mosaic Law, and so further indicating that the list is a Christian list.
- Dan is omitted. This is probably because Judges 18:30 notes the tribe's idolatry and so would not be fit to be included in a Christian list.
- Ephraim is omitted and appears to have been replaced by a never-before-existing tribe of Joseph.

These accumulated factors seem to indicate that John was presenting an arrangement very different to that of ethnic Israel and therefore giving subtle clues that ethnic Israel is not in view here, but rather this list is really a Christian transformation of the Jewish military census lists given in Numbers.

3. In Revelation 7:3 the 144,000 are called *"the servants of our God."* By the 90s C.E., to the Christian mind, this term would not have referred to unbelieving ethnic Jews or even to Christian ethnic Jews.

4. The fact that the 144,000 are *"ransomed from the earth" (14:3)* and *"were ransomed from the mankind" (14:4)* links them with Revelation 5:9 which concerns Jesus' being told that: *"by your blood you ransomed people for God from every tribe, language, people, and nation."* And therefore they are a multi-ethnic group of Christians.

Revelation 14 and the "Great Multitude" Show the 144,000 to Be Christians

❖ "Then, as I watched, there was the Lamb standing on Mount Zion. With him were 144,000 who had his name, and his Father's name written on their foreheads. Then I heard a sound out of heaven, like the sound of a torrent of waters, and like the sound of loud thunder. And the sound I heard was like that of harpists playing their harps. They are singing a new song in front of the throne and in front of the four living creatures and the elders, but no one was able to learn the song except the 144,000 who had been ransomed from the earth. These are the ones who haven't contaminated themselves with women—indeed they are virgins. It is these who follow the Lamb wherever he goes. These were ransomed from among mankind as first fruits to God and to the Lamb, and no deceit was found to come from their mouths. They are blameless" *(14:1-5)*.

To understanding these passages the *"great multitude"* must also be taken into account. So John tells us in *7:9-17* that:

"After these things I looked, and there was a vast crowd that no one was able to count, made up from every race, tribe, nation, and language. They were standing in front of the throne, and in front of the Lamb, dressed in white robes, and with palm branches in their hands. [10]They were shouting out in a loud voice, "Salvation belongs to our God, who sits on the throne, and to the Lamb!" [11]And all the angels who were standing around the throne and the elders and the four living creatures, fell down with their faces to the ground in front of the throne and knelt in worship of God, [12]saying, "Amen! Blessing and glory, and wisdom and thanksgiving, and honour and power and strength be to our God for ever and ever! Amen!" [13]Then one of the elders asked me, "Who are these people dressed in white robes, and where have they come from?" [14]"My lord," I replied, "you know the answer!" So he said to me, "These are the ones who <u>have come out of the great tribulation</u>. They have washed their robes and <u>made them white in the blood of the Lamb</u>. ¹⁵For this reason they are in front of God's throne, devotedly serving Him day and night in His sanctuary. The One seated on the throne will spread His tent over them. ¹⁶They will hunger no more, and thirst no more, and the sun won't beat down on them, or any scorching heat, ¹⁷because the Lamb in the centre by the throne will caringly guide them and lead them to fountains of living waters, and God will wipe away every tear from their eyes."

THE GREAT MULTITUDE ARE CHRISTIANS – BOTH JEWISH AND GENTILE

Indeed, this is a picture of multi-ethnic Christians "who have come out of the great tribulation," and their white robes are as a result of their having "washed their robes and made them white in the blood of the Lamb." For this reason they are "before the throne of God, and serve him day and night in his temple" (Rev. 7:14, 15). Individually they would have made their robes "white in the blood of the Lamb" at the time of their acceptance of Jesus as Messiah and their subsequent baptism, but now they thank God and the Lamb for their salvation (Rev. 7:10).

There is nothing in the full passage on the "great multitude" or anywhere else in Scripture to indicate that Jewish Christians have been excluded from this "great multitude."

NOTE: Please see Appendix C which shows that the "great multitude" will not be literally in heaven.

THE GREAT MULTITUDE ARE NOT RESURRECTED CHRISTIANS

Indeed, these Christians are also living in the end-time because they are shown as having just *"come out of the great tribulation."* This means, according to all scholars, that they have <u>survived the great tribulation;</u> bearing in mind that the word "tribulation" means "persecution," and the great persecution is from the wrath that Satan pours out on them and is certainly not God's wrath (Rom. 5:9; 1 Thess. 5:9). So these are the Christians who did not get killed by Antichrist—they are not resurrected Christians.

Furthermore, the great tribulation occurs before the pouring out of God's wrath on wicked mankind (Matt. 24:29, Joel 2:31); yet the indications of the timing of the resurrection are that it occurs near the end of the time when God pours out his wrath. This is shown by Jesus' interjection in the description of the pouring out of the sixth bowl of wrath, so that Christians have not yet been caught up to Jesus:

77

❖ "The sixth angel poured out his bowl… demonic spirits, performing signs, who go out to the kings of the whole world to assemble them for battle on the great day of God the Almighty. ("Behold, I am coming like a thief! Blessed is the one who stays awake and keeps his clothes at hand, so that he will not be caught naked and his shameful condition be seen.") And the spirits gathered the kings to the place that in Hebrew is called Armageddon" *(Rev. 16:12-16).*

In New Testament Terms the "Sons of Israel" Is Strongly Indicated as Referring to the "Israel of God"

On the side of those who propose that the 144,000 must be ethnic Jews, the argument is made that the term "Israel" is only used of the Jewish people in both Testaments. However, although this is true of the Old Testament it is not true of the New Testament. Indeed, in the New Testament the term "Israel" and its cognates concerning "Jews" and "the true circumcision" all have reference to multi-ethnic Christians.

1. "The Vine" was a symbol of Israel (Ps.80:8ff; Jer. 2:21). So Jesus as *"the true vine"* is the true Israel. Therefore, his followers, as the branches, are part of the true Israel (John 15:1-6)—the *"Israel of God."* So Grant Osborne states that: "Jesus most likely chose twelve disciples to signify the righteous remnant embodying the true Israel…" *Revelation (Baker Exegetical Commentary)* p.312.

2. In Philippians 3:3 the apostle Paul calls Christians, *"the true circumcision"* which puts multi-ethnic Christians in the place of ethnic Israel, at least in terms of its functions.

3. Paul makes this same contrast in Romans when he says: *"But he is a Jew who is one inwardly"* (Rom. 2:9) and *"For they are not all Israel who are descended from Israel"* (Rom. 9:6) i.e. of what is Israel by faith and not ethnic Israel. Also Paul described this as a tree to which Gentiles were starting to be grafted in (Rom. 11:17, 18).

4. The term *"the Israel of God" (Gal. 6:16)* refers to Christians and is contrasted with *"Israel according to the flesh" (1 Cor. 10:18).* So Longenecker writes that: "all of the views that take "the Israel of God" to refer to Jews and not gentiles…fail to take seriously enough the context of the Galatian letter itself."

The following modern versions show that *"the Israel of God"* in Galatians 6:16 refers to Christians:

❖ "As for all who will follow this rule—may peace and mercy be upon them, **even** upon the Israel of God" (Mounce).

❖ "...**even** upon the [true] Israel of God!" (AMP); "...**even** upon the Israel of God!" (Moffatt; Wuest); "...**that is,** on the true Israel of God!" (Williams); "**even** to the Israel of God" (NIV1984); "...to the true Israel of God... (Phillips); "...to God's true Israel" (Knox); "They are the true people of Israel and they belong to God" (WE); "they are the new people of God" (NLT).

5. In Galatians, Paul does not allow for any distinctions between Jewish and Gentile Christians*: "there is no longer Jew or Greek...you are all one in Christ Jesus"* (Gal 3:28). So there is no elitism.

6. The letter of James was written no earlier than 44 C.E., when the scattered church was predominantly Jewish; yet in the introduction to his letter James' address is: *"To the twelve tribes who are dispersed abroad" (Jas.1:1 NASB).* This is unlikely to refer only to Jewish Christians, because conversion of the Gentiles had already begun by then under the command of Jesus when he said that Christians were to be his *"witnesses...to the remotest part of the earth" (Acts 1:8).* So the first Gentile family to be converted was that of Cornelius, probably in the late 30s and no later than 41 C.E.

   So the phrase *"the twelve tribes who are dispersed abroad"* "is most readily understandable as an ideal description of the Christian community in its role as the new, or true Israel in the world (cp, Gal 6:16; Heb. 4:9; 1 Pet. 2:9-10; and for all Christians as the "dispersion"'" according to *The Anchor Bible Dictionary* Volume 3, p.624. So evidently James saw these mainly Jewish Christians as *"the Israel of God"* (Gal 6:16) that would expand to include more and more Gentiles. So James didn't write his letter to be only for Christians who were Jewish; it was for the new Israel made up of spiritual Jews.

7. The apostle Peter applies to the Christian Community what was originally applied to Israel as *"a chosen people"* (Isa 43:20) and *"a Kingdom of priests and a holy nation"* (Ex.19:6) when he calls Christians *"a royal priesthood, a holy nation"* (1 Pet. 2:9). So, now

this Christian *"holy nation,"* is very largely the focus in the New Testament, rather than any focus on ethnic Israel.

8. Peter also shows that the original function of Israel has been transferred to the Christian Community when he says: *"you also, like living stones, are being built up as a spiritual house, to be a holy priesthood to offer spiritual sacrifices..." (1 Pet. 2:5).*

9. The Christian Community is central throughout the Book of Revelation. Indeed, just as with Peter's comments above, the lyrics of the song about Christians say: *"And you [God] have made them a kingdom and priests to our God, and they will reign on the earth"* (Rev. 5:10), thus showing the application being transferred from ethnic Israel to the Christian community.

10. A further part of the context of the 144,000 is the set of seven letters written to the seven Christian communities. These never distinguish between ethnically Jewish and Gentile Christians. They were written to multi-ethnic Christians who are to *"overcome"* (Rev. 2:7, 11, 17, 26; 3:5,12, 21) and who are true Jews in contrast to *"those who claim that they are Jews, but are not" (Rev. 2:9; 3:9).* This fact implies that Christians are the *true* Israel. So in explaining this expression George Eldon Ladd says:

> These "Jews" are without question Jews by race and religion, who met together in the synagogue to worship the Lord. But in reality, inwardly, they are not Jews, because they have rejected Jesus as their Messiah...true Jews are people of the Messiah.
>
> *A Commentary on the Revelation of John*, p.43.

So, these biblical facts indicate that by the time of the writing of Revelation in the mid 90s C.E., Jesus, as the immediate source of the Revelation to John, would be focused on those who are Jews *"inwardly"* (Rom. 2:9, Rev. 2:9, 3:9), that is, the multi-ethnic *"Israel of God"* (Gal. 6:16), *"the true circumcision"* (Phil. 3:3), rather than ethnic Israel. So in the *Encyclopedia of Biblical Prophecy* J. Barton Payne states:

> The group cannot be national Israel, Israel after the flesh, because the Jews are converted only after the outpouring of the wrath of God, and specifically at the time when they look directly upon the Messiah whom they have pierced (Zech 12:10). p. 612.

In summary the relevant factors are:

- The irregularity and peculiarity of the list of the tribes and so discounting ethnic Israel as being the 144,000.
- The details that are common to Revelation 14:1-5 and the Great Multitude as all concerning Christians.
- The New Testament usage of the term "the Israel of God" for Christians.

These factors all indicate that the 144,000 is a reference to spiritual Israel i.e. Christians. This also shows that we can discount Views #3 and #4 concerning ethnic Israel. Further proof of these points can be seen by a comparison of other details described in Appendix A along with the comments of scholars such as George Eldon Ladd who states that:

> "There are good reasons to believe that by the 144,000 John means to identify spiritual Israel—the church. This view is suggested by certain irregularities in the list of the twelve tribes of Israel."
>
> *A Commentary on the Revelation of John*, p. 114.

Answering the Objection to the Interpretation
That the 144,000 are Christians

Jesus said to his apostles:

- ❖ "I can assure you,"…"In the age when everything is renewed, when the Son of Man is seated on his glorious throne, you who have followed me will also sit on twelve thrones, justly governing the twelve tribes of Israel" *(Matt. 19:28 and Luke 22:30).*

So is Jesus here using the phrase "the twelve tribes of Israel" as a reference to ethnic Jews or is he referring to spiritual Israel?

Certainly, to apply this to spiritual Israel would be an unnatural way of taking the phrase "the twelve tribes of Israel" in this particular context. So Jesus is referring here to a time when the twelve apostles will judge ethnic Israel, presumably for its general rejection of Jesus as the Messiah. However, in Revelation 7 there is no statement concerning any judgment of those spoken of there. Furthermore, there are the many factors detailed earlier which either prove or strongly indicate that Revelation 7 speaks of Christians.

"Factors Indicating that the Number 144,000 Is Symbolic

1. Throughout the Scriptures the number twelve is used for God's people. Examples are: the twelve tribes of Israel, the twelve apostles, twelve of various structures and utensils used in the tabernacle and temple, 12,000 valiant warriors (Judges 21:10), and many others. So the figure of 12,000 serves well as a symbolic number of spiritual Israel (Please see Chapter 3 How Numbers Are Used in Revelation).

2. The number 144,000 is the squared number of 12 x 12 magnified by being multiplied by 1000. This is based on the twelve tribes of Israel as a complete nation. Indeed, twelve for the number of God's people, squared for completeness and multiplied by a thousand to suggest the vast numbers is the meaning of 144,000 as a symbolic number. These combined factors also show this number to indicate completeness so that not one of the redeemed Christians is missing. So Bible commentator Grant Osborne states in *Revelation (Baker Exegetical Commentary)* p.312 that:

    > The purpose here is to stress the perfect completeness of the whole (note "every tribe") "number" of the persevering of the church in a threefold way: taking 12 (the number of completeness), then squaring it, and then multiplying it by 1000, another symbol of completeness in the book (note also the "24 elders" of 4:4, the "12,000 stadia" of 21:16, the "144 cubits" of 21:17, and the "twelve crops of fruit" of 22:2).

Adding to this Richard Bauckham states that:

> The number of the Israelite army in Revelation 7 of 12,000 from each of the twelve tribes is, of course, a symbolic number, a 'square number' of perfection, like the perfect dimensions of the new Jerusalem (21:16). *The Climax of Prophecy* p. 218

Furthermore, Robert Gundry states that:

> The number 144,000 doesn't set a numerical limit. It signifies innumerability. The listing of twelve tribes doesn't set an ethnic limit. It signifies a theological status. That is to say, the 144,000 don't replace the church on earth during the tribulation. They *are* the church on earth during the great tribulation.
>
> *First the Antichrist* pp 92-93.

3. The extremely large dimensions of the New Jerusalem in Revelation 21 are evidently symbolisms to describe the city (city being a reference to a large population i.e. people). Its dimensions are about 1,500 miles each for the length, the breadth, and the height of the city, and having a wall that is 210 feet (144 cubits) thick. If taken literally this seems to be an impossibly large structure that would protrude 1,500 miles into outer space and could not fit on the land of Israel. This indicates that only a hyperbolic/figurative interpretation for the city seems plausible, and that the wall's thickness of 144 cubits is symbolic and so indicating that the number 144,000 is also symbolic.

4. Because John *"hears"* the number 144,000, yet he *"sees"* the *"great multitude that no man could number"* it is notably indicated that the 144,000 group are the same group as the multi-ethnic *"great multitude"* and so being a strong indicator that the number 144,000 is symbolic.

5. If one recognises that the term *"the sons of Israel"* is to be interpreted symbolically as being the Christian *"Israel of God"* (Gal. 6:16) then, for consistency, the number 144,000 must also be interpreted symbolically.

Furthermore, the fact that 144,000 is a fixed number in contrast to *"a great multitude which no man was able to number"* may be because it is God's way of saying to John that not a single one is missing.

All of this means that we can further discount View #2 as well as Views #3 and #4 as described in Chapter 14. This leaves View #5 as appearing to be the basically correct one. However will other factors change our understanding of this view?

Chapter 16

Examining Variations on the View of 144,000 as Christians

Now that we have established the basic factors about the 144,000 as a reference to Christians in the end-times and with the number 144,000 as being symbolic, we can look further at other details about them. These concern views #6, #7, and #8 which are variously detailed at the end of Chapter 14 as all concerning Christians with the symbolic number of 144,000.

The Questions on These Views to Consider

View 6. Are these 144,000 a special group that is taken from the "great multitude" or from "the sons of Israel"?

View 7. Are these 144,000 the true church, but who are taken from the professing church i.e. the "great multitude"?

View 8. Does the 144,000 group of Revelation 7 exist throughout the world or only in Judea?

View 6. The 144,000 Are Taken Out from "The Sons of Israel," but Not Taken Out from the "Great Multitude"

In Revelation 7:5-8 the 12,000 each are sealed "from" or "out of "(Gk *ek*) each tribe and therefore are only part of a whole number. So in the *Word Biblical Commentary* David Aune quotes Caird who says:

> 144,000 were marked from every tribe of the sons of Israel; i.e., those who are sealed are part of a larger group, for ek + genitive here is a partitive genitive, indicating that a limited number are separated from the larger group. Whatever "the tribes of the sons of Israel" represents, 12,000 from each tribe can only mean a portion of those who make up the whole "tribe."

So, when tallied the entire 144,000 must also be only part of a whole number of spiritual Israel that have existed since the first century. There is no indication in the passages or their context that the 144,000 are taken as a group from the "great multitude," but only from "the sons of Israel" as mentioned in Rev. 7:4. So we can discount View #6.

View 7. The 144,000 Are Not Simply the True Church as Separated Out from the Professing Church

The idea that the 144,000 are the true church, but are taken from the professing church i.e. the "great multitude" is very similar to View #6 above. Therefore, this proposal does not work for the same reasons given in #6. Furthermore, the "great multitude" is not simply a professing church which lacks genuine faith, but is described as fully devoted to God and Jesus. According to 7:14 and 15 they have:

❖ "...come out of the great tribulation. They have washed their robes and made them white in the blood of the Lamb. For this reason they are in front of God's throne, devotedly serving Him day and night in His sanctuary."

So we can discount View #7.

View 8. Where Do the 144,000 Appear on the Scene?

Although the many end-time prophecies in the Hebrew Scriptures, along with Jesus' description of end-time events concern the local area in Jerusalem and Judea (Matt. 24, Mark 13, Luke 21), the book of Revelation contains much universal language so that some features of the end-times will be earth-wide, including the pouring out of God's wrath upon all of wicked mankind who support the Antichrist at the time of Jesus' return. Indeed, Revelation 3:10 speaks of *"the hour of trial which is about to come upon the whole world."*

Although in Revelation 14 the 144,000 are shown to be standing on Mount Zion i.e. Jerusalem in Judea, it is evident that in 7:1ff they are seen throughout the entire earth because John says he, "saw four angels, standing at the four corners of the earth, holding back the four winds of the earth." Certainly, throughout the Scriptures this phrase "four corners of the earth" is a reference to the entire earth. So clearly the 144,000 are sealed in protection from the damage that is to occur to "the earth and the sea" in their entirety and so must exist world-wide at this early point in time described in Revelation 7. However, the scene changes by the time we get to Revelation 14 because the 144,000 are then shown to be in Judea on Mount Zion at that later time.

▲

The examination of all these views leaves only View #5 as giving this full picture of Revelation 7:3-8 which noted that it is a **symbolic number of 144,000 of the multi-ethnic group of Christians** existing **world-wide** in the **end-time**. These have come from all of spiritual Israel i.e. the entire age-long Christian *"Israel of God."*

The further details of this view are that the 144,000 are presented in their role as the Messianic army of Jesus—*"the Lion of the tribe of Judah."* So this prompts us to ask our last questions about the 144,000 and concerning "the great multitude."

§

Chapter 17

Are the 144,000 and the Great Multitude the Same Group?

We have already noted the many factors showing that the 144,000 group:

* Appears only in the end-time.
* Is sealed for protection during the pouring out of God's wrath.
* Is taken from *"the sons of Israel"* which in New Testament terms is the Christian *"Israel of God"* (Gal 6:16).
* Is in a very irregular and peculiar list, and therefore is indicated as being part of the multi-ethnic Christian *"Israel of God."*
* Is not seen as literally numbered at 144,000, this figure being symbolic of organizational completeness.
* Exists throughout the earth (Rev.7), but only later arrives on Mount Zion (Rev. 14).

We have also noted that the *"great multitude"* is comprised of Jewish as well as Gentile Christians and therefore is not distinct from the 144,000 in that sense.

Our final questions on the 144,000 are:

* Are the 144,000 and "the great multitude" pictures of the same group from different perspectives?
* What are the roles of the 144,000 and of the "great multitude"?

Along the way in our studies we have seen hints concerning the answer to the first question. But now is the time to look in much greater detail regarding our understanding of this aspect of Revelation Chapter 7. To do this we must note other statements about Christians that are mentioned in the Revelation, especially wherever the term "God's holy people" (the holy ones or saints) is mentioned.

The 144,000 Have Some of the Same Characteristics and Experiences as the *"Great Multitude"*

The purpose of this section is to show the common factors found in the Revelation statements concerning the 144,000, the great multitude, and the holy ones. These common factors are:

1. They are involved in the end-times trials.
2. They are sealed for protection.
3. They are multi-ethnic followers of Christ.
4. They are the redeemed from all nations.
5. They sing the new song (Rev. 5:9, 14:3).

Because the *"great multitude"* is the body of the holy ones we can deduce that the 144,000 have some of the same characteristics and experiences as the great multitude of holy ones [*saints i.e. Christians*] as shown in the following summaries:

1. *THEY ARE INVOLVED IN END-TIMES TRIALS.*

    The **144,000**, are *"sealed against the four winds"* (7:1, 3) of the coming wrath of God and Jesus (6:17) so that, as the **holy ones** (saints), they are kept protected *"from the hour of trial coming upon the whole world"* (3:10). This shows that the 144,000 and the holy ones i.e. the *"great multitude"* are protected when God pours out His wrath on the wicked.

2. *THEY ARE SEALED FOR PROTECTION*

    The **144,000** have *"[Jesus'] name and the name of his Father written on their foreheads"* (14:1) and so are *"sealed"* for protection (7:3, 4) before the coming wrath of God (6:17, 7:1, 3). The **holy ones** (saints) have the *"seal of God"* (9:4) for protection against the locust attack. This is an indicator that the 144,000 may be the same as the multi-ethnic group of Christian holy ones (saints) and therefore the same as the *"great multitude."*

3. *THEY ARE MULTI-ETHNIC FOLLOWERS OF CHRIST.*

    The **144,000** are "the bond-servants of our God" (7:4), having "[Jesus'] name and the name of his Father written on their foreheads" (14:1) and "are following the Lamb wherever he goes" (14:4) just as "the Lamb...will guide" the **great multitude** (7:17). This indicates that the 144,000 and the great multitude are all Christian holy ones and so may be different descriptions of the one same group.

4. *THEY ARE REDEEMED FROM ALL NATIONS.*

    Because there are not two different groups of 144,000 in the passages of chapters 7 and 14, the "tribes of the sons of Israel" (7:4) must refer to "the Israel of God" (Gal. 6:16) as shown earlier.

88

So as the **144,000**, these are the multi-ethnic Christians "redeemed from mankind" (14:4), just as the **holy ones** are "ransomed from every tribe, tongue, peoples, nation" (5:9) and the **"great multitude"** are "from every nation, tribe, peoples and tongues" (7:9). Again this indicates that the 144,000 are to be multi-ethnic.

5. THEY SING A NEW SONG

The **144,000** are singing "a new song...no one could <u>learn</u> the song except the 144,000" (14:3) and yet in Revelation 5:8-10 we read that the 24 elders sang this new song about the holy ones (saints) who were "ransomed from every tribe, tongue, peoples, and nations (kingdom/priests)" (5:8, 9). Evidently these multi-ethnic Christians had learned the new song from the 24 elders/heavenly beings and so the 144,000 are also to be Christians from every nation. This appears to be "the song of Moses and the song of the Lamb" (15:2, 3) sung by the holy ones who are the "great multitude." Furthermore, these multi-ethnic Christians are described in 5:10 as "priests to our God." This gives a further connection to the **"great multitude"** in 7:9-17 who are also described as priests to our God because they are in the temple and are bound to praise Jesus in song because of his redeeming sacrifice.

So because the "great multitude" are multi-ethnic Christians i.e. the holy ones (saints) as the 144,000, they are Christian followers of the Lamb who have been redeemed from mankind in general and are sealed for protection before God's wrath is poured out on wicked mankind.

The Strong Indicators That the 144,000 Are the Same Group as the Great Multitude

1. With the background of the above factors concerning the 144,000 and the "great multitude," and the fact that John **hears** the number 144,000 in 7:4, but **sees** the "great multitude that **no one could count**" in 7:9 (so that the number 144,000 is uncountable because it is symbolic), it is logical to conclude that there is a strong indication that the 144,000 and the *"great multitude,"* are exactly the same group of Christians, but from different perspectives. Indeed, theologian Richard Bauckham states that:

The vision of the 144,000 and the innumerable multitude in chapter 7 forms a parallel to that of the Lion and the Lamb in chapter 5. Just as in 5:5-6, John heard that the Lion of Judah and the Root of David had conquered, but saw the slaughtered Lamb, so in chapter 7 he hears the number sealed (7:4) but sees an innumerable multitude (7:9). It seems likely, therefore, that the relation between the 144,000 and the innumerable multitude is intended to be the same as that between the Lion and the Lamb. Moreover, there are specific links between the Lion and the 144,000 and between the Lamb and the innumerable multitude. To the Lion of the tribe of Judah corresponds the list of the sealed of the tribes of Israel, headed by those of the tribe of Judah. To the Lamb standing (5:6), who has ransomed people from every tribe, tongue, people and nation (5:9), corresponds the multitude from all nations, tribes, peoples and tongues, standing before the Lamb (7:9). *The Climax of Prophecy* p. 216

2. If the *"great multitude"* is a completely separate group, then the statements concerning protection of the 144,000 from God's wrath are not shown as applying to them in Revelation 7. Yet the fact that all Christians will be protected during the time of God's wrath (2 Thess. 5:9, Rom. 5:9) indicates that the "great multitude," as "the holy ones" (saints) in Revelation 9:4, do also have the "seal of God" for protection against the locust attack during the fifth trumpet. This gives a further strong indicator that the "great multitude" are the same body of people as the 144,000 who are also sealed for protection.

3. The 144,000 have many of the same characteristics and experiences as the "great multitude." The fact that the singing of the new song is common to both the 144,000 (14:2-4) and the multi-ethnic holy ones (5:8, 9; 15:2, 3) who are the Christian "great multitude," is an especially strong indicator that the 144,000 and the "great multitude" are one and the same group.

Christians Presented from Different Perspectives

In Revelation 5:10 the four living creatures and the twenty-four elders state concerning Christians: "You *[Jesus]* have made them a kingdom and priests for our God..." So clearly Christians will have two major roles

90

and so here the 144,000 are described in their role of being a Messianic army organized in military marching order and led by Jesus—"the lion of the tribe of Judah" (5:5, 7:5); whereas the "great multitude" are described in their role of being a body of priests positioned "before the Lamb." So from the above strong indicators that the 144,000 and the "great multitude" are the same body of people they are clearly being presented in their two different roles, as was Jesus in Revelation 5 i.e. as the Lion and then as the Lamb.

So the picture of end-time Christians as the 144,000 shows them as an army organized in military marching order; whereas the picture of them as the "great multitude that no one could count" shows them in their priestly role.

Indeed, it is only by putting all the factors together that this leads to the almost certain conclusion that the 144,000 is simply a different picture of the same survivors of the great tribulation who have been "sealed" (7:3) as protected in preparation against the coming wrath of God which follows immediately after the great tribulation.

From all this information and reasoning we can now get a clear and full picture of who exactly the 144,000 are.

The Roles of the 144,000 and the Great Multitude

THE 144,000 IS PRESENTED AS A MESSIANIC ARMY

Because the 144,000 in Revelation 7 can be only part of the age-long "sons of Israel/the Israel of God," the question would be: In what capacity do they serve? The indicators from the Scriptures seem to be that they serve as a holy army and the reasons for this are listed below:

1. The list in Revelation 7:4-8 has the literary form of a military census of the tribes of Israel as with the military census lists in Numbers chapter 1 and 2:3 and 10:14.

2. An Israelite army composed of twelve equal tribal contingents conforms to Old Testament practice e.g. one thousand troops from each of the twelve tribes was dispatched against Midian (Num. 31:4-6).

3. The fact that Messiah's tribe of Judah is listed first in Revelation 7 indicates that the 144,000 are to be led by Messiah. Judah is also listed first in the military order of the tribes in the camp (Num. 2:3; 7:12; 10:14), showing that there is a Messianic military order to the tribes in Revelation 7.

91

4. According to Revelation 14:4, the 144,000 are symbolically shown to be all adult males as would be found in an Israelite army.
5. The new song of Revelation 14:3 belongs to holy-war terminology.
6. The description of the 144,000 males as being "the ones who did not defile themselves with women; in fact, they are virgins" (14:4) may be regarded symbolically as reflecting the purity regulations required of participants in a holy war (Lev. 15:16; Deut 23:9-10; 1 Sam. 21:5). (Please see NOTE below).
7. The term, "the armies of heaven" (as in most modern versions) in Revelation 19:14 indicates a military scene by referring to those Christians who ride alongside the Messiah in the eschatological battle when the enemies "will make war on the Lamb, and the lamb will conquer them...and those with him are called and chosen and faithful" (Rev.17:14).
8. The symbolic aspect to the number 144,000 [12 x 12 x 1000] indicates an 'organizationally complete army.'

NOTE: That they "did not defile themselves with women; in fact, they are virgins" (14:4) is not a literal comment because legitimate sexual relations is never a defilement. It may simply mean that they have remained undefiled spiritually and in their teaching just as with Paul's desire to present believers to Christ as a "pure virgin" (2 Cor. 11:12) i.e. undefiled spiritually.

But what kind of Christian army will this be? Please note the following possibilities:

a. A literal fighting army at the battle for Jerusalem as Christ destroys the armies that were gathered at *"the place called Armageddon"* (Rev.16:16).

COMMENT: Nowhere do the Scriptures indicate that Christians will need to fight. In fact, conscientious objection has been a hallmark of Christians. Even for ancient Israel's deliverance from Egypt: "Moses said to the people, *"You must not be afraid. Stand still and see the salvation of Yahweh, which he will accomplish for you today, because the Egyptians whom you see today you will see never again."* (Ex. 14:13). Indeed, Richard Bauckham makes the point that:

> "The lamb really does conquer, though not by force of arms, and his followers really do share in his victory, though not by violence."
>
> *The Climax of Prophecy*, p. 230.

b. An army of martyrs having given their faithful witness.

COMMENT: Certainly Christians would be willing to die for their faith and indeed some, but not all, become martyrs during the great tribulation as evidenced with the opening of the fifth seal in Revelation 6. However, the "great multitude...have come out of the great tribulation," that is, they are survivors as a body, and so are not all martyrs.

c. To do the special work of preaching the gospel during the great tribulation.

COMMENT: Although the prime mandate of a military army isn't the function of speaking/preaching, it is possible that because it concerns witnessing Christians that the 144,000 might actually be preachers.

d. The military marching order.

COMMENT: This parallels ancient Israel marching out of Egypt in highly organized fashion. It also fits with the reason for the census in Numbers 1 i.e., a military marching order.

It seems that a combination of points **c**, and **d** are the most likely scenarios.

THE GREAT MULTITUDE IS PRESENTED AS CHRISTIAN PRIESTS

To understand how Christians, as the "great multitude," are in a priestly role, we need to appreciate the fact that the temple mentioned throughout Revelation is called the *naos* in Greek. This building housed the Holy and the Most Holy compartments and was called the sanctuary; whereas the word used elsewhere in the New Testament for the whole temple complex (courtyards etc) is *hieron*.

Also, the statement that: "before the throne there was a sea of glass, like crystal" (4:6) means that "the throne" also must be associated with the sanctuary. So the description of the "great multitude" of the multi-ethnic body of Christians, who are living immediately after the great tribulation, shows them "standing before the throne and before the Lamb, dressed in white robes" (7:9). Such robes were worn by the priests of Israel and so the "great multitude" is shown here as serving figuratively as priests "before the throne of God... and they serve him day and night in his sanctuary" (7:15).

§

Chapter 18

The Completed Identification of the 144,000

The weight of the evidence in our analysis of all the various factors presented above indicates that View #5, listed in Chapter 14 of this book, is the most likely best view in identifying the 144,000 and in giving the full description of them. This view is that, in Revelation 7, the 144,000 will be a symbolic number of a multi-ethnic body of end-time Christians and so protected during the time of God's wrath. They will exist world-wide. However, these same Christians are shown in Revelation 14 as standing on Mount Zion. They have come from all of spiritual Israel i.e. the entire age-long Christian *"Israel of God"* and are presented in their role as the Messianic army of Jesus—*"the Lion of the tribe of Judah."* Furthermore, this same body of Christians is presented in their priestly role as the "great multitude" in Revelation 7:9-13.

This view is supported by the many definite factors and the connected factors listed earlier. This view has been arrived at by seeking to ask all of the relevant questions. These questions concern the timing of these events, the location of the individuals concerned, the common factors among the 144,000, "the great multitude," and other statements about Christian "holy ones," including the fact that the Book of Revelation focuses on Christians of all races with no separate mention of Jewish Christians. Then the process of searching the Scriptures for the answers to these questions was begun, as well as to note if the theologians had helpful points to make.

No assumption was made that the 144,000 and the great multitude were the same group. Nevertheless, the answers to each of the relevant questions have led strongly to that conclusion. Furthermore, the answers to those questions also led to understanding that the other views definitely could not be correct even if they failed because of only one of the definite factors. (Please see Appendices A and B).

Although it is no proof of the correctness of the above understanding, the views of others with a professional scholarly background should be noted on any subjects that are particularly difficult, as is this one concerning the 144,000.

Conclusions of Numerous Scholars on the Identity of the 144,000

The interpretation of the 144,000 in Revelation 7 as a picture of the Christian community, inclusive of both Jewish and Gentile Christians, is the view held by the majority of scholars since the early part of the twentieth century. We also note that a very large number of these professional scholars give good reasons as to why the number 144,000 should be taken as symbolic. These are: Metzger, Bauckham, Osborne, Ladd, Gundry, Mounce, and many more.

Furthermore, the general concept of View #5, or some close variation of it, is also held by Lohmeyer, Farrer, Caird, Beasley-Murray, Schussler, Fiorenza, Chilton, Harrington, Giesen, and Michaels. This view details how the 144,000 are end-times Christians of the age-long multi-ethnic body of the Christian "Israel of God." They are sealed for special protection during the day of God's wrath and are the same people as those in the "great multitude," only presented from a different perspective, that is, as organized in military marching fashion to give a faithful witness.

God's Plan for a Remnant of Natural Israel in God's Kingdom

The above view in no way attempts to negate Paul's statements that there will be a body of Jews who become Christians in the future <u>after Christ returns</u> "if they do not continue in their unbelief" *(Rom. 11:23)*, so that he says "and in this way all Israel will be saved" *(Rom. 11:26)*. This plan is detailed in the following Scriptures: Isa. 61:2b-11; Jer. 23:23; Hos. 3:4-5; Mic. 2:12; Zech. 13:8, 9; Matt. 19:28 (Luke 22:29); 23:39; Rom. 9:27; 11:1-2, 11, 23, and 25-26.

...

We will now move on to examine the events from which the 144,000 are to be protected.

Chapter 19

Breaking of the Seventh Seal
—The First Four Trumpet Blasts
Revelation 8

TEXT

When he broke open the seventh seal, there was silence in heaven for about half an hour. **²**Then I saw the seven angels who stand in the presence of God. Seven trumpets were given to them. **³**Another angel, who was holding a golden censer, came and stood at the altar. He was given a large quantity of incense to offer up on the golden altar that is in front of the throne. It was offered along with all the prayers of God's holy people. **⁴**So the smoke from the incense, with the prayers of God's holy people, ascended from the angel's hand to God. **⁵**Then the angel took the censer, filled it with fire from the altar, and threw it down on the earth, and there were thunderclaps, rumblings, flashes of lightning, and an earthquake. **⁶**Then the seven angels who had the seven trumpets got ready to blow them.

The First Trumpet

⁷The first angel blew his trumpet. Hail and fire mixed with blood were thrown onto the land, so that a third of the land was burned up, a third of the trees were burned up, and all the green grass was burned up.

The Second Trumpet

⁸Then the second angel blew his trumpet. Something like a massive mountain of burning fire was thrown into the sea. A third of the sea became blood, **⁹**and a third of the creatures living in the sea died, and a third of the ships were destroyed.

The Third Trumpet

¹⁰Then the third angel blew his trumpet. A huge star, blazing like a torch, fell from the sky. It fell on a third of the rivers and on the springs of water. **¹¹**The name of the star is Wormwood. So a third of the waters became wormwood, and many people died from these waters because they had been made bitter.

The Fourth Trumpet

¹²Then the fourth angel blew his trumpet. A third of the sun was struck, and a third of the moon, and a third of the stars, so that a third of [their light] was darkened. A third of the day was without light and a third of the night also.

¹³Then I looked, and I heard an eagle flying in mid-air, saying with a loud voice, "What calamity! What calamity! What great calamity awaits those who live on the earth, because of the remaining sound-blasts of the trumpets, that the three angels are about to blow!"

Overview

We now return to the sealed scroll for the breaking of the seventh and final seal. The first three seals concerned the first half of Daniel's 70th "seven" during which the early activities of the Antichrist take place. The fourth and fifth seals concerned the great tribulation (persecution) as Satan's wrath against God's people resulting in many Christian martyrs and paralleling the latter half of Daniel's 70th "seven." The sixth seal concerned the sign of the end of the age (Matt 24:29) with the phenomena of earth-wide darkness for a time. Finally we saw the interlude for the sealing of the 144,000.

This seventh seal pictures the events of God's retribution upon the wicked followers of Antichrist—"the earth-dwellers," firstly with the warning judgments of the seven trumpets and then with the plagues of God's final punishment poured out from the seven bowls of plague.

When we come to Revelation 8:7-12 we see that the first four trumpet blasts involve plagues of elemental forces. However, it speaks of only "a third of" earth, sea, fresh waters, and physical luminaries as being affected by these plagues. So these appear to refer to the effects on the various environments of Antichrist's kingdom as a literal approximation of a large land area occupied by his kingdom and so only affecting those who live in that area. However, when we later come to the pouring out of the bowls of plague this appears to encompass all those who worship the Antichrist world-wide. (Please see Appendix C for the evidence that Antichrist's Kingdom will not be world-wide although its influence will be world-wide and his worshippers will exist world-wide).

Comment on the First Four Trumpets

8:1: "When he broke open the seventh seal. There was silence in heaven for about half an hour." Here no plague or judgment message is given with these opening words about the seventh seal. In fact, this is the seal which, when broken, allows the scroll to be opened and so revealing the judgments of the seven trumpets, the seventh of which reveals the seven plagues poured from the bowls. Therefore, the blowing of the seven trumpets actually constitutes the seventh seal. These judgments do not appear to be poured out on absolutely all of mankind but only "on those who had the mark of the beast, and who had worshipped his image" *(Rev. 16:2).* They have the purpose of driving these people to repent (Rev. 9:20). So the area upon which these plagues are poured involves only the kingdom of "the ferocious beast" (the Antichrist) i.e. approximately one third of the world.

This "silence" simply refers to a dramatic pause of a brief time of silence. It represents the anticipation of God's coming judgments (Zech. 2:13) as the seven trumpets are about to be blown.

8:2: "**Then I saw the seven angels who stand in the presence of God. Seven trumpets were given to them**." As with Gabriel as one "who stands before God" *(Luke 1:19)* which is a reference to his being one of the archangels, so, too, these seven angels are also archangels. They are identical with "the seven spirits of God" mentioned in 1:4 and 4:5.

The blasting of these trumpets concerns judgment and follows the 4 + 2 + 1 pattern as similar to the seals.

Interestingly, each trumpet continues to sound, but over a short period of time. (Please see Appendix D).

The first four trumpet blasts affect the environment of Antichrist's direct kingdom i.e. approximately one third of those who worship the Antichrist i.e. one third of the land, sea, springs, and the atmosphere. Trumpets five and six concern the demon attacks upon those within the Beast's kingdom. Trumpet seven, which includes the bowl judgments, concerns the final battle leading to the destruction of all who are worshippers of Antichrist.

8:3: "**Another angel, who was holding a golden censer, came and stood at the altar. He was given a large quantity of incense to offer up on the golden altar that is in front of the throne. It was offered along with all the prayers of God's holy people**." This is not one of the "seven angels" or even Messiah Jesus, but rather an angel with a priestly function, a common understanding in Jewish thought.

This golden censer pictures intercessory prayers. It was a portable shallow golden pan for burning incense and likely in the form of a ladle or small shovel with a long hand-shaped handle. It was used for carrying burning coals on which the incense would be burned. One example of the usage of incense is that on the Day of Atonement the High priest would use such a censer to carry burning embers along with a container of incense in his other hand into the most holy compartment and then to pour the incense onto the burning embers for the scent to rise into the air. The incense would be a mixture of resin droplets, galbanum gum, mollusc scent with an equal amount of frankincense, and so producing an aromatic odour. In contrast with the description in Rev. 5:8 of the twenty four elders offering of incense, this incense here only accompanies the prayers of the holy ones.

This altar is the altar of incense which, in the earthly temple, was placed in the holy compartment. The burning embers of coal were topped up from the altar of burnt offering.

The throne likely refers to the Ark of the Covenant placed in the most holy compartment of the tabernacle. It was viewed as God's throne and so is a reference to God's presence.

8:4: "**So the smoke from the incense, with the prayers of God's holy people, ascended from the angel's hand to God.**" This smoke rises with the prayers of God's holy people and so adds fragrance to those prayers. These prayers trigger a response from God to bring His judgments upon the world (6:9-11).

8:5a: "**Then the angel took the censer, filled it with fire from the altar, and threw it down on the earth.**" This fire would be in the form of glowing embers taken from the altar of incense. However, it now becomes the fire of judgment, rather than for the burning of incense as linked with prayers.

8:5b-6: "**Thunderclaps, rumblings, flashes of lightning, and an earthquake. Then the seven angels who had the seven trumpets got ready to blow them.**" As expressing God's majesty and power this atmospheric phenomena is described for the second time. The first mention is in 4:5, but without the earthquake. The third mention is in 11:19 with the addition of "severe hail." The final mention is in 16:18 concerning the pouring out of the seventh bowl, but again with no mentioning of hail. This is one of the indicators that the seventh seal, seventh trumpet, and seventh bowl of plague are all connected as the same event.

Once again we see that these are God's seven archangels. Their trumpet blasts are announcements of what devastations God is to bring upon those who fight against His purpose for the earth.

8:7: "**The first angel blew his trumpet. Hail, fire and blood thrown onto the land, so that a third of the land was burned up, a third of the trees were burned up, and all the green grass was burned up.**" This attack upon the land represents the destruction of agriculture in the Antichrist/ferocious beast's kingdom.

The land represents the kingdom of "the ferocious beast" (Dan. 7:7-8, 19-22). This is indicated when "the fifth poured out his bowl on the throne of the beast, so that darkness enveloped his kingdom" (16:10). This kingdom of the Beast occupies the area from the Euphrates River (9:14) right up to where John sees the symbolic mountain falling into the eastern Mediterranean.

This first trumpet blast is a replicating of the seventh plague on ancient Egypt in the time of Moses which the Israelites, who lived in the area called Goshen, did not suffer. Also when leading the Israelites into the land of Canaan, God rained down huge hailstones upon the Amorite army (Josh. 10:11). Furthermore, in Job 38:22-33, we find that God reserves "storehouses of hail" to rain down on His enemies.

The fire here could be the fire (glowing embers) thrown from the golden censer. So the fire which first sent prayers up to God now switches to being fire of judgment. However, in reality it could be flashes of lightning as in 8:5.

"Blood" mixed with fire was often used to indicate God's bringing of destruction at the end of the age (Joel 2:30-31; Acts 2:19-20).

So this first trumpet blast concerns the literal burning up of Antichrist's economy based upon agriculture, thereby wrecking part of his economic plan. Indeed, it says "all the green grass" of his kingdom is burned i.e. to emphasize the totality of this destruction.

8:8: **"Then the second angel blew his trumpet. Something like a massive mountain of burning fire was thrown into the sea. A third of the sea became blood."** This trumpet continues to sound, but over a short period of time. *(Please see 8:7).*

This description is only "like" a massive hill and therefore is symbolic, most likely of an angelic being as in 1 Enoch 18:13 where "seven stars are like great burning mountains." Again the fire is that of judgment and the serious damage done to the economy of the sea merchants is quite literal as with the plagues upon Egypt.

8:9: **"A third of the creatures living in the sea died, and a third of the ships were destroyed."** This represents the destruction of the Beast's economy from the various seas closest to Antichrist's kingdom i.e. the Mediterranean Sea, the Black Sea, and the Caspian Sea. However, the effect no doubt will concern trade in all of the world's oceans.

8:10, 11: "Then the third angel blew his trumpet. A huge star, blazing like a torch, fell from the sky. It fell on a third of the rivers and on the springs of water. ¹¹The name of the star is Wormwood. So a third of the waters became wormwood, and many people died." This trumpet also continues to sound, but over a short period of time and represents the destruction of the economy from the inland waterways of the Beast's kingdom. Indeed, from this there will be a shortage of drinking water.

The star called Wormwood is most likely symbolic of a descending angel. In scripture stars are often symbols of angels (Job 38:7). In fact, wormwood is not literally directly poisonous, but is more of a symbol of bitter sorrow, especially in connection with death. Furthermore, wormwood is also associated with sins of the flesh and idolatry. So this angel is allowed to literally devastate a third of the world's sources of fresh water, specifically the waters of the Beast's kingdom. The fact that "many people died" is because the water is now undrinkable.

8:12: "Then the fourth angel blew his trumpet. A third of the sun was struck, and a third of the moon and a third of the stars, so that a third of their light might be darkened. A third of the day was without light and a third of the night also." As with the other trumpets this continues to sound, but over a short period of time. *(Please see 8:7).* This very apocalyptic event affects the atmosphere and brings about deep darkness on the Beast's kingdom.

This fourth trumpet blast is a replicating of the ninth plague on ancient Egypt in the time of Moses, a plague which the Israelites did not suffer. At first sight this description defies the known laws of physics. However, in apocalyptic literature such effects do occur.

8:13: "Then I looked, and I heard an eagle flying in mid-air, saying with a loud voice, What calamity! What calamity! What great calamity awaits those who live on the earth, because of the remaining sound-blasts of the trumpets, that the three angels are about to blow!" This cannot be a literal eagle because it is capable of human speech. In the Hebrew Scriptures the eagle can be a symbol of any of the following:

- Power and swiftness of flight for deliverance (Ex. 19:4; Prov. 23:5).
- Portents of death and destruction (Jer. 48:40-42).
- Youthful vigour and strength (P. 103:5).

Evidently this particular eagle is flying in mid-air for the purpose of

101

announcing the coming death and destruction of the earth-dwellers who do not repent. It is possible that this messenger is one of the four living creatures i.e. a cherub or seraph and would be the one that "looked like a flying eagle" (4:7).

So these four events from the blowing of these first four trumpets will bring destructive plagues on all parts of the physical environment of Antichrist's kingdom.

The rather out-of-date term "woe" really means a real calamity or disaster. So the angel is really saying "What calamity!" three times for emphasis. It does not simply mean sorrow on the part of sufferers. Indeed, these three calamities match with the blasting of each of the final three trumpets, so that the first calamity is that of the fifth trumpet and the second calamity is that of the sixth trumpet etcetera. Once again these affect those who are the "earth-dwellers" i.e. the one third who live in the area of Antichrist's kingdom. Also the imminence of these disasters is shown in the statement that the angels with trumpets "are about to blow."

Chapter 20

The First Calamity on Antichrist's Followers
(Fifth Trumpet)
Revelation 9:1-12

TEXT

Then the fifth angel blew his trumpet. I saw a star that had fallen from the sky to the earth. The key to the shaft of the abyss was given him. ²He opened the shaft of the abyss, and smoke rose out of it like smoke from a huge furnace. The sun and the air became darkened by the smoke from the shaft. ³Then locusts appeared out of the smoke and onto the earth. They were given abilities like those of earth's scorpions. ⁴They were told not to damage the grass of the land or any green plant or tree, but only those people who don't have the seal of God on their foreheads. ⁵They weren't allowed to kill them, but only to inflict severe pain on them for five months, and their inflicting of severe pain is as when a scorpion strikes a person. ⁶In those days, people will seek their own death, but will never find it. They will long to die, but death will escape them.

⁷The locusts looked like horses equipped for battle. On their heads were things like crowns, gold in appearance, and their faces were like human faces. ⁸They have hair like women's hair and their teeth were like lions' teeth. ⁹They have breastplates like iron breastplates and the sound of their wings was like the thunder of many horse-drawn chariots charging into battle. ¹⁰They also have tails with stingers, just like scorpions; so that with their tails, they have the ability to harm people for five months. ¹¹They have as their king the angel of the abyss, whose name in Hebrew is "Abaddon," and in Greek he has the name "Apollyon." ¹²The first calamity has passed. But take note: two more distressful calamities are to come after these things!

Overview

The earlier four trumpet blasts of plagues of elemental forces affected only the environment of Antichrist's kingdom. Indeed, those humans who will have taken the mark of the Beast within Antichrist's kingdom have not yet been shown to be directly attacked. It is with the blowing of the fifth and sixth trumpets that we first see devastating demonic attacks directly upon these ones.

Comment on the Fifth Trumpet

9:1a: "**Then the fifth angel blew his trumpet and I saw a star that had fallen from the sky to earth.**" This continues to sound, but again over a short period of time. *(Please see 8:7).*

As with the other trumpets which involve stars, so too, we have here the involvement of an angelic being—a messenger from God. Some commentators even feel that this could be Satan because of Jesus' comment that he, "saw Satan fall like lightning from heaven" (Luke 10:18). However, this is unlikely because the phrase, "had fallen from the sky" does not mean that he is a fallen angel, but simply that he had descended to the earth. So this "star" is not to be identified with "the angel of the Abyss" in 12:9.

9:1b: **"The key to the shaft of the abyss was given him."** The abyss (Gk *abyssos*) is wrongly and illogically thought of as a "bottomless pit." The meaning is gained by examining all of the occurrences of "abyss" in the Scriptures. In fact, the Greek Septuagint never renders the Hebrew word *sheol* as *abyssos*, although it is used of the place where Jesus' body was after his death (Rom. 10:7). So unlike *sheol/hades*, as meaning the general grave, the meaning here is that of "unfathomable" and "an exceedingly deep" and vast place of restraint often with reference to the sea. It is so deep that only God can bring someone back from it. The term is further defined as "a prison" in Revelation 20:7. However, it is not a literal place but is figurative of an infinite void of absolute restraint and so can apply to a good person (Jesus—Rom. 10:7) and those who are evil (the demons—Luke 8:31; 2 Pet. 2:4; Jude 6). It is also the place from which Antichrist will emerge in the future (11:7; 17:8) and where Satan will be imprisoned for the one thousand years (20:1-3).

So the "key" and the "shaft" to the abyss are also symbolic and simply show the angel's control over imprisonment by such total restraint or release from it.

9:2: **"He opened the shaft of the abyss, and smoke rose out of it like smoke from a huge furnace. The sun and the air became darkened by the smoke from the shaft smoke rose out of it."** This smoke as symbolic of the wicked portends God's wrath and points to the coming destruction in the lake of fire of those who unrepentantly worship the Antichrist.

9:3: **"Then locusts appeared out of the smoke and onto the earth. They were given abilities like those of earth's scorpions."** These locusts are symbols of demons. They are symbolic because their behaviour is nothing like literal locusts and they also appear as very strange looking horses. Furthermore, they are indicated as being demons because they are released from the abyss, the very location that demons feared being thrown into: "They [*the demons*] implored him [*Jesus*] not to command them to go away into the abyss" *(Luke 8:31).* Furthermore, they have "Abaddon" as their king (9:11, this likely being a name for Satan. They are further linked with the Antichrist because, just as he ascended from the abyss (11:7, 17:8), so too, do they.

This releasing of these symbolic locusts reflects the eighth plague on ancient Egypt as well as the literal locust plague described by Joel 1:2-2:11, this latter plague showing the approach of "the great and awesome day of Yahweh" (Joel 2:31).

9:4: "**They were told not to damage the grass of the land or any green plant or tree, but only those people who don't have the seal of God on their foreheads**." On the surface this seems to contradict what is said about the destructive effects on the grass and trees from the first trumpet blast when the vegetation was consumed by fire. However, this command in 9:4 is said only to emphasize the purpose of these "locusts" as being to harm actual humans, rather than to consume a locust's natural food of vegetation. It is therefore, a further indication that we are seeing demon activity in this passage of Revelation. Furthermore, this may even be a reference to the grass etc. in the rest of the world outside of Antichrist's own kingdom.

God's punishment falls specifically upon those who have "the mark of the Beast" (14:9; 16:2); yet Christians were sealed for their protection back in Revelation 7 and so are totally unaffected by this demonic attack.

The purpose of these demon attacks upon the earth-dwellers is to prove to them that the false gods that they have worshipped, namely, the antichrists and the final Antichrist are forces promoted by Satan. These ones are really the hateful enemies of mankind.

9:5: "**They weren't allowed to kill them, but only to inflict severe pain on them for five months, and their inflicting of severe pain is as when a scorpion strikes a person**." The purpose of this excruciating pain is to intimidate, terrorize and demoralize "the earth-dwellers," but not to kill them. It has repentance as the goal and allows the people an opportunity to repent of their worshipping of the Beast.

This symbolic period of five months indicates that God has placed a strict limit on the time of inflicting severe pain on "the earth-dwellers." Literal locusts are restricted to the dry season between April and August (five months) in Palestine.

9:6: "**In those days, people will seek their own death, but will never find it. They will long to die, but death will escape them.**" This severe pain and terrorization of the people by the demons will be so horrific that they literally want to die to escape the pain and terror. However, it appears that God will not let them die at this time even if they attempt suicide. Indeed, they must suffer until they have fully experienced what is coming to them in the sixth trumpet. The reason for this restraining of them in death is that their terrible murderous crimes against God's people must be paid for as based on the law of retribution (*lex talionis*).

9:7-8: "**The locusts looked like horses equipped for battle. On their heads were things like crowns, gold in appearance, and their faces were like human faces. ⁸They have hair like women's hair and their teeth were like lions' teeth.**" This imagery is taken from the description of the locusts in Joel 1 and 2 and indeed, horses in the ancient world were seen as the most devastating of weapons when used for war. In the imagery given here what they wear on their heads only look like crowns of gold and are simply a symbol of victory. Also the descriptions of the human faces, the long hair like the hair of Parthian warriors of the east, and the fierce teeth like lion's teeth (Joel 1:6), as features of these locusts, further show that these are not literal locusts because these are attributes of intelligent beings along with the cunning of fierce lions for catching and devouring of prey.

9:9: "**They have breastplates like iron breastplates and the sound of their wings was like the thunder of many horse-drawn chariots charging into battle.**" This feature shows that these war horses are totally invulnerable to earthly enemy weapons and that the horrifying sound would terrify the earth-dwellers.

9:10: "**They also have tails with stingers, just like scorpions so that with their tails, they have the ability to harm people for five months.**" In this description we find a further indication that these locusts with tails like scorpions represent demons. In fact, Jesus even used the phrase "snakes and scorpions" as symbols of demonic forces (Luke 10:19).

9:11: "**They have as their king the angel of the abyss, whose name in Hebrew is "Abaddon," and in Greek he has the name "Apollyon."**" This angel is most likely a reference to Satan. His names "Abbadon" (Heb.) or Apollyon (Gk) mean "destroyer." This one is unlikely to be the Beast i.e. "the son of destruction" (2 Thess. 2:3) because the Beast is never classified as an angel/messenger. Possibly, because of the use of the article with the word "angel" this one is shown to be the well-known leader, and the most well-known one is Satan.

Although it is true that literal locusts have no leader (Prov. 30:27) these are not literal locusts and so, as demons, these ones do have a leader—a king. Indeed, in Jesus' time it was generally accepted that Satan (Beelzebul) is "the ruler of the demons" (Matt. 12:24).

9:12: "**The first calamity has passed. But take note: two more distressful calamities are to come after these things!**" This is a reminder of the three calamities (woes/disasters) announced in 8:13. Because "the first calamity has passed" these calamities clearly do not overlap.

§

Chapter 21

The Second Calamity on Antichrist's Followers
(Sixth Trumpet)
Revelation 9:13-21

TEXT

The Sixth Trumpet

¹³Then the sixth angel blew his trumpet. I heard a single voice coming from the four horns on the golden altar that is in front of God. ¹⁴It said to the sixth angel, who was holding the trumpet, "Release the four angels who are held bound at the great river Euphrates!" ¹⁵So the four angels who had been kept ready for the hour, day, month, and year were released to kill a third of the human race. ¹⁶The number of troops of cavalry was 200 million; I heard their number. ¹⁷This is how I saw the horses and the riders in the vision: they had breastplates that were fiery red, hyacinth blue, and sulphur yellow. The heads of the horses looked like lions' heads, and fire, smoke, and sulphur came out of their mouths. ¹⁸By these three plagues a third of mankind was killed: by the fire, smoke, and sulphur coming out of their mouths.¹⁹The horses' power is in their mouths and in their tails, because their tails are like snakes with heads that inflict injuries.

²⁰The rest of mankind—those who hadn't been killed by these plagues—didn't change their ways concerning their activities. They didn't give up worshipping demons and idols made of gold, silver, bronze, stone, and wood—idols that aren't able to see, hear, or walk. ²¹Nor did they have a change of mindset leading them to turn away from their murders, their occult practices, their sexual immorality, and their stealing.

Comment on the Sixth Trumpet

9:13: "**Then the sixth angel blew his trumpet. I heard a single voice coming from the four horns on the golden altar.**" This trumpet continues to sound for a time as with the earlier trumpets, but only over a relatively short period of time *(see 8:7)*.

The four horns symbolize God's power. The altar was mentioned in 8:3 with the opening of the seventh seal. So this voice is most probably the voice of the angel who presented the prayers of God's people to Him for the avenging of their blood (8:3-5; 6:10).

9:14: "**It said to the sixth angel, who was holding the trumpet, "Release the four angels held bound at the great river Euphrates.**" These are four demon angels of high rank who have been "held bound" i.e. restrained by God or one of His agents until this appointed time.

It is possible that these four are "the [demon] princes" of four eastern (Euphrates) end-time nations (Dan. 10:13, 20-21), but are placed as leaders over the 200 million demon cavalry.

The events described for this sixth trumpet blast are very similar to those of the fifth trumpet blast, only more devastating. The key difference between the events of the two trumpet blasts is that, whereas no "earth-dwellers" die as a result of the fifth trumpet blast, one third of mankind i.e. "the earth-dwellers" do die as a result of the sixth trumpet blast. Indeed, the limit to one third of mankind is seen in the statement about the Euphrates which indicates the eastern boundary of Antichrist's kingdom and that it is a symbol of foreign invasion. Please note that 16:12 shows that with the sixth bowl the Euphrates, "dried up in order to prepare the way for the kings from the east."

9:15: "So the four angels who had been kept ready for the hour, day, month, and year were released to kill a third of the human race." The fourfold aspect to this shows how definite God is about the pouring out of this plague and with His predestined will for the major parts of His end-time program.

As with the earlier trumpet blasts affecting only one third of the environment, namely, Antichrist's kingdom, so this one third of mankind appears to be a literal approximation of "the earth-dwellers" living within the boundaries of Antichrist's kingdom.

Earlier, at the breaking of the fourth seal, Death and Hades "were given authority over a quarter of the earth, to kill…" (6:8). However, 6:8 is a reference to the great tribulation and the killing of Christians, but now in Revelation 9 we have moved into the time of the pouring out God's wrath and we see the killing of "the earth-dwellers." Throughout these events Christians are totally protected from these expressions of God's wrath (Rom. 5:9, 1 Thess. 5:9) by their sealing in 7:1-4. This is just as the Israelites were protected during the last seven plagues poured out on ancient Egypt.

9:16: "The number of troops of cavalry was 200 million." This is a further picture of the demon hordes and is most probably a figurative number to show an innumerable horde. Some have proposed that these are human armies; however, because of the descriptions that have factors in common with Joel 1 and 2 and the fifth trumpet description of the demonic locust attack, it seems more likely that these cavalry also picture a demon attack.

109

9:17: "This is how I saw the horses and the riders in the vision: they had breastplates that were fiery red, hyacinth blue, and sulphur yellow. "The heads of the horses looked like lions' heads and fire, smoke, and sulphur came out of their mouths." The grammar here indicates that both the riders and their horses have these breastplates. The colours correspond to the "fire, smoke, and sulphur" which came out of the lion-like mouths and result in "a third of mankind" being killed (vs.18).

Lions were the most dangerous creatures in the Middle-East in John's time, and so this description shows the ferocity and destructiveness of these demon-horses. Also because the heads are like lions' heads they would have lions' teeth just as the locusts do in the fifth trumpet scene (9:8).

9:18: "By these three plagues a third of mankind was killed: by the fire, smoke, and sulphur coming out of their mouths." John, of course, would be thinking in terms of the results of bombardment by the ancient Roman weapons of war, such as their siege engines which hurl fire into enemy strongholds rather than modern-day weapons.

Earlier, during the blasting of the fifth trumpet, death was forbidden to these "earth-dwellers" in Antichrist's kingdom (9:6); but now they literally die. In fact, the term "mankind" here is used in the same way "world" and "earth-dwellers" are used in referencing those who worship Antichrist as ones who are totally opposed to God as well as persecuting His people. So in being "one third" the reference is to those worshippers of Antichrist who die by the action of these demonic cavalry at the blasting of the sixth trumpet.

9:19: "The horses' power is in their mouths and in their tails, because their tails are like snakes with heads that inflict injuries." This feature connects the sixth trumpet blast to the stinging of the scorpions' tails in the fifth trumpet blast. So once again it is evident that a picture of demon attack is being described here. As with the scorpion tails, the snake bite only severely harms "the earth-dwellers," rather than killing them. It is from the lion-like mouths that death comes by means of the three plagues of "fire, smoke, and sulphur."

9:20: "The rest of mankind—those who hadn't been killed by these plagues—didn't change their ways concerning their activities. They didn't give up worshipping demons and idols made of gold, silver, bronze, stone, and wood—idols that aren't able to see, hear, or walk." All of this terror

110

from God still has a merciful purpose, that is, to move those of "the rest of mankind" world-wide i.e. the remaining supporters and worshippers of Antichrist to repent of the worship of their idols and their immoral life-style. The stubbornness of humans to change is quite amazing. One would imagine that "the rest of mankind" i.e. the remaining "earth-dwellers" world-wide would learn the lesson from all that they will have seen of God's activity against Antichrist's kingdom, that is, seeing what has happened to the one third who had been killed because of this plague of demon attack at the blasting of the sixth trumpet. One would imagine that they would repent of these disgusting activities and particularly of their worship of lifeless material wealth as well as the worship of the Antichrist. Of itself "an idol in this world is really nothing" (1 Cor. 8:4) and has no power. However, from another perspective, demons are viewed as standing behind the worship of idols and so idolaters become partners with the demons (1 Cor. 10:20).

9:21: "**Nor did they have a change of mindset leading them to turn away from their murders, their occult practices, their sexual immorality, and their stealing.**" This shows that at this point in the sequence of events God is still hoping for repentance on the part of these idolaters who are also living immoral lives. This description follows the pattern of Paul's words in Romans 1:29-31:

> "They were filled with all kinds of injustice, wickedness, greediness, and depravity; they became full of envy, murder, quarrelling, deceitfulness, and spitefulness. They also became gossips, character assassins, God-haters, insolent, arrogant, and boastful. Furthermore, they invent ways to be cruel; they are disobedient to parents; [31]they have no conscience; they don't keep their promises, and they show no kindness or care to others."

Chapter 22

The Small Unrolled Scroll
Revelation 10

TEXT

Then I saw another powerful angel coming down from heaven. He was wrapped in a cloud, and had a rainbow over his head. His face was like the sun, and his legs were like pillars of fire. **2**He had in his hand a small scroll that had been unrolled, and he placed his right foot on the sea and his left on the land. **3**Then in a loud voice he shouted out, just like a lion roaring. When he shouted out, the voices of seven thunders answered. **4**When the seven thunders spoke, I was about to write, but then I heard a voice from heaven saying, "Seal up the things which the seven thunders spoke, and don't write them down." **5**Then the angel that I saw standing on the sea and on the land raised his right hand to heaven. **6**He swore an oath by the One who lives forever and ever—the One who created heaven and everything in it, and the earth and everything in it, and the sea and everything in it. So he said, "There will be no further time interval! **7**But in the days of the sounding of the seventh angel, when he blows his trumpet, God's secret plan will be completed, just as He has announced to His bond-servants the prophets."

8Then the voice that I had heard from heaven began speaking to me again, saying, "Go and take the unrolled scroll from the hand of the angel who is standing on the sea and on the land." **9**So I went to the angel and asked him to give me the small scroll. "Take it and eat it," he told me, "and it will be bitter in your stomach, but it will be as sweet as honey in your mouth." **10**So I took the small scroll from the angel's hand and ate it. It was as sweet as honey in my mouth, but after I had eaten it, it became bitter in my stomach. **11**Then he said to me, "You must prophesy again about many nations, races, languages, and kings."

TRANSLATION POINTS

10:6: The phrase "no further time interval" is poorly rendered in the KJV as "that there should be time no longer" or "no more delay" in most modern versions. Both of these give a wrong sense to the context because God's plan does not suffer delays. "No further time interval" or similar is better.

10:7: "But in the days of the sounding of the seventh angel, when he blows his trumpet, God's secret plan will be completed." The KJV renders this as, "when he shall *begin* to sound." Most modern translations render it as, "when he is *about to* sound" *(NASB).* These also are not good renderings because they imply that the end will come just before the seventh angel blows his trumpet which does not fit the context. The RSV and the HCSB do not make this translation mistake.

Comment on the Angel and the Unrolled Scroll

10:1a: "**Then I saw another powerful angel coming down from heaven. He was wrapped in a cloud.**" This interlude brings a temporary halt to the describing of the events concerning God's day of wrath, but these events are resumed in Chapter 13. So the angel now returns to speaking about things connected with the great tribulation which will occur before God's day of wrath.

This is an angelic special herald of Christ and he is similar to or the same as the strong angel in 5:2. Although this gives the impression of similarity with the description of Christ in 1:13-16, it is not Christ himself. The *differences* are that Christ has:

- a golden sash, eyes like flames of fire,
- a voice like the sound of many waters,
- seven stars in his hand,
- a sharp two-edged sword protruding from his mouth,

The only similarities are that this powerful angel has "legs...like pillars of fire" which is similar to Jesus' "feet...like burnished bronze refined in a furnace" (1:15). This angel also has a face like the sun as does Jesus (1:16). However, Jesus is never called an angel in the entire New Testament (Heb. 1:4, 5, 13), but this angel's appearance does display the glory of Christ.

NOTE: the Woman of Revelation 12 and the angel of 19:17 are also associated with the sun.

10:1b: "**And had a rainbow over his head. His face was like the sun, and his legs were like pillars of fire.**" This rainbow is a crown and signifies glory and mercy. In Ezekiel 1:28 and Revelation 4:3 God is encircled by a rainbow. So here, the mercy and glory of God and Jesus are represented.

In being similar to Jesus' "feet...like burnished bronze refined in a furnace," this also shows this angel's power, stability, and purity with judgments of perfect justice. He is a reflection of Jesus in these ways.

10:2a: "**He had in his hand a small scroll that had been unrolled.**" This appears to be the seven-sealed scroll of 5:1. Evidence for the two descriptions of the scroll in 5:1 and 10:2 as referring to the same scroll is as follows:

- Regarding the word "small" theologian Richard Bauckam, who is one who shows that this scroll is the same one as in Rev. 5 ff, notes that, "in the Greek of this period words which are diminutive in form frequently no longer carry diminutive meaning. None of the diminutive forms in Revelation seem to be intended to be diminutive in meaning" *The Climax of Prophecy* p.243. However, if the diminutive form is relevant it still does not mean that this is a different scroll from the seven-sealed scroll, but rather that the seven-sealed scroll is physically small.

- Both scroll descriptions are similar to the scroll written on the front and the back as described in Ezekiel 2:9 to 3:1-3. So in the description given in Revelation 5:1, we are shown the first half of the scroll *(written on the front and the back)* and in 10:2, 8-11 we are shown the second half *(by the eating of it)* as a resuming of and expansion of the information in the now unrolled scroll. So the handling of the scroll runs as follows: God holds the scroll in His right hand (5:1); Jesus takes it from God's hand (5:7); Jesus, as the Lamb, breaks each of the seven seals (6:1-17); the scroll is unrolled revealing the seven trumpets (8:1, 2); then John takes the unrolled scroll from the hand of the angel representing Jesus (10:1, 8, 9). This is the same order of handling of the revelation in 1:1, namely, from God to Jesus to the angel to John, and finally to the Christian community.

- The opening words of each passage (5:2 and 10:1) are almost identical: "And I saw a powerful angel..." This indicates that the passages are likely to refer to the same situation.

As with Ezekiel's already unrolled scroll, these latter contents of the scroll could not be revealed until they had been ingested by John. The idea of closing and sealing of a scroll containing visions occurs several times in Daniel (8:26; 12:4, 9). Indeed, Revelation 5:1 and 10:2, 8-11 seem to resume discussion of Daniel's scroll (Dan. 12) also. This scroll was sealed to Daniel's understanding and will only be revealed to him at his resurrection at the time of the end. However, it was no longer sealed to John's understanding when handed to him by the angel. So when John receives this scroll it has been supplemented and clarified over and above all that Daniel had been given.

The formula "nations, tribes, peoples, and languages" is used only in reference to the diversity of the community of believers prior to chapter

10. After this point it is used specifically with reference to whole nations showing that Revelation 10 is an important transition point with God's focus more significantly on them.

The three and a half year time period appears only after Revelation 10 after John has ingested the scroll and then reveals its contents. So the scroll concerns God's secret purpose for establishing His kingdom on earth. It gives details of the great tribulation and God's day of wrath upon the earth-dwellers, starting with the blowing of the seventh trumpet which concerns the pouring out of the bowls of wrath.

10:2b-3: **"And he placed his right foot on the sea and his left on the land. When he shouted out, the voices of seven thunders answered"** Because this powerful angel is Christ's representative his foot action indicates Christ's possession of and authority over the entire world.

The reference to voices is an allusion to Psalm 29 which speaks of the voice of Yahweh which thunders and causes tremendous damage to forests, mountains, and the wilderness. Additionally, in all other references to thunder in Revelation, thunders form a precursor to coming judgments of divine wrath.

10:4: **"When the seven thunders spoke, I was about to write, but then I heard a voice from heaven saying, Seal up the things which the seven thunders spoke and don't write them down."** This does not refer to the sealing up of prophecy as with Daniel, but simply to affirm God's sovereign control over all the sets of judgments described in Revelation.

10:5: **"Then the angel that I saw standing on the sea and on the land raised his right hand to heaven."** To stand on the complete planet as God's representative shows that God, through Jesus, is in ultimate control of the world. Raising one's right hand is in the familiar gesture of an oath.

10:6: **"He swore an oath by the One who lives forever and ever—the One who created heaven and everything in it, and the earth and everything in it, and the sea and everything in it. So he said, "There will be no further time interval!"** Such a swearing of an oath in the eternal God's name shows the imminence of all that follows.

The phrase "the One who created heaven and everything in it" shows that Jesus was neither the creator of the universe, nor the agent of its creation (Isa.44:24), although Jesus is the agent of and reason for the new creation (Col. 1:13-20; 1 Cor. 8:6b).

115

10:7: "But in the days of the sounding of the seventh angel, when he blows his trumpet God's secret plan will be completed just as He has announced to His bond-servants the prophets." This shows that the using of the seventh trumpet will not be a single blast, but will be over a period of time—enough for all seven bowls to be poured out.

This secret plan, which is later revealed, is the good news of the Kingdom of God which is God's plan of salvation with it's granting of immortality for faithful Christians.

10:8: "Then the voice that I had heard from heaven began speaking to me again, saying, "Go and take the unrolled scroll from the hand of the angel who is standing on the sea and on the land." This is most likely the voice of Messiah Jesus and shows that John has moved back from heaven to earth vision-wise.

Just as Jesus, as the Lamb, had to take the scroll from God's right hand (5:7), John is asked to replicate this action by taking it from the angel's hand as a form of commissioning of John.

10:9-10: "It will be bitter in your stomach, but it will be as sweet as honey in your mouth. So I took the small scroll from the angel's hand and ate it. It was as sweet as honey in my mouth, but after I had eaten it, it became bitter in my stomach." The eating of the scroll symbolizes John's assimilation and digesting of the remaining prophetic message contained in the scroll. This was perhaps sweet as he begins to take it in, but then becomes bitter as he realizes its implications. An alternative way to see this is that it is bitter because it involves much suffering, but sweet as the Christian community emerges triumphant.

10:11: "Then he said to me, you must prophesy *again* against many peoples and nations and languages and kings." The term "again" is a reference to the first of the prophesying to the Christian communities in chapters two and three. Unlike Ezekiel whose message was only for Israel John must now reveal *the message concerning the nations* that is contained in the scroll. The subject matter of the scroll also involves the prophecy of Daniel 7 which gives the first reference to the 3½ years of Daniel's seventieth "seven" (Dan.7:25). Indeed, the theme of Daniel 7 is the transfer of sovereignty over "all peoples, nations and languages" to God through Jesus.

§

116

Chapter 23

Measuring God's Sanctuary
Revelation 11:1-2

TEXT

Then I was given a measuring rod like a staff. "Get up," said a voice, "and measure God's sanctuary, including the altar [area], and count those who are worshipping there; ²but don't measure the outer court beyond the sanctuary. Exclude it because it has been given to the nations and they will be permitted to trample on the holy city for forty-two months.

Overview

This interlude passage and some later passages in Revelation concern the events of the great tribulation. However, the main issue here concerns whether this refers to a literal or a symbolic "sanctuary."

Because the Revelation was given to John in the mid 90s AD this means that the last literal temple had lain in ruins for over twenty years. Certainly, the fact that Paul speaks of a future literal sanctuary in which the Antichrist will seat himself (2 Thess. 2:3-12) indicates that the Revelation must also be speaking of a literal sanctuary in the future. Furthermore, the trampling of "the holy city for forty-two months" is the same time period mentioned in Daniel's statements of a literal "time, times, and half a time" (1260 days) as the latter half of the last "seven" of Daniel's 70 "sevens."

A further factor is that the term city also refers to the people dwelling there and so the "holy city" of Jerusalem is a literal city of people.

Comment on Measuring God's Sanctuary

11:1a: "**Then I was given a measuring rod like a staff. "Get up," said a voice, and. measure God's sanctuary.**" Such a measuring reed was about 10 feet 4 inches or about three meters long (Ezek. 40:3-5). Biblically the act of measuring is a prophetic action to determine the boundaries of a structure and its appropriation (Ezekiel 40-42) for preservation and protection. So for any long-time neglected temple sanctuary the measuring or surveying of it implies that it is about to be inhabited once again. Indeed, in the future Millennium Yahweh will arrive to dwell in His sanctuary once again according to Ezekiel 43 and Zechariah 2:1-4, 13.

However, instead of a millennial sanctuary, Revelation 11 is speaking

117

of an end-times sanctuary in which Antichrist places himself. This is clear from Jesus' statement about the "Sacrilege which causes desolation…standing in the holy place" (Matt. 24:15) or "where he shouldn't" stand (Mark 13:14). Furthermore, Paul also spoke of the Antichrist ("the man of lawlessness") as seating himself in the literal sanctuary (2 Thess. 2:3-12). So this is a sacrilegious misuse of the sanctuary by Antichrist.

11:1b: "**Including the altar** [area]**, and count those who are worshipping there.**" According to theologian David Aune this involves the whole area containing the altar. Indeed, the majority of modern-day commentators interpret this as referring to "the altar of burnt-offerings" which is set outside in the court of the priests, rather than the altar of incense which is set inside the sanctuary.

Although many scholars treat this as applying to Christian worshippers because they treat the sanctuary as symbolic, it is clear that in a literal interpretation these worshippers must be Jewish and in an end-time Jewish temple. Because they are worshiping in the court of the priests where the altar is and in the sanctuary these ones must also be priests. The counting of these ones simply shows they are a complete number.

11:2a: "**But don't measure the outer court beyond the sanctuary. Exclude it because it has been given to the nations.**" This court is the Court of the Gentiles. In the pattern of events, as described by Daniel, Jesus, and Paul, it seems that these priests must finally leave or be removed from the temple because Antichrist stops the burnt-offering sacrifices (Dan. 8:11; 11:31; 12:11) and sets up "the sacrilege which causes desolation" (11:31; 12:11) at the middle point of the 70th "seven." Indeed, Antichrist seats himself in the sanctuary i.e. he forces his way into the sanctuary and harasses these Jewish "holy ones." In fact Daniel foretold that the Antichrist:

❖ "…will speak words against the Most High. He will harass the holy ones of the Most High continually. His intention will be to change times established by law. They will be delivered into his hand for a time, times, and half a time" *(Dan. 7:25 NET).*

11:2b: "**And they will be permitted to trample on the holy city for forty-two months.**" Here John is alluding to the trampling down of "the host of heaven" in Daniel 8:11-14. Indeed, this is the first mention in Revelation of the 3½ year (42 months) period as the second half of the last seven years of the prophecy of the 70 "sevens of years" as described in Daniel 9:24-27. This period is mentioned also in Revelation 12:6, 14 and 13:5.

This trampling down of the literal city of Jerusalem was earlier prophesied about in Zechariah 12:3 (as correctly rendered in the Greek Septuagint). It reads:

❖ "I will make Jerusalem a stone trampled by all the nations; everyone who tramples it will utterly mock it. And all the nations of the earth will be gathered against it."

In his Olivet discourse, as recorded by Luke, Jesus referenced this passage from Zechariah when he said:

❖ "When you see Jerusalem being surrounded by armies, then you will know that her desolation is imminent...²²These are days of vengeance, when all that is written in the Scriptures will be fulfilled... ²³There will be great distress in the land and punishment of this people. ²⁴They will fall by the edge of the sword, and be led away captive into all nations. <u>Jerusalem will be trampled down by the pagans</u>, until the times of the pagan nations have run their course" *(Luke 21:20-24 KGV)*. Also note Zechariah 13:8-14:2.

Because this sanctuary spoken of in Revelation 11 was written about in 90 C.E. and is connected with the statements in Zechariah 13 and Luke 21 it is evident that the Roman attack upon Jerusalem in 70 C.E. did not fulfil Jesus' words in Luke 21.

These "times of the pagan nations" i.e. "times of the Gentiles" will be 42 months long. For several reasons, including the statement in Revelation 11:2, this awaits a future fulfilment. Certainly it could not have started in 70 C.E. because Jerusalem did not continue to be trampled. In fact, in later times the city was peaceably held through the long Turkish and later British occupations.

§

119

Chapter 24

The Two Witnesses
Revelation 11:3-14

TEXT

³I will give authority to my two witnesses, dressed in sackcloth, to prophesy for 1,260 days. ⁴These are the two olive trees, the two lampstands, which stand in front of the LORD of the earth. ⁵If anyone wants to harm them, fire comes out of their mouths and destroys their enemies. This is how anyone who wants to injure them must be killed. ⁶These two have the authority to shut the sky, so that it will not rain during the days of their prophesying. They also have the authority over the waters, to turn them to blood, and to strike the earth with every kind of plague as often as they wish. ⁷When they have completed their testimony, the ferocious beast who comes up from the abyss will make war on them, and defeat them and kill them. ⁸Their dead bodies will lie in the street of the great city which, in a spiritual sense, is called Sodom and Egypt, where their lord was crucified. ⁹And those of the nations, tribes, languages, and races will keep looking at their dead bodies for three and a half days. They won't allow their bodies to be laid in a tomb. ¹⁰And those who live on the earth will gloat over them, and celebrate, and send gifts to each other, because these two prophets had caused severe pain to those who live on the earth. ¹¹But after three and a half days breath of life from God entered them, and they stood up on their feet, and tremendous fear gripped those who saw them. ¹²Then they heard a loud voice from the sky saying to them: "Come up here!" So they went up into the sky in a cloud, while their enemies watched them. ¹³And in that hour a powerful earthquake occurred, and a tenth of the city collapsed; 7,000 people were killed in the earthquake, and the survivors were terrified, and they glorified the God of heaven.

¹⁴The second calamity is over. But take note: the third calamity is coming quickly!

Comment on the Two Witnesses

11:3a: "**I will give authority to my two witnesses...**" These are also called "these two prophets" in verse 10. They have the combined characteristics of Moses and Elijah including several factors involving High Priest Joshua and Governor Zerubbabel (Zech. 4:1-3). The identification of the two witnesses has been one of the most debated identifications concerning the book of Revelation through the centuries.

There have been various suggestions in the distant past concerning their identity, such as Peter/Paul, Stephen/James, and John the Baptist/Jesus, as well as several conceptual theories such as that these

120

two witnesses refer to the Old Testament and the New Testament or to "the law and the prophets." However, the modern-day understandings involve:

A. That the two witnesses are the still alive Enoch and Elijah waiting in heaven and then appearing in the end-times.

WHY THIS INTERPRETATION FAILS

The reason for the suggestion that Enoch and Elijah are the two witnesses is that they supposedly were taken to heaven and are presently alive there waiting to return to engage in their activities as the two witnesses. However, this is not a scriptural position because such would be based on the false teaching of an intrinsic immortal soul as well as the fact that Jesus said, *"no one has ascended into heaven"* (John 3:13, also Acts 2:34). In fact, these ones were simply taken away through earth's atmosphere to a new location on earth, as with Elijah (2 Kings 2:11, 12; 2 Chron. 21:12), and later died just as all mortal humans die. So there is no reason to suppose that Enoch and Elijah themselves could be the 'two witnesses.'

B. That the two witnesses are the resurrected Moses and Elijah or High Priest Joshua and Governor Zerubbabel (Zech. 4:1-3).

WHY THIS INTERPRETATION FAILS

The reason for interpreting this as Joshua and Zerubbabel is because they are described as "a lampstand" and "two olive trees" in Zechariah 4:2-3 and as "the two anointed ones" (4:14). However, this suggestion does not fit because it would mean that either of these two pairs, that is, Moses/Elijah and Joshua/Zerubbabel would be resurrected at the beginning of the great tribulation and so before the first resurrection which occurs after that tribulation when Jesus returns (Matt. 24:29, 1 Cor. 15:22-23). Nowhere in the rest of the Scriptures is there a hint of anyone being resurrected before that great event. So this suggestion also fails.

C. That the two witnesses are two individual Christians in the future roles of Moses and Elijah with added features of High priest Joshua and Governor Zerubbabel.

WHY THIS INTERPRETATION FAILS

Sadly this view sometimes leads to individual Christians claiming that they are one of the two witnesses or others making that claim about them. Although this is a more feasible suggestion than the earlier views there are problems with it as with all views concerning simply two individuals. This is because the events described in Revelation 11 contain much that is symbolic. Also, there are strong indicators that Revelation 11 presents a corporate view of the two witnesses as many theologians and scholars show. For example G.R. Beasley-Murray states concerning the two witnesses that, "They represent the churches fulfilling their vocation to bear witness to Christ in the final time of tribulation." *The New Century Bible Commentary,* Revelation, p. 178.

D. That the two witnesses are symbolic of a body of Christians in the end-times within Antichrist's kingdom.

In this interpretation there is a combining of the character and activities of Moses and Elijah with features that are noted in Zechariah 4:1-14.

BACKGROUND TO THE TWO WITNESSES INVOLVING SYMBOLISMS

Malachi had prophesied that Elijah would return "before the coming of the great and awesome day of Yahweh!" *(Mal. 4:5).* Later, Jesus showed that this was initially fulfilled in John the Baptist (Matt. 11:14) who "went in the spirit and power of Elijah" *(Luke 1:17)* and so showing that Elijah had served as a symbol of a future great prophet, in this case John the Baptist.

Further background to Revelation 11 concerns God's statement that He would, "raise up for the [Jews] a prophet like you (Moses) from among their brothers" *(Deut. 18:18).* This statement led the Jews to expect this Prophet like Moses (John 6:14) and so making Moses a symbol of "the Prophet," who turned out to be Jesus.

Finally, as background to Revelation 11, Jesus' transfiguration vision had both Moses and Elijah appearing in it (Matt. 17:1-13) as symbolic of the forerunners to the coming of the kingdom (Matt. 16:28). So bearing in mind that the work of Elijah had symbolized the work of John the Baptist and that the work of Moses had symbolised the work of Jesus as the greatest prophet, we can understand how the two prophets in Revelation 11 also serve as symbols along with so many other symbols in that passage. Furthermore, the purpose of the transfiguration was to show that Jesus has authority superior to that of Moses and Elijah who served as symbols in that vision.

Regarding two witnesses, Deuteronomy 17:6 shows that "whoever is deserving of death shall be put to death on the testimony of two or three witnesses; he shall not be put to death on the testimony of one witness" *(NKJV)*. So, as recognized by many scholars the number "two" is used as the symbol of witness. In fact, in the end-times there must be at least two witnesses to the idolatry of those who worship the Antichrist beast before the convicting and sentencing of them can be carried out i.e. the drinking "of the wine of the wrath of God, which is poured out full strength into the cup of His indignation" (Rev. 14:10).

The following factors show why the identification of the two witnesses is likely to be understood as being **a symbol of a body of Christians in Antichrist's kingdom in its role of witness and martyrdom (Rev. 6:9-11) in the end-times.**

THE TWO WITNESSES ARE SYMBOLIC

Primarily there is a great amount that is symbolic in Revelation 11 e.g. Jerusalem is described symbolically in being called Sodom and Egypt. So regarding the two witnesses the key symbols are their description as "the two olive trees and the two lampstands" as well as fire coming out of their mouths as clearly symbolic of God's fiery denunciations of the idolatrous worshippers of Antichrist. Indeed, it would be strange and physically damaging to the two witnesses if this were literal fire. So, the many symbolic descriptions throughout Revelation 11 provide us with a basis to understand that the description of the two witnesses is entirely symbolic and particularly that the most significant miracles done through the hands of Moses and Elijah were so that the hearers and or readers of this passage will think of those activities of Moses and Elijah when they think of the two witnesses.

THE TWO WITNESSES ARE CORPORATE

Leading commentators such as Metzger, Mounce, Beale, Aune, Ladd, Osborne, and others, take the two witnesses as a symbol for the witnessing church. So based on Beale's work (quoted by Grant Osborne in his book *Revelation-Baker Exegetical Commentary p. 418),* we find that any interpretation involving only individuals is ruled out and that the two witnesses must be corporate because:

1. The symbolic two lampstands are connected to "the seven lampstands" of Revelation 2 and 3, which are the seven Christian communities" i.e. the complete community. However, because "two" is the symbolic number of witness "the two lampstands" show the Christian communities in their single role of witness (Num. 35:30; John 8:13-18).

123

2. The two witnesses function as a combined Moses and Elijah, so the stress is not on the individual, but on the group. This is a compelling reason for a corporate function of the two witnesses.

3. The event when the ferocious beast overcomes the two witnesses points to Revelation 13:7 where, "he *(Antichrist)* was permitted to wage war against God's holy people and to conquer them" and in Daniel 7:21: "...that horn *(Antichrist)* was waging war with the holy ones and overpowering them." So this further indicates that the two witnesses are corporate and not simply two individuals.

4. This "witnessing" parallels the witnessing community of believers elsewhere in the book of Revelation e.g. "...the souls of those who had been slain because of the word of God, and because of the testimony which they had maintained" *(Rev. 6:9)* and "...because of the word of their testimony...and [they] hold the testimony of Jesus" *(Rev. 12:11, 17: also19:10; 20:4).*

5. The two lampstands and two olive trees also point to a corporate aspect. Indeed, they have a two-fold ministry: judgment (11:5-6) and witness (11:7). In his book *Revelation* (p. 418) Grant R. Osborne comments that:

> The context of this interlude (10:1-11:13) makes it probable that *the two witnesses* do stand for the witnessing church in it's suffering and triumph (as in 10:8-10 and 11:1,2).

6. Those who watch the defeat and the resurrection of the witnesses are found throughout Antichrist's kingdom ("those who live on the earth") because Revelation 11:9-13 speaks of these observers as being from the "nations, tribes, languages, and races" (vs. 9). Indeed, in the first century setting this means they are found throughout that kingdom, and so must be a body of people, rather than simply two individuals.

A lesser factor in a corporate interpretation of the two witnesses is that Revelation 2:13 earlier introduced Antipas of Pergamum as the "faithful witness" who was most likely representative of the entire Christian community which had remained faithful and so indicating that the two witnesses are also representative of others.

In summary, because of all the above factors involved it seems most likely that the two witnesses are a symbol of the single community of

Christians, within Antichrist's kingdom, in its role of witness in the end-times, but become martyrs at the beginning of and during the great tribulation. However, not all Christians are killed during the great tribulation, because Revelation 7:14 speaks of those "who come out" of it. Also Jesus' Olivet discourse shows the local picture of end-times events (Matt. 24:15-22; Luke 21:20-24). So this does not speak of the entire Christian community as being the two witnesses.

11:3b: "...**Dressed in sackcloth, to prophesy for 1,260 days**." Being dressed in sackcloth is a sign of mourning and deep sorrow.

A careful reading of the flow of events in verses 3-12 shows this period of 1,260 days (verses 3-6) will occur during the <u>first half</u> of Daniel's 70th "seven," as suggested by Victorinus, Hyppolytus, and other early Christians. Indeed, the prestigious *Word Biblical Commentary* states that:

> "when the three and one half year ministry of the two witnesses is concluded, the beast will spend the remaining three and one half years of the full week of seven years fighting the saints."

Furthermore, Grant Osborne in his commentary on Revelation says that:

> "This passage breaks naturally into two sections. The prophetic ministry of the witnesses is described in 11:3-6, and 11:7-13 details their death and resurrection."

So these two commentaries express the view that the ministry of the two witnesses is in the first half of the 70th "seven" and the war against them i.e. the persecution of the great tribulation is in the second half of the 70th "seven" at which point they are killed. This is because, in the first half, these two witnesses are free from Antichrist's oppression until the end of their time of prophesying when he begins to "make war upon them" (vs. 7). So the events from verse 7 onward concern the great tribulation during the <u>second half</u> of Daniel's 70th "seven" when Antichrist "will make war on them." Evidently it is only those in "the great city" who are killed, after which they are resurrected when all Christians are resurrected (also see chapter 10).

11:4: "**These are the two olive trees, the two lampstands, which stand in front of the LORD of the earth**." These two olive trees and two lampstands may refer to the anointing and commissioning of the two witnesses with holy spirit, hence the metaphor of olive trees supplying oil to the lampstands. As two lampstands these ones are light-bearers. Indeed, this verse alludes to Zechariah 4 concerning the work of Zerubbabel and High Priest Joshua in the restoration of Jerusalem, its temple and its worship and so indicating the full restoration of true worship prior to the establishment of the Kingdom.

11:5: "**If anyone wants to harm them, fire comes out of their mouths and destroys their enemies. This is how anyone who wants to injure them must be killed.**" The fire is from their mouths and so is metaphorical for God's fiery judgments (Jer. 5:14). So this fire does not literally burn up or destroy their enemies, but condemns and destroys the wrong thinking and teaching of these enemies. However, this ability is only used whenever someone "wants to harm them;" yet having it symbolizes their immunity to attack so that they can complete their testimony.

11:6: "**These two have the authority to shut the sky, so that it will not rain during the days of their prophesying. They also have the authority over the waters, to turn them to blood, and to strike the earth with every kind of plague as often as they wish.**" These ones simply have authority for using these miraculous abilities. The text does not say that they actually use those abilities right through this period, but perhaps it simply demonstrates that they have the power to do so. Therefore, these abilities simply give warning of coming divine judgment and the sackcloth indicates that their message is one showing that all should repent.

11:7: "**When they have completed their testimony the ferocious beast who comes up from the abyss will make war on them, and defeat them and kill them.**" This is the first mention in Revelation of this one who is the Antichrist—known as "the little horn" (Dan. 7:7-8; 8:9). However, he does not necessarily come up from the abyss during the time of the prophesying of the two witnesses, but as they finish. Regarding the abyss please see *9:1* which shows that it is not a literal place but is figurative of an infinite void of absolute restraint primarily used for the demons and Satan.

11:8: "**Their dead bodies will lie in the street of the great city which, in a spiritual sense, is called Sodom and Egypt where their lord was crucified.**" Because the two witnesses are symbolic of a body of people, this symbolism carries through to when their corpses are lying on the street so that even as two dead witnesses they are still a symbol of a single body with the combined characteristics of Moses and Elijah.

This city refers initially to the people of the city of Jerusalem, but extends to all within Antichrist's kingdom. The primary reference must be to Jerusalem because that is "where their lord *[Jesus]* was crucified." The reason that the terms Sodom and Egypt are applied to Jerusalem in this spiritual sense is because this city will become wicked and spiritually depraved like Sodom (Isa. 1:10) as well as idolatrous and a place of enslavement as with ancient Egypt. Indeed, Theologian George Eldon Ladd says that: "It is obvious that that the city of Jerusalem is intended..." And, in quoting Hanns Lilje, he says:

> "Jerusalem is not merely mentioned as an empty theoretical metaphor. In some way or another, the earthly, geo-historical Jerusalem will have its place in the history of the last days,"
> *Commentary on the Revelation of John* p.157.

Also, Professor David Aune adds to our understanding when he writes:

> "Where their Lord was crucified...the great city as Jerusalem" and that "the author has transformed the historical Jerusalem into a symbol of an unbelieving world."
> *Word Biblical Commentary* Vol. 52B, pp.619, 620.

Furthermore, Grant Osborne also feels that a literal city is what is spoken of here, but with an added dimension when he says:

> It must refer to Jerusalem in this context, however, for 11:8 describes it as the place 'where also the Lord was crucified,' and in 11:13 the population of the city is 70,000, the size of Jerusalem ... In a secondary way, it also represents all cities that oppose God."
> *Revelation (Baker Exegetical Commentary)* p. 426-7.

11:9: **"And those of the nations, tribes, languages, and races will keep looking at their dead bodies for three and a half days. They won't allow their bodies to be laid in a tomb."** This appears to show that it is not only the non-believing inhabitants of Jerusalem who rejoice over the deaths of these witnesses, but all the nations within Antichrist's kingdom.

This time period of 3½ days is certainly not an allusion to the time Jesus was in the tomb, because this was only a period of parts of three days and three nights as seen in the statement that he would be raised up

127

"on the third day" (Matt. 16:21; 17:23; 20:19; Luke 9:22; 18:33; 24:7, 46). Instead this period is an allusion to the three and a half years noted in both Daniel and Revelation in its different forms and as symbolic of that period to show the relative shortness of it (See Aune in the *Word Biblical Commentary Vol. 52b p.609)*. So this period likely refers to the relatively short period of 3½ years during which the two witnesses are killed and later raised up some time "after 3½ days" or years (vs. 11) of the great tribulation.

11:10: "**And those who live on the earth will gloat over them, and celebrate, and send gifts to each other, because these two prophets had caused severe pain to those who live on the earth.**" "Those who live on the earth" is once again a reference to the followers and worshippers of Antichrist. So the witnessing message of "the two witnesses" had also been a rebuke to and denunciation of these nations within Antichrist's kingdom. So naturally, along with the inhabitants of Jerusalem, these all rejoice at the deaths of the two witnesses. Indeed, the sending of gifts to each other indicates that those in Jerusalem have entered into a sympathetic alliance with those nations.

11:11: "**After 3½ days breath of life from God entered them and they stood up on their feet, and tremendous fear gripped those who saw them.**" In this interlude passage we have a proleptic (anticipatory) statement of the literal resurrection of these Christian two witnesses along with all other Christians during the blowing of the seventh trumpet (11:18). In fact, the first resurrection is not shown to take place in stages. So when the two witnesses are resurrected all Christians must be resurrected at the same time when Messiah returns (Mark 13:24-27; 1 Cor. 15:23; 1 Thess. 4:17) at the end of the approximately 3½ year period of the great tribulation. This, therefore, shows the first resurrection to be post-tribulational (Matt. 24:29).

11:12: "**Then they heard a loud voice from the sky saying to them, "Come on up here. So they went up into the sky in a cloud, while their enemies watched them.**" This is either the voice of Christ or that of his angelic emissary.

If it is the case that the two witnesses are a symbol of a section of the Christian community, then Revelation 11:12 would seem to be focusing on the resurrection and rapture of those Christians who, as the two witnesses in Judea, suffered and died through the great tribulation. This is really a divine rescue and a vindication of them as with Enoch and Elijah; but it is not a taking of them to God's location in heaven because it involves "a cloud" and so is within earth's atmosphere ("the clouds" and "the air" in 1 Thess. 4:17) with no further mention of their being literally in God's heaven as was the case with Jesus. Furthermore, clouds are used in the Bible to indicate either God's presence or divine transportation, and in this context divine transportation is meant. So the passage references the catching up of this body of "the two witness" into the air to meet Jesus i.e. the rapture. Also 1 Thessalonians 4 indicates that there is only one time of ascension for Christians and which closely follows on after the first resurrection.

11:13a: "**And in that hour a powerful earthquake occurred and a tenth of the city collapsed; 7,000 people were killed in the earthquake**." The passage is still speaking of events occurring in Jerusalem. Indeed, this earthquake occurs at the same time as the call to the two witnesses to "Come up here," and so is also at the time of Jesus' return.

If "the city" is a reference to people and the "collapse" is not speaking of city walls, then if a tenth of the population equals approximately 7,000 then the population would have been around 70,000, a population which fairly well represents the historically estimated population of Jerusalem in the first century. However, because 7,000 die this would mean that approximately 63,000 survive.

11:13b: "**The survivors were terrified, and they glorified the God of heaven**." This seems to be a case of genuine repentance and conversion to the worship of God by those in Jerusalem and the area of Judea. It seems that nine out of ten of the remaining population of Jerusalem repent (Zech. 12:10; Rom.11:25-27). Yet because it is after the first resurrection these people will not have immortality at this time, but remain as mortals during the Millennium.

11:14: "**The second calamity is over. But take note: the third calamity is coming quickly!**" This is simply an editorial comment by John after the interlude concerning the measuring of God's sanctuary and the activity of the two witnesses. So this second disaster for Antichrist's followers is stated as being now over in preparation for the third and final calamity to come upon them.

Chapter 25

The Seventh Trumpet - The Final Calamity
Revelation 11:15-19

TEXT

15Then the seventh angel blew his trumpet. Loud voices were heard in heaven saying: "The kingdom of the world has become the Kingdom of our LORD and of His Messiah, and He will reign for ever and ever."

16Then the twenty-four elders who were sitting on their thrones in front of God fell down with their faces to the ground, kneeling in worship of God **17**saying:

"We thank you, LORD God, the All-Powerful, the One who is and who was, because you have taken your great power and begun to reign. **18**The nations were enraged, but your time to punish them has arrived, namely the time for the dead to be judged; and to reward your bond-servants the prophets and holy ones, that is, those who revere you—both lowly and prominent. Now is the time to destroy those who are destroying the earth."

19Then God's sanctuary in heaven was opened, and the ark of His covenant appeared in His sanctuary. And there were flashes of lightning, rumblings, thunderclaps, an earthquake, and severe hail."

TRANSLATION POINT

Verse 18 is rendered "your time to punish them has arrived, <u>namely</u> the time for the dead to be judged" rather than "your time to punish them has arrived <u>and</u> the time for the dead to be judged." This is because Grant Osborne points out that this is "not chronological time but eschatological time, so that the Greek word *kairos* (time) borrows the verb from the previous clause, and the *kai* (and) that introduces it is probably epexegetical, thus yielding the translation" above i.e. "namely" instead of "and."

Comment on the Seventh Trumpet

11:15: "**Then the seventh angel blew his trumpet. Loud voices were heard in heaven saying, 'The kingdom of the world** (Gk *kosmou*) **has become the Kingdom of our LORD and of His Messiah and He will reign for ever and ever."** After the interlude of 11:1-14 John resumes writing about the blowing of the seven trumpets. So now the blowing of the seventh trumpet brings the third and final "calamity" or disaster upon the followers of Antichrist. However, this is not simply a momentary event, but introduces the period of the end which concerns the pouring out of the seven bowls including the plagues upon Babylon and its destruction as detailed in Revelation chapters 17 and 18.

The phrase "The kingdom of the world" is singular because by this time all the world's kingdoms will be strongly influenced by Antichrist as if they are one kingdom in opposition to God. As with many other occurrences in the New Testament the term "world (Gk *kosmou*)" is a reference to the human world in opposition to God and therefore belonging to Satan (Matt.4:8; 2 Cor.4:4).

"The Kingdom of our LORD and of His Messiah" concerns the beginning of God's Kingdom as being the new government of Earth administered by Messiah Jesus, and which will be established at a point in time during the blowing of the future seventh trumpet. However, this statement and those in verse 17-18 are all part of an isolated synopsis of what will happen through the remaining chapters of Revelation up to and including Revelation 20:6. So even though the verbs here are in the past tense, what is said here is proleptic i.e. in anticipation, but concerning the near future i.e. "in the days of the sounding of the seventh angel, when he blows his trumpet..." (Rev. 10:7). Indeed Christians are certainly not caught up into the air to meet Jesus at the beginning of the blowing of the seventh trumpet; but rather this event will not be likely to occur until a point in time after the warning given in Rev. 16:15 which says: "I am coming like a thief. Blessed is the one who stays awake and keeps his clothes." This is said during the outpouring of the sixth bowl, which means that Christians are still mortals on earth at a time near the end of the blowing of the seventh trumpet, and so indicating that 11:15; 17-18 are proleptic statements.

The phrase, "He will reign for ever and ever" is a reference to God's reign, but by extension to the reign of Messiah (Luke 1:33; Heb.1:8).

11:16: "**Then the twenty-four elders who were sitting on their thrones in front of God fell down with their faces to the ground, kneeling in worship of God.**" Please see 4:4 to see that these ones are angelic beings. Their sitting on thrones indicates that they are now ruling angels.

11:17: "**Saying: We thank you, LORD God, the All-Powerful, the One who is and who was, because you have taken your great power and begun to reign.**" Although this hymnic section is presented in the past tense it is, as shown above, the prophetic past and so is used in anticipation of the future events. God's having "begun to reign" also anticipates the pouring out of the seven bowls of His punishment on the wicked world.

131

11:18a: "**The nations were enraged, but your time to punish them has arrived, namely the time for the dead to be judged.**" This anticipates the outpouring of the seven bowls of God's wrath and when combined with the previous hymnic phrase, this is an allusion to Ps. 98:1 from the Greek Septuagint—"the Lord has begun to reign; the people are enraged." However, this passage in 11:18 also reflects Psalm 2:2 where we find that, "The kings of the earth establish themselves, and the rulers conspire together against Yahweh and his anointed."

Because of this linking of "the dead" with the enraged nations it would seem that the reference is to those living, but spiritually dead persons (John 5:25). Certainly, it does not refer to dead Christians who are already judged. Indeed, Peter shows that it was from his day that the, "time for judgment [was] to begin with God's household; and if it begins with us, what will be the outcome for those who don't obey God's good news? (1 Pet. 4:17). However, if the reference is to what will occur at the end of the 1000 years i.e. the Great white throne judgment (20:11-15), then the reference could well refer to the literal non-Christian dead.

11:18b: "**And to reward your bond-servants the prophets and holy ones, that is, those who revere you—both lowly and prominent.**" This seems to be speaking of a single group of persons, namely Christians, including those faithful servants prior to Christ's first coming. The statement implies the resurrection of all those who have been faithful through time and concerns the first resurrection. In fact, the rewards are those that were stated to the seven communities, namely:

1. To "grant for them to eat of the tree of the perfect life, which is in the paradise of God."
2. That they "will never be harmed by the second death."
3. That they will be given "some of the hidden manna"…and "a white stone with a new name written on it."
4. That they will be given "authority over the nations, to rule them with an iron sceptre"…and be given "the morning star."
5. That they will be "clothed in white clothing"…and there will never be an erasing of "their name from the book of the perfect life"…and Jesus "will confess their name in the presence of my Father and of His angels."
6. That they will be made, "a pillar in the sanctuary of [Jesus'] God, and they won't go out of it anymore"…Jesus "will write on them the name of my God and the name of the city of my God, the New

132

Jerusalem, which comes down out of heaven from my God, and my new name."

7.   Jesus will "give permission for them to sit with [him] on [his] throne."

Additionally there will be the further rewards that are stated in the Gospel accounts and in the rest of the New Testament.

11:18c: **"Now is the time to destroy those who are destroying the earth."** The "earth" here is not the physical planet, but by metonymy, "the people of the earth." They are destroyed by those within Babylon the great which is spoken of in Jeremiah 51:25 as "you who destroy the whole earth" and therefore includes all who follow the ferocious beast—the Antichrist. Because all of this description is anticipatory we will find that it is expanded in chapters 15 and 16 concerning the pouring out of the bowls of wrath.

11:19: **"God's sanctuary in heaven was opened, and the ark of His covenant appeared in His sanctuary and there were flashes of lightning, rumblings, thunderclaps, an earthquake, and severe hail."** This symbolic language parallels 4:1 where a door is opened for John. This is the door in the sanctuary building that leads to the holy of holies containing the ark of His covenant i.e., God's throne and therefore His very presence. It is also a symbol of His faithfulness to His covenant promises. So here God is revealing deep heavenly truths to John.

These flashes of lightning etc. are conventional ways of expressing the majesty and power which attend the divine presence. This is the third mention of this phenomenon and is connected to the seventh trumpet blast. The first mention is in 4:5, but without the earthquake. The second mention, connected to the seventh seal, is in 8:5, but without the addition of "severe hail." The final mention is in 16:18 concerning the pouring out of the seventh bowl, but again with no mention of hail. Therefore, this is one of the indicators that the seventh seal, seventh trumpet, and seventh bowl of plague are all connected as the same event.

§

Chapter 26

The Woman, the Child, and the Dragon
Revelation 12:1-6

TEXT

Then a spectacular sign appeared in the sky: a woman clothed with the sun, and with the moon under her feet. On her head was a crown of twelve stars. [2]She was pregnant and was crying out in the agony of labour to give birth. [3]Then another sign appeared in the sky: a formidable fiery-red dragon that had seven heads and ten horns. On each head were seven diadem crowns, [4]and his tail swept down a third of the stars in the sky and hurled them to the earth. Then the Dragon stood in front of the woman who was about to give birth, so that he could devour her child as soon as it was born. [5]So she gave birth to a son—a male child—who is going to rule all the nations with an iron sceptre. Her child was snatched away to God and to His throne. [6]Then the Woman escaped into the desolate wasteland, where a place has been prepared for her by God, so that she could be nourished for 1,260 days.

Overview

This is an interlude passage with 12:1 being a clean break with the earlier chapters of Revelation, although it does expand on the details of the two previous interludes of 7:1-17 and 10:1 to 11:13.

This passage contains many symbolisms and is perhaps one of the more difficult in Revelation to interpret. In fact, although many commentators understand this part of the vision as concerning the age-long conflict between Satan and God's people there are good reasons to view this as concerning primarily the future. One reason is that in 4:1 everything concerns "what must happen" i.e. in the future. Another reason is the mention of the 1260 days in 12:6 and the time, times, and half a time in 12:14 which period concerns the future time period of the 70th "seven" noted in Daniel chapter 9.

Furthermore, it is only by assumption that some commentators take these descriptions to refer to Jesus' birth and his ascension to heaven. Again there are good reasons why this is not so. These include the fact that, as a vision, this could not refer to past events which had taken place some sixty years earlier. Certainly, Jesus' life, crucifixion, resurrection, and ascension to God's right hand had all occurred long before this prophecy. Also, there is the fact that Mary had died long before this prophecy and so excluding her from the woman of this scene.

Everything concerning the two primary signs, namely the Woman and the Dragon that John "sees," he sees happening in the sky rather than on the earth at the time he sees it. Indeed, it should be thought of in terms of a preview or short trailer for the future last seven years of this age and ending with the great tribulation. Indeed, because the time period of 1260 days is stated then the location of these events must be in or near to Jerusalem.

Interestingly, verses 7-17 seem to be a resumption and expansion of the details in verses 1-6 i.e. the same event, but with added details and from a different perspective.

Comment on the Woman, the Child, and the Dragon

12:1: "**A spectacular sign appeared in the sky: a woman clothed with the sun and with the moon under her feet. On her head was a crown of twelve stars**." The majority of scholars recognize that this is the ideal faithful Woman—a symbol of true Israel, that is, the believing messianic community through all of time. Therefore, this is a corporate Woman and links with her description in the prophecy of Genesis 3:15. From that prophecy she developed into the twelve tribes from the twelve sons of Jacob ("stars" in Gen. 37:9-11) and is now the Christian "Israel of God," (Gal. 6:16) "seated...in the heavenly places incorporated into [Messiah]" (Eph. 2:6). For this reason she can be seen simultaneously in heaven (the sky) and on the earth. However, although the vision is in the sky, we do not have to imagine the woman as actually being in the sky and then coming down to earth. Rather, she is actually on the earth because she is later shown as pursued by the Dragon after he has been thrown down to earth. This is similar to the vision in chapter 19 when John sees horses riding in the sky, and yet the actual events happen on earth. Certainly the Woman is seen on earth in verse 6.

Referring again to the "stars" these, along with the sun and moon are light bearers and the crown that she wears is a *stephanos* i.e. a crown of victory. Indeed, the believing messianic community has been and is a light-bearer of God's truth.

12:2: "**She was pregnant and was crying out in the agony of labour to give birth**." This does not refer to Mary's pregnancy with Jesus. It is also not a reference to the Jewish community's bringing forth of the Messiah at his literal birth; but rather this will occur at the "beginning of the birth pangs" of the Messiah (Matt. 24:4-8) as detailed in Jesus' Olivet discourse, that is, the agonies for Christians even immediately before the great tribulation begins (Matt. 24:9-22). Because the Woman is the ideal

THE WOMAN, THE CHILD, AND THE DRAGON

faithful Israel i.e. the believing messianic community, she is in anguish to give birth to the "male child" noted in verse 5. Similarly, Isaiah 66:7-8 speaks of the birth of the nation of Israel.

12:3: "**Then another sign appeared in the sky: a formidable fiery-red dragon that had seven heads and ten horns. On each head were seven diadem crowns.**" This is a symbol of Satan—the Serpent of Genesis 3:15. The connection is Isaiah 27:1 concerning: "Leviathan the twisting serpent...the dragon that is in the sea."

The seven heads, ten horns and seven diadems are to indicate who was (and still is) the true ruler of these seven kingdoms (see 17:10). These heads, horns, and crowns are the same as for the ferocious beast (Antichrist) in 13:1-2. These are either a reflection of Satan's symbolic appearance or his transference of his authority to Antichrist at the time Antichrist comes out from the abyss (11:7; 17:8). These heads are all symbols of rulers and are also the same as the seven heads on the four beasts that Daniel was shown in Daniel 7:2-7. The seven heads with seven diadem crowns indicate Satan's and later Antichrist's pretension to sovereignty over the earth. The ten horns are the ten that are on the fourth beast of Daniel 7:7 and are later seen in Revelation 17:12 as the ten kings connected with Antichrist.

The Dragon is red because of all the blood of the martyrs that he has caused to be shed. (Please note "the red horse" in 6:4 as a reference to the bloodshed in warfare).

12:4a: "**And his tail swept down a third of the stars in the sky and hurled them to the earth.**" This may be a reference to the "twelve stars" in the crown (12:1) and therefore to "true Israel." Although some commentators understand these "stars" as being demons or angels, it is more likely that this is an allusion to Daniel 8:9, 10 concerning the future when "some of the host and some of the stars [little horn (Antichrist)] threw to the ground and trampled on." Certainly, the term "stars" is often a reference to spirit beings, either angels or demons. However, on a few occasions the Bible uses the term "stars" as a symbol for certain humans. This understanding fits better as parallel with the details of the expanded description of this event in Rev. 12:7-17. So this "third of the stars" most likely refers to one third of or a large section of the entire body of Christians through time and perhaps concerning the end-time Christians living in Judea or within Antichrist's kingdom who are to be trampled on during the great tribulation.

136

12:4b: "**Then the Dragon stood in front of the Woman who was about to give birth, so that he could devour her child as soon as it was born.**" This is a picture of hostility. It shows Satan's desire to destroy the body of Christians living in Judea or within Antichrist's Kingdom just prior to the great tribulation i.e. the time of Satan's wrath, which he then proceeds to pour out on them. His goal is to stop the establishment of the Messianic Kingdom.

12:5a: "**She gave birth to a son—a male child—who is going to rule all the nations with an iron sceptre.**" The term "male-child" is a figure of youthful vigour and authority. As with the "Woman" this figure is also a corporate entity. So, this "male-child" is a picture of the Christians living within Antichrist's kingdom and more specifically in Judea. This description fits with the Daniel's 70th "seven," and occurs during the second half of it i.e. during the great tribulation.

Although this clause about the male child shows the judicial authority that Messiah will have (Ps. 2:9) it seems that here it is applied only to those Christians who will become "overcomers" by the end of the great tribulation and who will also "rule all the nations with an iron sceptre" (2:26-27).

12:5b: "**Her child was snatched away to God and to His throne.**" To restate the point, this is not a reference to the ascension of Messiah Jesus to heaven because his rapture did not have the purpose of escaping Satan's hostility. Furthermore, there is no mention of a resurrection of the holy ones. It is, however, a simple symbolism of those who are incorporated in Messiah as being snatched away and into God's protection. Although similar to the rapture events of both Enoch and Elijah this is not a literal rapture, but symbolically shows that, as a body, these living Christians will have God's spiritual protection and as a body they will survive. However, Seal five described in 6:9-11 shows that there will be some individuals who will literally die as martyrs during the great tribulation.

12:6: "**The Woman escaped into the desolate wasteland where she has a place prepared by God, so that she could be nourished for 1,260 days.**" This statement is repeated in verse 14, and in apocalyptic literature this is merely a pictorial way to show that, even during the great tribulation, true Christians will be spiritually protected and nourished by God.

The picture here is based upon the fact that in all of biblical history it was the wilderness or desolate wasteland containing Mount Sinai (Horeb—"the mountain of God" in Midian, Arabia (Gal.4:25) that was the place of safety, preservation, and nourishment to flee to: *1)* for Moses (Ex. 3:1), *2)* for Israel's escape from Egypt (Deut. 1:6), and *3)* for Elijah (1 Kings 19:8). Indeed, just as the natural Israelites under Moses were fed and nourished with manna, so too, the spiritual "Israel of God" i.e. true Christians will be spiritually sustained (Rev. 2:17 and John 6:31-35, 47-51) as a body through the 1,260 day long great tribulation caused by the Dragon. Accordingly, Jesus said regarding his community of believers that, "the gates of the common grave will not overpower it." (Matt.16:18).

However, this spiritual protection and spiritual nourishment doesn't mean that they are spared the wrath of Satan which wrath will lead to some Christians becoming martyrs.

§

Chapter 27

War in Heaven and Persecution of the Woman
Revelation 12:7-18

TEXT

7Then war broke out in heaven: Michael and his angels went to war against the Dragon, and the Dragon and his angels fought back. **8**But he couldn't win, and there was no longer any place for them in heaven. **9**So the formidable Dragon—the ancient Serpent, the one called the Devil and the Satan, who deceives the whole inhabited earth—was thrown down to the earth, and his angels with him. **10**Then I heard a loud voice in heaven saying,

"The time of [God's] victory and His power has arrived: the Kingdom of our God with the authority of His Messiah! The accuser of our brothers and sisters has been hurled down, the one who accuses them day and night in front of our God. **11**But they triumphed over him through the blood of the Lamb and through the message of their testimony, because they didn't love their lives even when facing death. **12**So be glad, you heavens and all who live in them! But what great calamity awaits the earth and the sea, because the Devil has come down to you, filled with terrifying anger, and knowing he has only a short time left."

13When the Dragon realized that he had been hurled down to the earth, he began to pursue the woman who gave birth to the male child. **14**But the woman was provided with the two wings of a huge eagle so that she could fly away from the Serpent into the desolate wasteland, to the place where she is nourished for a time, times, and half a time. **15**But the Serpent spewed water like a river from his mouth after the woman, in order to sweep her away by a torrent. **16**But the earth helped her when the ground opened its mouth and swallowed the river that the Dragon had spewed from his mouth. **17**So the Dragon became angry at the woman, and went away to wage war on the rest of her children, those who obey God's commandments and hold to Jesus' testimony.

Comment on the War in Heaven and the Persecution of the Woman

12:7-8: "**Then war broke out in heaven: Michael and his angels went to war against the Dragon, and the Dragon and his angels fought back. But he couldn't win, and there was no longer any place for them in heaven**" This verse begins the retelling of the events just given in 12:1-6 i.e. a resumption and expansion of those events. Here the Greek does not say that there "was war" (in older versions) as if in the past tense, but that "War broke out," (most modern versions) or "Now war arose in heaven"

(ESV) or "Then a war began" (NIV). Indeed, it is Satan who begins this war causing Michael to defend God's people because he is the appointed guardian of them. In fact, he "will arise" ready for guarding them during the great tribulation (Dan. 12:1, 2). This further sets the events in Revelation 12 immediately before the time of the great tribulation.

Satan and his demons will be expelled by God from their location in a lower heavenly realm so that this part of God's universe is cleansed of them. However, this is in preparation for his wrath to be poured out on Christians during the great tribulation.

12:9: "**Then the formidable Dragon—the ancient Serpent, the one called the Devil and the Satan, who deceives the whole inhabited earth—was thrown down to the earth, and his angels with him.**" Although Michael and his angels war against Satan, it appears from the grammar of a divine passive that God was the active force behind Michael in expelling Satan down to the earth.

The descriptive title "the Serpent" used here along with Satan's other titles indicates that "the Serpent" in the Garden of Eden (Gen. 3) was not a literal snake, but rather was a glorious spirit creature (Ezek. 28:12-19) and an intelligent deceiver (2 Cor.11:3). The Hebrew words *nachash* (serpent) and *seraph* (fiery serpent) are closely connected and so are further connected to the Seraphim—heavenly beings (Isa. 6:2-6).

12:10: "**Then I heard a loud voice in heaven saying, 'The time of [God's] victory and His power has arrived: the Kingdom of our God with the authority of His Messiah! The accuser of <u>our brothers and sisters</u> has been hurled down, the one who accuses them day and night in front of our God.**" This is a celebration of God's victory in His plan. He is now exerting His power fully against Satan. This voice could be angelic or it could be that of Christians living externally to Antichrist's kingdom. The latter is more likely because they are elated that, "the accuser of our brothers and sisters has been hurled down." A further possibility is that it is the metaphorical voice of the martyrs of 6:9-11.

12:11: "**But they triumphed over him through the blood of the Lamb and through the message of their testimony, because they didn't love their lives even when facing death.**" This is not a physical triumph, but one of faith, that is, faith in the sacrifice made by Jesus as the basis for a new administration of earth. This includes faith in God's promise of a resurrection to life in His kingdom.

12:12: "So be glad, you heavens and you who dwell in them! But what great calamity awaits the earth and the sea, because the Devil has come down to you, filled with terrifying anger, and knowing he has only a short time left" This exclamation of "you heavens" is symbolic of the Christian Holy Ones. (Please see Chapter 1 pages 4 and 5). So Christians can be glad because "the end" of Satan's rule is getting closer and therefore "the Kingdom of our God with the authority of His Messiah" is about to be established." Also this will bring an end to Satan's false accusations.

12:13: "When the Dragon realized that he had been hurled down to the earth, he began to pursue the woman who gave birth to the male child." This is similar to when Pharaoh pursued Israel into the wilderness. But here it is God's action of hurling Satan down to the earth that precipitates Satan's declaring his wrath upon Christians when he uses his agent the Antichrist to act as the very embodiment of Satan himself. This occurs in the middle of the 70th "seven" and so at the beginning of the 1,260 days. Hence Jesus warned:

❖ "So when you see *'the sacrilege which causes desolation'*—spoken about by Daniel the prophet—'standing in the holy place' (let the reader understand), then those in Judea must begin escaping to the hills...How terrible it will be for those who are pregnant and for those who are nursing their babies in those days! So pray that when you must escape it won't be in winter, or on a Sabbath. Certainly, at that time there will be *great tribulation unequalled* by anything that has happened since the beginning of the world until now, or will ever happen again. And if those days hadn't been cut short, no one would be saved. But for the sake of the chosen ones those days will be cut short." (Matt. 24:15-16, 19-22 also see Dan. 12:1).

12:14: "But the woman was provided with the two wings of a huge eagle so that she could fly away from the Serpent into the desolate wasteland to the place where she is nourished for a time, times, and half a time." "The two wings of a huge eagle" most probably refers to transportation by means of angels. Again when Israel was pursued by Pharaoh, God had "born [Israel] on eagles' wings and brought [her] to [Himself]" (Ex. 19:4). The narrative now switches from the term "Dragon" to that of "Serpent" and so focusing on Satan's deceptive nature.

141

This verse repeats what is said in verse 6 and is pictorial of God's care in the spiritual feeding and protection of His people during the great tribulation. However, this doesn't mean that they are spared the wrath of Satan which wrath will lead to some Christians becoming martyrs.

12:15: "But the Serpent spewed water like a river from his mouth after the woman, in order to sweep her away by a torrent." This is a metaphor for satanic propaganda leading to destruction. With poisonous water, as from a poisonous serpent, Satan attempts to destroy the faithful Christian *"Israel of God."* It is like the poisonous water at Mara in the wilderness for Israel (Ex. 15:23-25). According to Robert Gundry, rather than a "flood" of soldiers this will be a flood of Serpent-like deception and propaganda *"to deceive, if possible, even the chosen ones"* (Matt. 24:25)

12:16: "But the earth helped her (the woman) when the ground opened its mouth and swallowed the river that the Dragon had spewed from his mouth." Again according to Robert Gundry this is the personified earth which absorbs the Serpent-like deception and propaganda. It reflects the literal swallowing up by the earth of Korah, Dathan and Abiram (Num. 16:30-32). It also reflects the occasion where the poisonous water at Mara in the wilderness is changed to sweet water after Moses hurled a tree into it (Ex. 15:23-25). This means that the Serpent-like inspired deception, propaganda, and accusations will not succeed with these spiritually well protected Christians.

12:17: "So the Dragon became angry at the woman, and went away to wage war on the rest of her children, those who obey God's commandments and hold to Jesus' testimony." The scene shifts from the Serpent aspect of Satan's nature i.e. that of deception, back to his Dragon nature of ferociousness. His anger is directed at the entire believing community—the Woman, but the waging of war is against the physically unprotected individual Christians—"the rest of her children" who are in the rest of the world outside of Judea or outside of Antichrist's kingdom. Chapter 13 gives the details of Satan's waging war with them by means of the Beast.

§

142

Chapter 28

The Ferocious Beast from the Sea
—The Antichrist
Revelation 13:1-10

TEXT

12:18 And [the Dragon] stood on the sand of the seashore.

13:1 Then I saw a ferocious beast coming up out of the sea. He had ten horns and seven heads. On each of his horns there was a diadem crown, and on each of his heads there was a blasphemous name. **2**The beast that I saw was like a leopard, with a bear's feet, and a lion's mouth. The Dragon gave him his power, his throne, and total authority. **3**One of his heads appeared to have been fatally wounded, but his fatal wound was healed. And the entire world was in awe and followed the beast. **4**They worshipped the Dragon because he had given authority to the beast. They also worshipped the beast, chanting: "Who is like the beast?" and "Who is able to wage war against him?" **5**He was given a mouth speaking arrogant things and blasphemies, and he was allowed to exercise authority for forty-two months. **6**So he opened his mouth in blasphemies against God: to blaspheme His reputation and character and His dwelling place (that is, those who live in heaven). **7**He was permitted to wage war against God's holy people and to conquer them. He was given authority over every tribe, nation, language, and race. **8**And everyone living on the earth will worship him—everyone whose name hasn't been written in the scroll of life belonging to the Lamb who was [sacrificially] slaughtered from the foundation of the world. **9**Anyone who has ears ought to listen! **10**Anyone who is meant for captivity, will go into captivity. Anyone who is to be killed with the sword, with the sword they will be killed. This shows the patient endurance and faithfulness on the part of God's holy people.

TRANSLATION POINT

In verse 8 the Greek word order favours the rendering: "the Lamb who was [sacrificially] slaughtered from the foundation of the world" so that the antecedent for "the foundation of the world" is not the phrase "written in the scroll" but the word "slaughtered" even though many versions render it otherwise to match with Revelation 17:8.

Comment on the Antichrist

12:18: **"And [the Dragon] stood on the sand of the seashore."** This statement is not only part of all that follows in Chapter 13 but also acts as a link with 12:1-17. Here, Satan comes to a standstill in anticipation as he summons the beast coming up from the sea. He is waiting on the sand of the seashore which pictures the fleshly seed of mankind.

143

13:1: "**Then I saw a ferocious beast coming up out of the sea. He had ten horns and seven heads. On each of his horns there was a diadem crown, and on each of his heads there was a blasphemous name.**" This is the Antichrist and his kingdom. It parallels the picture of him as "the beast who comes up from the abyss" (Rev. 11:7) i.e. the metaphorical deep depths of the sea which have restrained him up to now. Furthermore, the sea can be symbolic of the politically agitated world (Isa. 57:20) and certainly waters can picture nations (Rev. 17:15).

The seven heads, ten horns and seven diadems on its heads are the same as for the Dragon—Satan in 12:3 except for a change of position for the diadems. On the Dragon the diadems are on the heads, but for the beast they are on the horns. Nevertheless, this description is either a reflection of Satan's symbolic appearance or the transference of his authority to Antichrist at the time Antichrist comes out from the abyss (11:7; 17:8). These heads are all symbols of rulers and are also the same as the seven heads on the four beasts that Daniel was shown in Daniel 7:2-7. The seven heads with seven diadem crowns indicate Satan's and later Antichrist's pretension to sovereignty over the earth. The ten horns are the ten that are on the fourth beast of Daniel 7:7 and are later seen in Revelation 17:12 as the ten kings associated with Antichrist. Therefore this ferocious beast is a political entity and, indeed, the world-power.

13:2: "**The beast that I saw was like a leopard, with a bear's feet, and a lion's mouth. The Dragon gave him his power, his throne, and total authority.**" This pictures a composite beast which derives its details from Daniel 7:2-7, where the four beasts, whose characteristics John combines, represent Antichrist's future kingdom. The total of heads on the four beasts in Daniel also adds up to seven.

Nevertheless, Satan can do nothing without God's permission. Indeed, it is with Satan's power that Antichrist will be able to perform powerful works to deceive even the chosen ones (Matt. 24:24; 2 Thess. 2:9).

However, in Revelation 2:13 we were told that Pergamum is "where the Satan's throne is." So could it be that some part of Antichrist's rule will be from Satan's throne in Pergamum in Asia Minor? Indeed, he seems to originate from Turkey according to Ezekiel 38, 39 with reference to Gog of Magog as the Antichrist.

13:3: "**One of his heads appeared to have been fatally wounded, but his fatal wound was healed. And the entire world was in awe and followed the beast.**" Although it is stated that he "appeared to have been fatally

144

wounded" this does not mean that he wasn't actually killed. It is not just one of the heads that is displayed as slain but the beast himself (13:12, 14). His death and his coming back to life seems to be a parody of Christ's death and resurrection, although in Antichrist's case it is simply a resuscitation, but with Satan being the one to make this happen, so that he has brought his son back from the dead.

13:4: "**They worshipped the Dragon because he had given authority to the beast. They also worshipped the beast, chanting: "Who is like the beast?" and "Who is able to wage war against him?"** These followers/disciples of Antichrist turn this into worship of him because they have been deceived by the miracle of his fatal wound being healed (2 Cor.4:4). This is a usurpation of the worship that rightfully belongs to God only and amounts to the worship of Satan himself.

13:5: "**He was given a mouth speaking arrogant things and blasphemies, and he was allowed to exercise authority for forty-two months.**" His mouth in being like "a lion's mouth" (verse 2) is used to produce the ongoing boastful blasphemies noted in verse 6. This echoes Daniel 7:8, 20 and 2 Thessalonians 2:4.

The 42 months is the period of the great tribulation and concerns Seals 4 and 5.

13:6: "**So he opened his mouth in blasphemies against God: to blaspheme His reputation and character and His dwelling place, (that is, those who dwell in heaven).**" God's "dwelling place" represents "the heaven-dwellers" who are the Christian Holy Ones (See 6:10). So these are blasphemies against the end-time Christians as well as against God.

13:7: "**He was permitted to wage war against God's holy people and to conquer them. He was given authority over every tribe, nation, language, and race.**" This war is the great tribulation when Satan pours out his wrath upon Christians (Dan. 7:21; 12:1; Matt. 24:21) through the Antichrist. However, the conquering of them is short-lived (6:8-11) through the 1260 days; and, in fact, they spiritually "triumph over him through the blood of the Lamb and through the message of their testimony, because they didn't love their lives even when facing death" (Rev. 12:11). Antichrist's authority is temporary and is largely within the confines of his own kingdom and the nations which follow him. So there is a spatial limitation to his kingdom, although his influence and authority is world-wide for a time. Please see Appendix D.

145

13:8: "**And everyone living on the earth will worship him** [*the beast out of the sea*]—**everyone whose name hasn't been written in the scroll of life**." These are "the earth-dwellers" as a symbol of the followers and worshipers of Antichrist. So this seems to indicate that it won't be literally everyone on earth who will worship the Antichrist, and certainly the true Christians would not do so.

This is the second mention in Revelation of the scroll of life. For those whose names are written in it there is very comforting security for them, as long as they remain "incorporated into Christ" (Rev. 3:5).

13:8b-9: "**Belonging to the Lamb who was [sacrificially] slaughtered from the foundation of the world. Anyone who has ears ought to listen!**" This shows that the Messiah as the sacrificial lamb was foreordained, at least from the time of the first prophecy in Genesis 3:15 which concerns Satan's bruising in the heel of "the seed of the Woman" i.e. the Messiah and those incorporated into him (Gal. 3:29). The importance of this message is emphasized in the last phrase here.

13:10: "**Anyone who is meant for captivity will go into captivity. Anyone who is to be killed with the sword, with the sword they will be killed. This shows the patient endurance and faithfulness on the part of God's holy people**." This is an allusion to the very similar thought in Jeremiah 15:2. Clearly, Christians have been persecuted throughout their history, including having been taken captive and killed. This will intensify during the Antichrist's great tribulation upon them (Matt. 24:9). So along with their maintaining of their faith and remaining patient as Christians, the Apostle Peter speaks of Jesus' example for Christians who are being persecuted when he writes:

❖ "When they hurled their insults at him, he never retaliated; when he suffered, he made no threats. Instead, he left his case in the hands of God who always judges justly" *(1 Pet. 2:23).*

§

146

Chapter 29

The Ferocious Beast from the Earth
—The False Prophet
Revelation 13:11-18

TEXT

¹¹Then I saw another ferocious beast coming up out of the earth; he had two horns like a lamb, but he was speaking like a dragon. ¹²He exercises all the authority of the first beast in his presence, and makes the earth and those inhabiting it worship the first beast whose fatal wound was healed. ¹³He performs spectacular signs, even causing fire to come down from the sky in full view of the people. ¹⁴He deceives those who live on the earth by the signs he was allowed to perform on behalf of the beast—directing those who live on the earth to make an image for worship of the beast who had the sword wound and yet came to life. ¹⁵He was allowed to impart breath of life to the image of the beast, so that it could speak, and to cause anyone who wouldn't worship the image of the beast to be put to death. ¹⁶He also compels everyone—lowly and prominent, rich and poor, free and bond-servant—to be branded on their right hand or on their forehead, ¹⁷so that no one can buy or sell things unless he has the brand-mark, that is, the beast's name or the number of his name. ¹⁸This requires wisdom. Let anyone who has sufficient insight calculate the beast's number, because it's a human's number, and his number is 666.

Comment on the False Prophet

13:11: **"Then I saw another ferocious beast coming up out of the earth; he had two horns like a lamb, but he was speaking like a dragon."** This beast is a separate individual to the first beast. This one comes "out of the earth" in contrast to the first beast who arises from the sea/abyss. In doing so, this second beast arises from the more stable parts of society generally governed by religious principles and systems. The two horns of power on this beast show that he is subordinate to the seven horned beast and is the one who bears witness to the first beast and derives his power from his association with the first beast. This beast is likely to arise from within religious circles because he appears to be as gentle as a lamb, but he is among the false prophets that Jesus spoke of who will lead many Christians into deserting the faith (Matt. 24:10-12, 24-28). Indeed, his satanic nature and character are seen in how he speaks i.e. as a dragon.

13:12: **"He exercises all the authority of the first beast in his presence, and makes the earth and those inhabiting it worship the first beast whose fatal wound was healed."** This second beast is a tool of the Antichrist.

147

He is Antichrist's minister of propaganda and high priest. Whereas the first beast is a civil political power—a false Messiah, this second beast is a false prophet and is later called "the false prophet" (Rev. 16:13, 14; 19:20; 20:10). Indeed, he "makes" the earth-dwellers worship the Antichrist who has set himself up as a god in the temple of God (2 Thess. 2:4), so he heads up a new organized religion.

13:13: "**He performs spectacular signs, even causing fire to come down from the sky in full view of the people.**" These are not fake miracles or mere tricks, but certainly something that Satan is quite capable of as he did in Job's case in calling down fire (Job 1:16). However, in 13:3 this is a parody of God's miracle working through Elijah (1King 18:38; 2 King 1:10) and the two witnesses in calling down fire as well as the spectacular signs God did through Jesus. So these counterfeit miracles in 13:3 seem to be those that will be produced by Satan and that will accompany "the royal coming of the lawless one"—the Antichrist (2 Thess. 2:9). These signs are performed for the purpose of promoting the worship of Antichrist so that even sceptics who do not believe in the supernatural must think again!

13:14: "**He deceives those who live on the earth by the signs he was allowed to perform on behalf of the beast—directing those who live on the earth to make an image for worship of the beast who had the sword wound and yet came to life.**" Here we have the divine passive, showing that such miracles are only allowed by God's permission. The deceiving here is that of making the earth-dwellers view the first beast as invincible and so to worship his image which is really the worship of the Antichrist himself. This is similar to the time when Nebuchadnezzar had a ninety foot high image built and commanded everyone to worship it (Dan. 3:1-6). This was likely an image of himself.

13:15: "**He was allowed to impart breath of life to the image of the beast, so that it could speak, and to cause anyone who wouldn't worship the image of the beast to be put to death.**" In the ancient world special effects equipment was used to produce speaking and moving idols. However, this image of Antichrist is shown to really speak as a miraculous action from Satan. Just as the Antichrist is supernatural so, too, is this image. The purpose of the speaking is to utter Antichrist's commands.

The sentence structure here indicates that it is the second beast who causes those who wouldn't worship this image to be put to death.

148

13:16: "He also compels everyone—lowly and prominent, rich and poor, free and bond-servant—to be branded on their right hand or on their forehead." This is the action of the second beast—the false prophet. Such a brand-mark indicates allegiance to the beast i.e. that they belong to him. The purpose is so that each person will have rejected all previous loyalties. Indeed, the general centralization of society could easily be turned against Christians to marginalize them so that there is a polarizing of people. The fact that it is applied to the "lowly and prominent, rich and poor, free and bond-servant" indicates social inclusivity i.e. truly everyone is compelled to have this mark.

However, the mark of the Beast is unlikely to be a physical mark, biometric identification, or implanted chip, although some sort of citizenship card or similar could be used in a "marking" application of each person.

Nevertheless, just as the mark of God is his seal i.e. the mind-set and values that Christians hold (2 Tim. 2:19) "sealed with the holy spirit of promise" (Eph. 1:13), so too, the mark of the Beast could be the counterfeit of God's mark—the mind-set and values of the Antichrist world or even a parody of the sealing of Christians. Certainly, all true Christians will resist having Antichrist's brand-mark. For this they may suffer the following economic problems.

13:17: "So that no one can buy or sell things unless he has the brand-mark, that is, the beast's name or the number of his name." Could this brand-mark of the Beast be the sin of "blasphemy against the spirit [that] will not be forgiven"? (Matt. 12:31). This possibility is because of the declarations against the followers of the Beast in Rev.14:9-11.

Because of this mark and this ruling it is likely that, at this time, Jesus' parable recorded in Matthew 25:31-40 concerning the actions of the sheep who are not yet Christians may come to apply. Furthermore, this ruling from this beast may be less severely enforced beyond the boundaries of Antichrist's own kingdom i.e. the area of the four kingdoms statue of Daniel 2:31-35, 45.

13:18: "This requires wisdom. Let anyone who has sufficient insight calculate the beast's number, because it's a human's number, and his number is 666." In modern terms the number 666 is called a triangular number, but no one has truly solved the meaning of this number. Modern commentators try to apply this to Nero Caesar based on the Nero redivivus legend that Nero died and came back to life. This approach to

149

the number 666 was done by the use of gematria, meaning "manipulation with numbers." It is a substituting of letters for the numbers to produce a code. However, this does not fit in the Greek, namely, the language that John was using and so this gives the result as being 1005. Therefore, many have assumed that John meant for it to be rendered in Hebrew/Aramaic, but this only works if an extra letter "n" is added to the Greek first i.e. *neron kaisar*, but John did not have Hebrew in mind. In fact, this method can be used to produce a variety of results, including applying it to "Hitler." Others have viewed the number as a reference to the papal system or Napoleon Bonaparte or some modern dictator such as Stalin, Pol Pot, or Saddam Hussein.

One likely feature is that the number simply refers to the Antichrist's human imperfection to the third degree and so intensifies his evil character. Nevertheless, it seems that speculation on how this number applies will remain fruitless until it becomes evident in the future.

§

Chapter 30

The Triumph of the Lamb and the 144,000 on Mount Zion
Revelation 14:1-5

TEXT

Then, as I watched, there was the Lamb standing on Mount Zion. With him were 144,000 who had his name, and his Father's name written on their foreheads. ²Then I heard a sound out of heaven, like the sound of a torrent of waters, and like the sound of loud thunder. And the sound I heard was like that of harpists playing their harps. ³They are singing a new song in front of the throne and in front of the four living creatures and the elders, but no one was able to learn the song except the 144,000 who had been ransomed from the earth. ⁴These are the ones who haven't contaminated themselves with women—indeed they are virgins. It is these who follow the Lamb wherever he goes. These were ransomed from among mankind as first fruits to God and to the Lamb, ⁵and no deceit was found to come from their mouths. They are blameless.

Overview

Chapter 14 continues the interlude between the seven trumpets and the seven bowls. However, the phrase "as I watched, there was..." indicates a new subject here which is presented in four units: 14:1-5; 14:6-12; 14:13; 14:14-20. These four units represent a pastiche of themes and motifs drawn from many places elsewhere in Revelation. Here, these 144,000 are the same as the earlier ones of 7:4-8 who were sealed with the name of the Lamb and of the Father.

Comment on the Lamb and the 144,000 Standing on Mount Zion

14:1: "**Then, as I watched, there was the Lamb standing on Mount Zion. With him were 144,000 who had his name, and his Father's name written on their foreheads.**" In Jewish apocalyptic Mount Zion is the centre of rulership (Heb.12:22-24), the place where Messiah will defeat his enemies and will judge them. So this is a picture of triumph for Messiah Jesus and will also fulfil the prophecy in Psalm 2. The fact that he is "standing" is an indicator of his actions as a divine warrior.

Because Mount Zion is differentiated from the "sound out of heaven" in verse 2, it is clear that this is the literal Mount Zion on earth upon which parts of the city of Jerusalem are built and which will be the capital of God's Kingdom. So the time of this picture is that of the return of Jesus to earth at the beginning of the Millennium and is therefore proleptic and only realized in chapters 19 and 20.

These 144,000 are shown to be sharing in Jesus' triumphant victory while standing with him on the literal Mount Zion. However, this is not a different group to the 144,000 in 7:4-8 and the "names" given here show that they are Christians and were sealed with those names in 7:2-4. As shown earlier the number 144,000 should be taken as symbolic. Indeed, Galatians 4:27 shows that Christians, in their totality, are to be finally more numerous than the ancient nation of Israel (millions) and so vastly more than a literal 144,000. These ones are the living end-times Christians of the age-long multi-ethnic body of the Christian *"Israel of God."* They are sealed for special protection during the day of God's wrath (Ps.27:5) and are the same people as those in the *"great multitude,"* (7:9-17) only presented from a different perspective, that is, as organized in military marching fashion to give a faithful witness.

14:2: "**Then I heard a sound out of heaven, like the sound of a torrent of waters, and like the sound of loud thunder. And the sound I heard was like that of harpists playing their harps.**" Because the voice that John hears is out of heaven, John is evidently on earth vision-wise. So he hears the voice of the angelic choir like the sound of the thunderous music of celebration for the great victory of the Messiah.

Harps are first mentioned in 5:8 and are there shown to be more like lyres with 10 or more strings each, rather than like the Welsh harp.

14:3: "**They are singing a new song in front of the throne and in front of the four living creatures and the elders, but no one was able to learn the song except the 144,000 who had been ransomed from the earth.**" The harps mentioned in verse 2 are the musical accompaniment to the singing of the new song which relates to "the age to come" and is sung by the heavenly court of angels. This is similar to the singing of the "new song" in 5:9 by the four living creatures and the 24 elders (see TRANSLATION POINT on 5:10). However, out of all of mankind only the 144,000 could learn this song from the angelic beings. The reason for this is that only the 144,000 are Christians and have experienced the recent events as well as having overcome Satan's deceptions. So their being "ransomed from the earth" does not mean that they are literally taken away from the earth, but as in verse 4b it shows they are ransomed or redeemed from among mankind.

14:4a: "**These are the ones who haven't contaminated themselves with women—indeed they are virgins** *(Gk parthenoi i.e. the masculine form)."* This does not make these a special group separate from all other Christians. The very rare use of *parthenoi* for men here indicates that this description is of a metaphorical nature. It does not mean that they literally have never had sexual relations with a wife because such would never been seen scripturally as a contamination or defilement. Although Jesus and Paul encouraged singleness for certain reasons and times they also showed that the married state was always the acceptable and normal state for Christians (1 Cor. 7:2-5, 32-33).

This, along with the statements about the 144,000 in Rev. 14:5, shows their moral and spiritual purity i.e. as pure as virgins just as Paul states that a Christian should be a "pure virgin" and meaning that they are to be undefiled, that is, uncontaminated by false teaching (2 Cor. 11:2). This means that they are spiritually chaste and have refused to participate in pagan worship, especially in the worship of the Antichrist beast. However, please note that today's idolatry also often involves money, possessions, success, and fleshly pursuits.

14:4b: "**It is these who follow the Lamb wherever he goes. These were ransomed from among mankind as first fruits to God and to the Lamb.**" Here we have further evidence that these are Christians. They are the 144,000 who have already been shown to be multi-ethnic Christians in the end-times. They follow Jesus because they know the shepherd's voice (John 10:3-4) and they prove this because they adhere to his instructions and promote him as Lord Messiah. This may even mean following Jesus into death if necessary.

Indeed, they have been ransomed because of accepting the sacrifice that Jesus made for them and for all mankind. This is similar to 5:9 where it is shown that "with your own blood you *[Jesus]* have ransomed people for God." Also the statement that they are "first fruits to God and to the Lamb" gives a sacrificial image. Obviously, the term *"first fruits"* refers to the first portion of crops that are presented to God, but there were also *"the first fruits of first fruits"* (Ex. 34:26; Ezek. 44:30). Nevertheless, this phrase *"first fruits to God"* does not refer to natural ethnic Jews because the focus of the New Testament, and indeed the Book of Revelation, is on multi-ethnic Christians. James calls his readers, "the first fruits of his *[God's]* creatures" (1:18) and so referring to the *"Israel of God"* when, as the *"great multitude,"* they *"have come out of the great tribulation."* (7:14). Therefore, this multi-ethnic group of Christians are the first fruits of God's harvest which guarantees the final harvest of all the Christian dead and the future believers.

Also please note that the phrase "to God and to the lamb" shows that Jesus is not God Almighty (please see my book entitled: *God, Jesus, and the Holy Spirit–It's No Mystery* in this series of *Concise Studies in the Scriptures*).

14:5: "**And no deceit was found to come from their mouths. They are blameless.**" Here again the moral and spiritual purity of the 144,000 is shown. In all of their preaching of the good news there is never any attempt to deceive others. In specific terms this could also refer to the major deception promoted by the worshippers of Antichrist about him as being mankind's saviour.

§

Chapter 31

The Three Angels Give Their Proclamations
Revelation 14:6-13

TEXT

6Then I saw another angel flying in mid-air. He had the good news of the age to come to proclaim to those who live on the earth, to every race, tribe, language, and nation. **7**He said in a loud voice: "Show reverence for God! Give Him glory! His judgment time has arrived, so worship the One who made the sky, the earth and sea and the springs of water!"

8Another angel, a second one, followed, saying: "Fallen, fallen is Babylon the great! She was the one who made all the nations drink the wine of the anger that comes upon her passion for sexual immorality."

9Another angel, a third one, followed them, saying in a loud voice: "If anyone worships the beast and his image, and receives a brand-mark on their forehead or their hand, **10**they will also drink of the wine of God's anger that has been mixed undiluted in the cup of His retribution. They will have severe pain inflicted upon them with fire and sulphur in the sight of the holy angels and in the sight of the Lamb. **11**And the smoke from their severe pain will go up forever and ever. Those who worship the beast and his image will have no respite day or night, along with anyone who receives the brand-mark of his name."

12This shows that the patient endurance of God's people involves keeping God's commands and keeping faithful to Jesus.

13Then I heard a voice from heaven saying, "Write: 'Blessed are the dead, those who die in solidarity with the Lord from now and onward!'"

"Yes," says the spirit, "so that they will rest from their hard work, because their deeds follow them."

Comment on the Three Angels' Proclamations

14:6: **"Then I saw another angel flying in mid-air. He had the good news of the age to come to proclaim to those who live on the earth, to every race, tribe, language, and nation."** This statement is addressed to "the earth-dwellers" i.e. those of Antichrist's kingdom and which links with Revelation 8:13 where the eagle announces the three calamities. The proclamations that are made by these three angels seem to fulfil Jesus' words in Matthew 24:14 and so likely occur during the last 3½ years of Daniel's 70th "seven" i.e. the time of the great tribulation.

14:7: **"He said in a loud voice: Show reverence for God! Give Him glory! His judgment time has arrived, so worship the One who made the sky, the earth and sea and the springs of water!"** This verse along with verse 6 is similar to Jesus' proclamation of, "The time is fulfilled and the Kingdom of God is now very near. Change your mindset and life-direction, and believe the good news!" *(Mark 1:15)*. This is a last chance appeal to repent for these "earth-dwellers," because it is judgment-time. If they do not change and show reverence for God, then they will suffer the consequences of following Antichrist rather than the creator of the universe.

Additionally, this points to "the One" who is the creator i.e. the Lord God and not to Jesus who is the Lord Messiah.

14:8: "**Another angel, a second one, followed, saying: "Fallen, fallen is Babylon the great! She was the one who made all the nations drink the wine of the anger that comes upon her passion for sexual immorality.**" This is the first direct mention of Babylon. Here the verb "fallen" is grammatically a proleptic aorist, showing the certainty of this fall because Babylon made the nations participate in her life-style—a reference to Jeremiah 51:7 which speaks of Babylon's "intoxicating all the earth. The nations have drunk of her wine." In fact, Rev. 14:8 is taken from Isaiah 21:9 but note Rev. 16:19 where God gives her the cup of the wine of His anger as punishment.

14:9: "**Another angel, a third one, followed them, saying in a loud voice: "If anyone worships the beast and his image, and receives a brand-mark on their forehead or their hand.**" It was the work of the false prophet in compelling many to accept the brand-mark of the Antichrist and causing them to worship him. This was done by means of the threat of economic sanctions and death for them.

14:10: "**They will also drink of the wine of God's anger that has been mixed undiluted in the cup of His retribution. They will have severe pain inflicted upon them with fire and sulphur in the sight of the holy angels and in the sight of the Lamb.".**" The term "undiluted" means full strength" i.e. the seven bowls of God's wrath in punishment are given to their maximum. Along with fire, this is one of the several symbols to indicate the destruction of the wicked.

The inflicting of severe pain does not concern wicked mankind in general, but the "earth-dwellers" i.e. those who are part of Antichrist's kingdom and worship him. This symbolically represents their sudden and irreversible destruction. It is similar to the <u>severe pain of destruction</u> of Babylon the great (18:7-8) as being destroyed "in one day...burned up by fire." (Please see my book *Delusions and Truths Concerning the Future Life* in this series).

156

14:11: "And the smoke from their severe pain will go up forever and ever. Those who worship the beast and his image will have no respite day or night, along with anyone who receives the brand-mark of his name." The smoke from this event goes on forever as shown in Isa. 34:9-10 as the background to Revelation 14:10-11 but not literally so. It symbolizes the permanent evidence of their eternal destruction. (Note Revelation 20:10).

14:12: "This shows that the patient endurance of God's people involves keeping God's commands and keeping faithful to Jesus." Keeping God's commands does not mean keeping the regulations of the Mosaic Law which were for Israel only, but keeping God's commands as given by Jesus along with his acceptance of the moral standards and principles given in the Mosaic Law (2 Tim. 3:16).

Contextually, rather than the "the faith of Jesus" this refers to "keeping faith with Jesus" (grammatically an objective genitive) as a common term used by Jewish Christians. So this does not refer to the doctrinal content of the Christian faith in this instance, but that of maintaining one's allegiance to Jesus.

14:13: "Then I heard a voice from heaven saying, "Write: 'Blessed are the dead, those who die in solidarity with the Lord from now and onward!'" "Yes," says the spirit, "so that they will rest from their hard work, because their deeds follow them"** This voice of an angel shows that, because of their maintaining their allegiance to Jesus many Christians have died and others will do so during the great tribulation. They are blessed because they have gained a victory in "keeping faithful to Jesus." However, the phrase to "die in solidarity with the Lord" refers to one's metaphorical dying to oneself and so includes all who are living and have maintained their allegiance to Jesus to the end, and so are also blessed.

The phrase "from now and onward!" indicates that the time of persecution i.e. the great tribulation is about to begin and so Christians must be determined to remain faithful.

The spirit here is "the spirit of Jesus," so it is really he who shows that all who maintain their allegiance to him, either right up to death or right up to his return, will have then proved worthy to receive their rewards. However, please notice that these rewards are for those involved in "hard work" and faithfulness toward Messiah Jesus.

§

157

Chapter 32

The Grain and the Grape Harvests
Revelation 14:14-20

TEXT

14Then I looked, and there was a white cloud, and sitting on the cloud was one like a son of man. He had a golden crown on his head and a sharp sickle in his hand. **15**Then another angel came out of the sanctuary, shouting with a loud voice to the one sitting on the cloud, "Use your sickle and reap, because the time to reap has come: the harvest of the earth is ripe!" **16**So the one sitting on the cloud swung his sickle over the earth, and the earth was reaped.

▲

17Then another angel came out of the sanctuary in heaven. He also had a sharp sickle. **18**Yet another angel—one who had authority over the fire—came from the [sanctuary] altar and called in a loud voice to the angel who had the sharp sickle, "Use your sharp sickle and gather the clusters of grapes from the vineyard which is the earth, because now its grapes are ripe." **19**So the angel swung his sickle toward the earth, and gathered the grapes from the earth's vintage. He threw them into the huge winepress of God's anger. **20**Then the winepress was trampled outside the city and blood flowed out of the winepress, up to the height of the horses' bridles, for a distance of 1,600 stadia.

Overview

Commentators are split concerning whether John took the grain harvest as a reference to the saving of Christians or the divine judgment of the wicked, which the other harvest—the grape harvest certainly is; or is it that both harvests concerned the judgment of the wicked. I take this to refer to the former i.e. the saving of Christians as indicated by the recent words in verse 13 of, *"Blessed are the dead, those who die in solidarity with the Lord from now and onward!"*

So here it appears that only the grape harvest alluded to in Joel 3:13 concerns divine judgment of the wicked. This is connected to the actions of the third angel described in 14:10-11 where there is the pouring out of the undiluted wine of God's anger of judgment on the wicked.

Comment on the Grain Harvest

14:14: **"Then I looked, and there was a white cloud, and sitting on the cloud was one like a son of man. He had a golden crown on his head and a sharp sickle in his hand."** This cloud pictures the *shekinah* glory of God. So as God's representative Jesus, who is never called or described as an

158

angel (Heb. 1:5, 13), is "one like a son of man...who comes with the clouds of heaven" as in Daniel 7:13—a clear reference to Messiah. Also Revelation 1:13 describes "one like a son of man" as referring to Jesus (1:17). So, this "one like a son of man" is shown to have a crown *(Gk stephanos—a laurel wreath)*, one that is golden and so further indicating that this refers to Jesus with his royal authority to judge the people of the nations (Matt. 25:31-46).

The white cloud is a signal for the second advent of the Lord Jesus as the coming of "God" in the sense of Jesus as being the prime representative of the almighty God.

Although the usage of a sickle generally had a significantly negative meaning, suggesting death, destruction, and judgment it was, nevertheless, used for all reaping and so is still appropriate for the harvesting of those who have God's favour. Its sharpness indicates the speed and efficiency of the gathering of this harvest.

14:15: "**Then another angel came out of the sanctuary, shouting with a loud voice to the one sitting on the cloud, "Use your sickle and reap, because the time to reap has come: the harvest of the earth is ripe!"** This is not "another angel" additional to "the one like a son of man" as if the one in verse 14 i.e. Jesus is also an angel. This is "another" as an addition to the angels mentioned in 14:6, 8, and 9.

The fact that the angel came out of the heavenly sanctuary shows that the command he gives to the "one like a son of man," namely, Jesus came from God. Therefore, it is not problematic for Jesus to obey such a command from an angel because the command originates from God.

Because Jesus is here shown as sitting on a cloud the same as in Matthew 24:30, it is evident that this harvesting occurs after the great tribulation (Matt.24:29) and therefore indicates a post-tribulation resurrection and rapture.

14:16: "**So the one sitting on the cloud swung his sickle over the earth, and the earth was reaped.**" This harvesting of the earth is a metaphor which involves the gathering of those having God's approval. Jesus illustrated this by speaking of the wheat as having been gathered into the barn i.e. resurrected and then gathered up with living Christians to meet the returning Jesus. The reality will be that this "harvest of the earth" occurs when Jesus "sends out his angels to gather his chosen ones from the four winds, from one end of the skies to the other" (Matt. 13:31; 1 Cor. 15:23, 35-49; 1Thess. 4:16-17).

Comment on the Grape Harvest

14:17: "**Then another angel came out of the sanctuary in heaven. He also had a sharp sickle.**" Again this coming out of the sanctuary indicates divine authorization for a mission, but this time it concerns the destruction of the wicked.

14:18: "**Yet another angel—one who had authority over the fire—came from the [sanctuary] altar and called in a loud voice to the angel who had the sharp sickle, "Use your sharp sickle and gather the clusters of grapes from the vineyard which is the earth, because now its grapes are ripe.**" It appears that this angel has brought fire in a censer with him from the altar of burnt offerings and alludes to Rev. 8:3-5. However, the focus is still on his coming from the sanctuary and so showing his authorization from God to give out the fiery judgment of God.

The "vineyard which is the earth" is a symbol of Antichrist and all who worship him (see 14:9) and is in direct contrast to Jesus as "the authentic vine" along with all those who are the branches (John 15:1-5).

14:19: "**So the angel swung his sickle toward the earth, and gathered the grapes from the earth's vintage. He threw them into the huge winepress of God's anger.**" The harvesting of the grapes is a first metaphor here for the destruction of the wicked worshipers of Antichrist during the day of God's wrath and is a picture taken from Joel's prophecy:

❖ "...put in your sickle for the harvest is ripe. Come, tread, for the wine press is full...For the Day of Yahweh is near in the valley of Decision" (Joel 3:11-16).

In this scenario "the huge winepress of God's anger" is a second metaphor for the destruction of the wicked of Antichrist's kingdom. Later, in 19:15, Jesus, as God's Messiah, is shown to be treading this winepress which will fulfil the prophecy given by Isaiah where God is asked:

❖ "Why is your apparel red, your clothes like someone treading a winepress? "I have trodden the winepress alone; from the peoples, not one was with me. So I trod them in my anger, trampled them in my fury; so their lifeblood spurted out on my clothing, and I have stained all my garments; for the day of vengeance that was in my heart and my year of redemption have come" *(Isa. 63:2-4).*

14:20: "Then the winepress was trampled outside the city and blood flowed out of the winepress, up to the height of the horses' bridles, for a distance of 1,600 stadia." The city mentioned is likely to be Jerusalem and all vineyards were located outside the city walls. However, the fact of this event as being outside the city may be that of poetic justice because of Jesus' execution having been "outside the gate/camp" (Heb. 13:12-13); or it may be because the prophecies in Zechariah show the final battle to be outside of those walls of Jerusalem (Zech 12-14). Nevertheless, the "blood" is taken from the picture of "the blood of grapes" i.e. the juice, but the height and distance (183 miles) of its flow is pure hyperbole indicating the completeness of God's judgment—40 x 40. This picture becomes even clearer in Revelation 16 and the latter half of Revelation 19. This destruction of the wicked repays all those who have been slaughtered throughout the ages.

§

Chapter 33

The Seven Angels with the Final Plagues
Revelation 15

TEXT

Then I saw another spectacular and awesome sign in the sky: seven angels bringing seven final plagues, which will bring God's anger to completion.

²Then I saw something like a glassy sea, mixed with fire. Those who had emerged victorious from the conflict with the ferocious beast, his image, and the number of his name were standing by the glassy sea. They had harps from God, ³and were singing the song of Moses, God's bond-servant, and the song of the Lamb:

"Spectacular and awe-inspiring are your deeds, LORD God, the All-Powerful! Just and true are your ways, King over the nations! ⁴Who will not revere you, O LORD, and glorify you in your entire being, because you alone are holy? All nations will come and worship before you, because your acts of justice have been revealed."

⁵After these things I looked, and the sanctuary in heaven—the tabernacle of the testimony—was opened. ⁶Then the seven angels bringing the seven plagues came out of the sanctuary, dressed in clean shining linen, wearing wide golden sashes around their chests.

⁷Then one of the four living creatures gave the seven angels seven golden drink-offering bowls filled with the anger of God who lives forever and ever. ⁸The sanctuary was filled with smoke from God's glory and from His power. No one was able to go into the sanctuary until the seven plagues of the seven angels were completed.

Overview

With Chapter 15 we move on from the interlude of chapters 12 to 14 and resume the events noted with the blowing of the seventh trumpet (11:15-19). These concern preparation for the outpouring of seven plagues. Once again these plagues are quite literal as with the ancient Egyptian plagues. Those ancient plagues act as the controlling image for all seven of the bowl plagues in Revelation. Furthermore, the first four plagues are of divinely directed natural disasters, whereas the last three are of direct judgments leading to destruction and in particular of Babylon the great.

It also appears that these judgments overlap each other and are therefore cumulative in their effects.

162

Comment on the Final Plagues

15:1: "**Then I saw another spectacular and awesome sign in the sky: seven angels bringing seven final plagues, which will bring God's anger to completion.**" This is the third "sign in the sky" that John saw, with the other two being in 12:1 and 12:3. As in 8:2 these seven angels are the archangels, but John doesn't actually see these angels until verse 6 when they come out from the sanctuary. The fact that these are the "seven <u>final</u> plagues" shows that the blasting of the trumpets also brought about actual plagues.

15:2a: "**Then I saw something like a glassy sea, mixed with fire.**" This shows that the entire scene is connected to the throne room (see 4:6) as with the seven seals and seven trumpets. So this glassy sea is likely a reference to the expanse of waters in Genesis 1:7, and perhaps to "the shape of an expanse, with a gleam like awe-inspiring crystal" beneath God's throne *(Ezek. 1:22-26),* and is simply to show the majesty and tranquillity of God's presence. So here we find that God's throne is set upon this glassy sea and in being "mixed with fire," as the cosmic counterpart to the lake of fire, it is seen to indicate the impending judgments about to fall upon wicked mankind.

15:2b: "**Those who had emerged victorious from the conflict with the ferocious beast, his image, and the number of his name were standing by the glassy sea.**" These holy ones are the "overcomers" detailed in Revelation 2 and 3, and who will receive the rewards detailed in those chapters. They are figuratively "standing beside the glassy sea on which God's throne sits in the temple, even as they are "heaven-dwellers," "seated in heavenly places incorporated into [Christ]" but existing on earth (Eph. 2:6). Nevertheless, this shows that they are privileged to figuratively stand before God on His throne.

15:2c, 3: "**They had harps from God and were singing the song of Moses, God's bond-servant, and the song of the Lamb: "Spectacular and awe-inspiring are your deeds, LORD God, the All-Powerful! Just and true are your ways, King over the nations!"**" The harps are a symbol of victory and rejoicing, but this is a single song which echoes the themes of liberation, victory, and restoration as found in the song of Moses (Ex. 15:1-19). However, John's is a new version of the song of Moses. It alludes to Isaiah 12 as an eschatological interpretation of Exodus 15 and several other verses from the Hebrew Scriptures. In other words it has been reworked by John through skilful use of the rabbinic technique of *gezara sawa* to portray the future victory by the Lamb's followers after the new exodus. It is because they have overcome and been delivered from the hostility and persecution dealt out by "the ferocious beast" during the great tribulation. This fact shows that the outpouring of the seven bowls of God's punishment, and therefore the seventh trumpet, occur after the great tribulation (please see chapter 9).

In praising the Lord God Almighty these words show that His "acts of justice have been revealed" and are about to be poured out on the entire unrepentant wicked world.

15:4: "**Who will not revere you, O LORD, and glorify you in your entire being, because you alone are holy? All nations will come and worship before you because your acts of justice have been revealed.**" This phrase, when taken in context, does not mean that there will be universal salvation. These words must be seen in the light of the full range of the biblical view of this subject (see my book, *How God Works in Human Affairs*). However, at this future time all nationalistic barriers will have fallen.

15:5: "**After these things I looked, and the sanctuary in heaven—the tabernacle of the testimony—was opened.**" As John sees these things his vision takes him right into the temple precincts to see the opening of the sanctuary which contains the most holy compartment and which has the Ark of the Covenant in it. This Ark is known as God's throne i.e. where God figuratively lives.

15:6: "**Then the seven angels bringing the seven plagues came out of the sanctuary, dressed in clean shining linen, wearing wide golden sashes around their chests.**" Their clothing shows their purity and therefore their right to be bearers of the coming judgment. The wide golden sash that they each wear indicates that they are also emissaries of Messiah Jesus who is also described with such a sash (see 1:13).

15:7: "**Then one of the four living creatures gave the seven angels seven golden drink-offering bowls filled with the anger of God who lives forever and ever.**" One of the cherubim (please see *4:6:*) hands each of the bowls to the archangels. The purpose of the pouring out of these bowls is that of judgment as a sacred offering to God, and therefore to remove those of mankind who are absolutely irredeemable in their opposition to God. So this is the beginning of "the day of God's wrath," also known as "the day of Yahweh," and "the day of the Lord."

15:8: "**The sanctuary was filled with smoke from God's glory and from His power. No one was able to go into the sanctuary until the seven plagues of the seven angels were completed.**" As with clouds, smoke also signifies the presence of God. Indeed, God's glory in a cloud filled the tabernacle in Moses' time when the tabernacle was completed (Ex. 40:35). It also filled the temple when it was completed in Solomon's time (1 Kings 8:11). So here, for the period of the outpouring of these seven bowls, God's glorious presence alone will be in the sanctuary and no one else will be able enter the sanctuary because of God's awesome holiness, majesty, and power.

After this preparation time we move on to the actual pouring out of these seven bowls of God's wrath or retributive punishment of the incorrigibly wicked.

§

Chapter 34

Pouring of the Seven Bowls of God's Wrath
Revelation 16

TEXT

Then I heard a loud voice from the sanctuary saying to the seven angels: "Go and begin to pour out on the earth the seven drink-offering bowls of God's anger."

The First Bowl

²So the first one went off and was pouring out his bowl on the land, with the result that a festering and painful sore appeared on those who had the brand-mark of the beast, and who had worshipped his image.

The Second Bowl

³The second was pouring out his bowl on the sea, and it became blood like that from a corpse, with the result that every living creature that was in the sea died.

The Third Bowl

⁴The third was pouring out his bowl into the rivers and the springs of water, resulting in their becoming blood. ⁵Then I heard the angel of the waters saying:

"You—the One who is and who was, the Holy One—are just. You have made these judgments, ⁶because they spilled the blood of holy ones and prophets, so you have given them blood to drink. This is what they deserve."

⁷I heard a voice from the altar saying, "Yes, LORD God, the All-Powerful, your judgments are true and just."

The Fourth Bowl

⁸Then the fourth was pouring out his bowl on the sun, and it was allowed to scorch people with fire. ⁹They were scorched by the intense heat, and they blasphemed the reputation and character of God, who has authority over these plagues. They wouldn't change their thinking and give Him glory.

The Fifth Bowl

¹⁰Then the fifth was pouring out his bowl on the throne of the beast, so that darkness enveloped his kingdom. Consequently, people began to chew on their tongues because of their pain. ¹¹They blasphemed the God of heaven because of their agonies and because of their sores. Nevertheless, they refused to turn away from their wrong activities.

166

The Sixth Bowl

12Then the sixth was pouring out his bowl on the great river Euphrates, causing its water to dry up in order to prepare the way for the kings from the east. **13**Then I saw three unclean spirits, like frogs, coming out of the Dragon's mouth and out of the beast's mouth and out of the false prophet's mouth. **14**In fact, they are spirits who are demons performing signs. They go out to the kings of the entire inhabited earth to gather them together to the battle of the great day of God, the All-Powerful. **15**("Take note: I am coming as a thief! Blessed are those who remain alert, and keep their garments on, so that they won't be walking around naked and be exposed to shame in public.") **16**So they gathered them into the place that is called *Harmagedon* in Hebrew.

The Seventh Bowl

17Then the seventh was pouring out his bowl into the air, and a loud voice came out of the sanctuary from the throne, saying: "It's finished!" **18**Then there were flashes of lightning, rumblings and thunderclaps, and a powerful earthquake—more powerful than had ever occurred since mankind has been on the earth. **19**The great city was split into three parts, and the cities of the nations collapsed. God remembered to give Babylon the great the cup of wine, namely, His fury and retribution. **20**Every island sped away, and the high hills disappeared. **21**Enormous hailstones, weighing as much as a hundred pounds, fell from the sky onto the people, but they blasphemed God on account of the plague of hail, because it was so extremely severe.

Overview

Revelation chapters 15 and 16 are a single unit with no interludes. Unlike the seven seals and seven trumpets, the pouring out of the seven last plagues will include no interlude sections, but are sequential and with an immediate throne-room scene. Similar to the seals and trumpets with their 4+2+1 pattern, these seven bowls are in a 4+3 pattern and constitute the third calamity of the seventh trumpet. Although the first four bowls parallel the first four trumpets in their targets of land, sea, springs, and atmosphere, there is a contrast with them because the trumpets will only affect one third of the world, namely, the area containing Antichrist's Kingdom and so only affecting those who live in that area; whereas, here the pouring out of the bowls of plague appears to encompass all those who worship the Antichrist world-wide. (Please see Appendix C).

Even more so than with the trumpets, the bowls include more of the same type of plagues that were poured out on ancient Egypt and in intensified form. These are: boils, water turned to blood, being scorched by the sun, darkness, and a massive hailstorm. The throne of the Beast, in 16:10 and already noted in 13:2, is a primary target when the fifth bowl is poured out and his followers are given their very last chance to repent. Most importantly, during the sixth bowl, there is a focus upon the responsibility of believers to be in the right spiritual condition at all times.

Comment on the Pouring of the Seven Bowls

16:1: "**Then I heard a loud voice from the sanctuary saying to the seven angels: 'Go and begin to pour out on the earth the seven drink-offering bowls of God's anger.'**" Only here and in verse 17 is there a voice from the sanctuary and so leading to the conclusion that this is God's voice; also because others had been temporarily excluded from the sanctuary (15:8b).

These bowl plagues are much more severe and intense than those from the trumpet blasts. They finally bring about the end of Antichrist's kingdom and affect the rest of his followers world-wide.

Similar to the first four trumpets, the first four bowl plagues fall on the environment of Antichrist's followers in the rest of the world. Again these plagues have the purpose of making these ones realize their dependence on the True God and to attempt to bring about their repentance.

16:2: "**So the first one went off and was pouring out his bowl on the land, with the result that a festering and painful sore appeared on those who had the brand-mark of the beast, and who had worshipped his image.**" In falling on the land there will be a complete desolation of the vegetation and so will completely destroy the world's economy gained from the land. The resulting lack of nutrition causes these people to suffer a literal "festering and painful sore"—an ulcerous infectious sore probably similar to Job's affliction with such sores (Job 2:1-13).

This is a replicating of the sixth plague on ancient Egypt—the plague of boils—(Ex. 9:9) in the time of Moses. The Israelites lived in the Egyptian province called Goshen and did not suffer this plague (Ex.8:22-23; 9:4, 6; 10:23; 11:7; 12:13; 19:5). So, too, Christians, while still not having experienced the rapture, will be exempt from the effects of this plague as shown by Isaiah:

❖ "Go, my people, enter into your chambers and shut your doors behind you; hide for *a very little* while, until *the* wrath has passed over. [21] For look! Yahweh *is* about to come out from his place to punish the iniquity of the inhabitants of the earth against him, and the earth will disclose her blood and will no longer cover her slain."

(Isa. 26:20, 21).

16:3: "**The second was pouring out his bowl on the sea, with the result that it became blood like that from a corpse. Every living creature that was in the sea died.**" This second bowl plague is greater than the first plague upon ancient Egypt which did not have the sea turned into blood, but only the Nile river (Ex. 7:19). This literal plague represents the complete destruction of the world's economy from the sea i.e. the food supply from the sea as well as trade in that food supply.

16:4: "**The third was pouring out his bowl into the rivers and the springs of water, resulting in their becoming blood.**" This third bowl is also a replicating of the first plague (Ex. 7:19) on ancient Egypt. It literally deprives those who worship the Beast in the rest of the world of drinking water as well as representing the destruction of the world's economy from the inland waterways.

16:5-6: "**Then I heard the angel of the waters saying: "You—the One who is and who was, the Holy One—are just. You have made these judgments, [6]because they spilled the blood of holy ones and prophets, so you have given them blood to drink. This is what they deserve.**" This doxology in praise of God shows his justice in pouring out these plagues on unrighteous mankind to avenge the murders of God's people. This also answers the prayer of the martyrs described in 6:9-11.

In Matthew 23:31 and 37 Jesus had also shown that murder of the prophets was a reason for divine judgment as well as implying this in the parable of the murder of the only son (Mark 12:1-12).

16:7: "**I heard a voice from the altar saying, "Yes, LORD God, the All-Powerful, your judgments are true and just.**" "LORD God, the All-Powerful" is the primary title for God. Although some think that this voice is a representative voice from the martyrs under the altar noted in 6:9-11, it is more likely that it is the angel who presented the prayers of God's people in 8:3-5.

169

16:8-9: "Then the fourth was pouring out his bowl on the sun, and it was allowed to scorch people with fire. They were scorched by the intense heat, and they blasphemed the reputation and character of God, who has authority over these plagues. They wouldn't change their thinking and give Him glory." This plague is not linked with the ancient Egyptian plagues. However, in this plague God overrules the laws of nature to produce extreme heat from the sun. This will actually "scorch people with fire" as if these are massive tongues of fire as with solar flares. Indeed, fire is God's basic weapon of judgment and destruction. Indeed, the prophet Isaiah had prophesied that, "a curse devours the earth, and its inhabitants suffer for their guilt; therefore the inhabitants of the earth are scorched, and few men are left" (Isa. 24:6 ESV).

This event is recognized by the followers of Antichrist as God's work because they blaspheme Him when they realize that He "has authority over the plagues." Nevertheless, God's purpose here is also to move those worshippers of Antichrist to recognize their real dependence upon Him as the one True God, and so to repent. However, their failure to do so is shocking in the face of God's obvious power and authority. Such failure to repent portends their coming destruction.

16:10-11: "The fifth was pouring out his bowl on the throne of the beast, so that darkness enveloped his kingdom. They blasphemed the God of heaven because of their agonies and because of their sores. Nevertheless, they refused to turn away from their wrong activities." This plague is similar to the ninth plague upon Egypt of "a darkness that can be felt" and lasting three days (Ex.10:21-29). Again the Israelites were unaffected. This is a supernaturally caused intense darkness. Whereas the trumpet blasts will affect Antichrist's kingdom directly, this plague of total darkness in his capital city—his central administration—finally results in the complete dissolution of his kingdom (18:15-17, 19). Even symbolically darkness indicates judgment.

The throne of the beast is mentioned in 13:2 where the Dragon gives Antichrist "his power, his throne, and total power."

Once again Antichrist's followers blaspheme God and refuse to repent. However, they do this because of the pain of their agonies and sores, and so making it is evident that the effect is on-going and does not cease before the next plague is poured out on them.

16:12: "The sixth was pouring out his bowl on the great river Euphrates, causing its water to dry up in order to prepare the way for the kings from

the east." The Euphrates River, which flowed through ancient Babylon, is 1,800 miles long, from 300 to 1200 yards wide, and from 10 to 30 feet deep. It is scarcely fordable anywhere and has never been known to dry up; so here this is a miraculous drying up. Earlier, as one of the waterways in Antichrist's kingdom this was turned to blood for a time, but now it is completely dried up. This bowl, similar to the sixth trumpet, is different from the earlier bowls, inasmuch as it is not really a plague upon humans, but a preparation for the final eschatological battle. Indeed, the drying up of the River Euphrates symbolically removes the barrier holding back the pagan hordes. So these Kings, in being from the east, are perhaps linked with the statement in Daniel 11:44 concerning the end-time scenario when Antichrist is fighting against the King of the South and then hears, "reports from the east and the north [that] shall alarm him, and he shall go out with great fury to bring ruin and complete destruction to many" *(NRSV)*. So, could this scene indicate the crossing of the Euphrates by a literal Islamic coalition—one which will include a modern-day Media/Persia i.e. Iran (Isa. 13:17-20; Jer. 51:11-13, 28), and possibly Pakistan? Their purpose certainly seems to be to attack the capital of Antichrist's Kingdom, which is why Antichrist is alarmed at the reports he hears "from the east and the north." So the miraculous drying up of the Euphrates makes all of this possible.

16:13-14: "**Then I saw three unclean spirits, like frogs, coming out of the Dragon's mouth, out of the beast's mouth, and out of the false prophet's mouth. [14]In fact, they are spirits who are demons performing signs. They go out to the kings of the entire inhabited earth to gather them together to the battle of the great day of God, the All-Powerful.**" "The Dragon" here is, of course, Satan and "the beast" is Antichrist with the false prophet as earlier shown to be the "beast from the earth" (Rev.13:11) who promotes the worship of the Antichrist using propaganda. This prophet is later destroyed (19:20). So here we see propaganda from all three entities and with a hint of the plague of frogs upon ancient Egypt—the second plague. However, in Revelation these frog-like demons incite, deceive and persuade these kings to action by the use of counterfeit miracles. In being "kings of the entire inhabited earth" these ones rule over "the earth-dwellers," namely, those who follow Antichrist—these phrases are virtually synonymous. These kings appear to be the ten horns of 17:12-14.

171

16:15: "(Take note: I am coming like a thief. Blessed are those who remain alert, and keep their garments on, so that they won't be walking around naked and be exposed to shame in public"). Evidently this is the voice of Jesus in this parenthetical statement whose "coming like a thief" means that it will be sudden and unexpected (Matt. 24:43-44). This is a last warning for Christians to continue to remain awake i.e. spiritually prepared, because they do not know the hour of Messiah's return (Matt. 24:42), and must be spiritually diligent by refusing the Beast's brand-mark. So in regard to each Christian's remaining alert, it was the custom in biblical times that if a guard was caught sleeping he would be stripped of his clothes in disgrace, so too, for Christians metaphorically if they fail in this. Indeed, up to this point there is still a risk that Christians could be thrown out of Messiah's wedding feast for figuratively being shamefully naked and having lost all dignity. Failure by Christians at this point in time to "be awake" and correctly dressed figuratively could strip them of all opportunity to share in the kingdom privileges during the thousand year reign of Messiah. Please note the failure of the Christian communities in Sardis (3:2-3) and Laodicea (3:18) to keep spiritually awake.

Furthermore, this statement by Jesus shows that Christians have not yet been granted immortality. So, whether dead or alive they have not been caught up to meet Messiah in the air (1 Thess. 4:17) earlier than this point in time. This informs us that, not only will it be a post-tribulation resurrection/rapture, but that it will be only around the time of the pouring out of this 6th bowl that the resurrection and rapture take place. This also means that it will be during the pouring out of this bowl that Messiah descends to earth's atmosphere (1 Thess. 4:17) to meet with the ascending Christians for some short period before descending to Earth to battle with Antichrist.

16:16: "So they gathered them into the place that is called *Harmagedon* in Hebrew." The term *Harmagedon* (Mountain of Megiddo) is mentioned only once in the entire New Testament. Although some commentators view this as concerning the literal ancient battle ground of Meggido in the territory of Galilee, this seems unlikely to have been John's meaning. The reasons are: firstly, that Megiddo was never a mountain, but only a plain on an artificial mound reaching a height of only 75 feet, and secondly, that the future eschatological battle ground is stated to be near Jerusalem (Joel 3:2; Zech 14:2ff) which is a long way from Megiddo's location in Galilee. So a better understanding would be that the term is symbolic and does not refer to any specific geographical location. Rather, the term Harmagedon is based on the Hebrew verb *gaddad* meaning "to gather in troops or bands" (BDB, p. 151), and as converted into the noun *maged* it means "a place of gathering troops." This description fits well with the context of verses 14 and 16 as well as with the statements showing that the future eschatological battle ground will concern "the mountains of Israel" (Ezekiel 38:8; 39: 2, 4, 17). So although the term *Harmagedon may be* symbolic, the battle is quite literal as other relevant passages in the Hebrew Scriptures also show.

16:17: **"Then the seventh poured out his bowl into the air, and a loud voice came out of the sanctuary from the throne, saying: "It's finished!"** The loud voice may well be that of God Himself (Isa. 30:30 and 66:6 LXX), and with this bowl the climactic end of the series of plagues poured out by Him using these archangels has been reached.

In Greek thinking the four natural elements of the natural world were earth, water, fire, and air. Scripturally the air is described as being the domain of Satan and the demons with Satan being *"the prince of the power of the air"* (Eph. 2:2) and the demons as being *"the spiritual forces of wickedness in the heavenly places"* (Eph. 6:12). Because these demonic forces are represented by Antichrist it is clear that the eschatological punishment by God of Antichrist and his followers has come to completion, although such destruction of them is given more detail in Revelation chapters 17 and 18.

16:18: **"Then there were flashes of lightning, rumblings and thunderclaps, and a powerful earthquake—more powerful than had ever occurred since mankind has been on the earth."** This is the cosmic storm based on the Sinai phenomena (Ex, 19:16-18). It is also the final occurrence of these words concerning an event of such magnitude as to be unique in all of human history. The first mention is in 4:5, but without the earthquake. The second mention, connected to the seventh seal, is in 8:5, but without the addition of "severe hail." The third mention of this phenomenon is in 11:19 connected to the seventh trumpet blast. This final mention is immediately after the pouring out of the seventh bowl, but again with no mention of hail. Therefore, this is one of the indicators that the seventh seal, seventh trumpet, and seventh bowl of plague are all connected as the same event. Indeed, these phenomena are all conventional ways of expressing the majesty and power which attend the divine presence. So, at this point in time Jesus takes control of Earth's affairs.

16:19: "**The great city was split into three parts, and the cities of the nations collapsed. God remembered to give Babylon the great the cup of wine, namely, His fury and retribution.**" The identification of "the great city" is problematic. Is it Jerusalem or Babylon? Supporting the view that the city is Jerusalem is the fact that later in verse 19 the text refers to "Babylon the great" as if it is a separate city to "the great city." Also Jerusalem is separated from the cities of the pagan nations which collapse. Furthermore, Jerusalem is referred to on just the one occasion as "the great city" in 11:8.

However, for those who favour the identification of "the great city" as being Babylon there is much proof inasmuch as it is called "the great city" in many more place than Jerusalem is given that title. These references to Babylon are found in 17:18; 18:10, 16, 18, 19, 21. Additionally, Jerusalem has already been shown as having been overthrown during an earlier great earthquake (11:13) when 7,000 of her inhabitants were killed. So the overall evidence leads to the conclusion that Babylon is "the great city [that] was split into three parts."

The statement that "the cities of the nations collapsed" was because of the enormous earthquake (Isa. 24:1-4, 19-20). However, this may refer only to the destruction of those cities within Antichrist's kingdom and those who have given their support to the Beast, including those of the ten (horns) kings who later seem to be included with "the kings of the earth" (18:9).

God does not have a poor memory. So the statement that, "God remembered" is a Semitic euphemism with reference to Babylon's crimes and therefore to her just punishment. This is "His fury and retribution," the cup from which Babylon must drink in undiluted form and which results in her destruction. In the next chapter we will examine exactly what Babylon is. We will also note that her fall, described in Revelation chapters 17 and 18, plays out the same judgments as those of the seventh seal, seventh trumpet, and seventh bowl.

16:20: "**Every island sped away, and the high hills disappeared.**" This is a seismic phenomenon causing the disappearance of the islands and high hills and refers back to 6:14 with its poetic language showing the cosmic catastrophes from which the worshippers of Antichrist cannot escape—it is a judgment statement i.e. an apocalyptic motif. Clearly, this must be as a result of the massive earthquake and so cover a very significant area including much of the Mediterranean Sea. A similar statement is made in 20:11 concerning the earth and the sky.

174

16:21: "**Enormous hailstones, weighing as much as a hundred pounds, fell from the sky onto people, but they blasphemed God on account of the plague of hail, because it was so extremely severe.**" Supernaturally directed hailstones have been used in the past by God to bring punishment and destruction to His enemies (Isa. 28:2, 17) as He did to the Amorites (Josh. 10:11). However, these hailstones in Revelation are enormous and far exceed any naturally produced hailstones. In fact, the largest hailstones ever recorded weighed 2.25 pounds and fell upon Bangladesh in 1986, killing 92 people. However, these hailstones noted in Revelation weigh as much as a small person!

Like the seventh Egyptian plague of hail that further hardened Pharaoh's heart (Ex. 9:34), so too, with these followers of Antichrist—they remain unrepentant as in 2:21 and 16:9, 11. Even back at the time of the sixth trumpet "the rest of mankind didn't change their ways concerning their activities" (Rev. 9:20-21).

§

Chapter 35

The Key Prophecies Concerning
Babylon the Great

Some thousands of years before the time of Christ the man Nimrod founded the city of Babel on the plain of Shinar and on the banks of the Euphrates River. To the Hebrew reader the name of this city meant "confusion" because God confused the languages of the inhabitants after their refusal to populate the earth as per God's command. In time the city came to be called Babylon (Gen. 10:10; 11:2-3, 5, and 9) and formed a great world empire under Nebuchadnezzar. This king was used by God to punish His own disobedient people, namely, Judah, by putting them into captivity in Babylon; but prior to this captivity the prophets Isaiah and Jeremiah had prophesied that Babylon itself would eventually be destroyed. However, there are certain details in the book of Revelation that indicate that these prophecies have not yet been fulfilled—even up to today.

Isaiah, Jeremiah and Revelation
All Speak of the Same Features of Babylon

The importance of Babylon in the Hebrew Scriptures must not be underestimated. Isaiah and Jeremiah addressed the subject of Babylon vastly more than they did concerning any other nation outside of Israel and Judah. Isaiah speaks of Babylon three times, firstly in chapters 13 and 14 (45 verses), then in chapter 21:9, and finally in chapter 47 (15 verses); whereas Jeremiah allots 110 verses in chapters 50 and 51 to Babylon, compared to 47 verses to Moab as the next most focused upon nation. The following passages in Jeremiah and Isaiah are compared with similar passages in Revelation and so indicate that Jesus, in giving the Revelation to John, was largely referencing Jeremiah 50 and 51 for chapters 17 and 18 of Revelation and therefore speaking of events that were yet to occur regarding Babylon.

BABYLON SITS BESIDE MANY WATERS

❖ "A woman residing on abounding waters, abundant in treasures, your end has come" *(Jer. 51:13).*

❖ "...the judgment of the notorious prostitute who is enthroned beside abundant waters...The waters you saw, where the prostitute resides ... these symbolize nations, populations, races, and languages"
(Rev. 17:1, 15).

176

BABYLON MAKES EARTH DRUNK FROM A GOLDEN CUP
- ❖ "Babylon was a golden cup in Yahweh's hand, she made the whole world drunk" *(Jer. 51:7 NJB).*
- ❖ "Those who inhabit the earth were made drunk with the wine of her fornication ... The woman...had in her hand a golden cup that was full of disgusting things" *(Rev. 17:2, 4).*

Similarly for Revelation 18 many of its statements are drawn from the books of Jeremiah and Isaiah, and are entirely about the literal city of Babylon. The following are the comparisons:

BABYLON'S HAUGHTY ATTITUDE
- ❖ "Yet you said, 'I will be a queen forever'...The one saying in her heart: I am and there is nobody else. I shall not sit as a widow, and I shall not know the loss of children" *(Isa. 47:7, 8).*
- ❖ "For in her heart she keeps saying, 'I sit a queen, and I am no widow, and I shall never see mourning'" *(Rev. 18:7).*

BABYLON IS A DWELLING PLACE OF DEMONS
- ❖ "And goat-shaped demons themselves will go skipping about there" *(Isa. 13:21).*
- ❖ "She has fallen! Babylon the great has fallen and she has become a dwelling place of demons" *(Rev. 18:2).*

BABYLON IS GUILTY OF MURDER
- ❖ "Not only was Babylon the cause for the slain ones of Israel to fall but also at Babylon the slain ones of all the earth have fallen" *(Jer. 51:49).*
- ❖ "In her was found **the blood of prophets** and of holy ones and of all those who have been slaughtered on the earth" *(Rev. 18:24).*

Isaiah, Jeremiah and Revelation
All Speak of the Same Destruction of Babylon

TAKING VENGEANCE ON BABYLON
- ❖ "Take your vengeance on her just as she has done to you" *(Jer. 50:15).*
- ❖ "**Render to her** even as she herself rendered" *(Rev. 18:6).*

ILLUSTRATING BABYLON'S DESTRUCTION

❖ "...when you finish reading aloud this scroll, you must tie a stone on it, and you must throw it into the middle of *the* Euphrates. And you must say, 'this is how Babylon will sink down and never rise up"
(Jer. 51:63).

❖ "Then a strong angel lifted up a great stone like a millstone and hurled it into the sea, saying: thus with **a swift pitch** will Babylon *the great city* be hurled down, she will never be found again"
(Rev. 18:21).

❖ "She has fallen! Babylon the Great has fallen"
(Isa. 21:9; Jer. 51:8; Rev. 14:8; 18:2).

This fall is not something separate from her destruction. Revelation 16:19 shows this destruction to be when the seventh bowl of God's wrath is poured out, and so showing that this destruction occurs after the great tribulation.

BABYLON'S DESTRUCTION IS SUDDEN

❖ "To you these two things will come suddenly, **in one day**: loss of children and widowhood" *(Isa. 47:9).*

❖ "**Suddenly** Babylon has fallen, so that she is broken..." *(Jer. 51:8).*

❖ "For this reason, the plagues will come upon her **in a single day**: death-dealing disease, mourning, and famine. She will be burned up with fire...That is why **in one day** her plagues will come...she will be completely burned with fire...Woe, woe, the great city, Babylon...For **in one hour** your judgement has come...for **in one hour** such great wealth has been laid waste!...the great city...**in one hour** she has been devastated... *(Rev. 18:8, 10, 17, 19).*

BABYLON'S DESTRUCTION IS ACCOMPLISHED WITH FIRE

❖ "The warriors of Babylon have ceased to fight, they remain in the strongholds, their power has dried up, they have become as women. Her dwelling places are **set on fire**, her bars are broken ... The wall of Babylon...will be **set aflame with fire**" *(Jer. 51:30, 58).*

❖ "The ten horns which you saw and the beast will hate the prostitute and make her desolate and naked. They will devour her flesh and **burn her up with fire** ... What calamity, what calamity, O great city, Babylon the powerful city! Because in a single hour your judgment has come!" *(Rev. 17:16; 18:10).*

GET OUT OF BABYLON BECAUSE OF HER SINS!
* ❖ "For clear to the heavens her judgement has reached...Get out of the midst of her my people" *(Jer. 51:9, 45).*
* ❖ "Get out of her my people ... For her sins have massed together clear up to heaven" *(Rev. 18:4, 5).*

BABYLON IS NEVER TO BE INHABITED AGAIN
* ❖ *"Therefore* desert creatures will live *there* with jackals, and daughters of ostriches will inhabit her. And she will not be inhabited again *forever,* and she will not be dwelt in *for all generations"*
  (Jer. 50:39).
* ❖ "The exhortations of the tambourines has ceased, the noise of the highly elated ones has discontinued..." *(Isa. 24:8).*
* ❖ "In this way, Babylon the great city will be thrown down with force, and will never be seen again! Never again will the sound of harpists, musicians, flute players, and trumpeters be heard in you; never again will craftsman of any trade be found in you; never again will the sound of a millstone be heard in you. *(Rev. 18:21-22).*

Clearly, Babylon will be judged by God because of its wickedness right from the time of the tower of Babel event and throughout its history. It has always been an enemy of God and of His people!

However, it is evident from the above comparisons that when Jesus presented this subject of Babylon the great to John in the Book of Revelation he drew primarily from Jeremiah 50 and 51 and with thoughts from Isaiah 13 and 14. These are set "in the day of Yahweh" (13:6, 9) i.e. in the end times. Yet, problematically, most commentators follow the assumption made by Martin Luther and John Calvin that ancient Babylon was totally destroyed long ago and that the prophecies given by Isaiah and Jeremiah are already completely fulfilled. But is this assumption correct? Do these prophecies have no bearing on how one interprets the details concerning Babylon the great in Revelation?

Were These Prophecies Fulfilled
When the Destruction of Ancient Babylon Occurred?

After some seventy years of the captivity of the Jews in Babylon, the Medes and Persians conquered the city in 539 B.C.E. It was a sudden and crafty take over, but they did not destroy the city. Instead, Cyrus the Persian improved the city, but allowed the captive Jews their freedom to return to Judea. Nevertheless, most Jews chose to stay in this thriving city. So evidently the key prophecies of Isaiah and Jeremiah were not fulfilled at that time.

During the reign of Cambyses there were two revolts which were finally put down later by King Darius who was said to have destroyed Babylon's walls and gates. However, when the historian Herodotus visited Babylon in c. 450 B.C.E., he discovered that only a small portion of the walls had been destroyed and some gates were still intact along with the royal palace, the temple complex of Marduk, and the tower of Babel. So clearly, up to that time, Babylon had not been utterly destroyed as had been prophesied by Isaiah and Jeremiah.

More than one hundred years later Alexander the Great captured Babylon from the Persians, and made it his capital city. He repaired and rebuilt much of the city, including the digging of a harbour and the building of a theatre there that could seat 4,000. So Babylon remained the capital of the eastern Greek empire for a while after Alexander's death in 323 B.C.E.

In 312 B.C.E., Seleucus Nicator replaced Babylon as the capital of the Greek Seleucid Empire with his new city of Seleucia, but Babylon remained an important city in the empire. In fact, it was a metropolis according to the historian Strabo with this situation for the city existing even throughout the time when the Parthians controlled Mesopotamia from 166 B.C.E. to 122 B.C.E Indeed, Josephus, who was provably very familiar with the area, records that a large number of Jews still lived in Babylon throughout the time of Parthian rulership. However, even though Babylon began to decline from this period onward, the historians and visitors show that it was still a functioning city with buildings, houses, and inhabitants, but gradually declining. In fact, the historian Pliny points out that Babylon still maintained its religious significance in his day (A.D. 23-79) and therefore just after Jesus' time. So Acts 2:9-10 records that Jewish pilgrims from "Mesopotamia" (the land of Babylon) came to Jerusalem for the festival of Pentecost.

Most importantly, the Apostle Peter sent greetings (1 Pet. 5:13) from a community of Christians living in the literal city of Babylon (not Rome – please see the next chapter).

Indeed, long after the writing of the Book of Revelation the city of Babylon still had some inhabitants. For example, in the twelfth century C.E Babylon had grown and several mosques had been erected. Although a little later Babylon largely became ruins there was still some activity there and with three small villages having been established within the boundaries of ancient Babylon in the late 1900s.

The last real activity concerning Babylon was in the 1980s when, for political reasons, Saddam Hussein began and completed much restoration work on the city before the first Iraq war. That work has remained in tact at least into the 1990s and in recent time the United Nations Organization now plans to pump millions of dollars into Babylon to turn it into a tourist attraction and working city once again.

Conclusion

All of the above information hardly shows the utter destruction of Babylon as had been prophesied by Isaiah and Jeremiah. So from the above facts it is evident that the history of ancient Babylon indicates that the prophecies of Isaiah and Jeremiah concerning Babylon have yet to be fulfilled. The destruction is to be swift and in one short time *(Isa. 47:9; Jer. 51:8)* "and she will not be inhabited again *forever,* and she will not be dwelt in *for all generations" (Jer. 50:39).* So even in its demise in the past, the situation for Babylon does not fit with those prophecies of Isaiah and Jeremiah. Indeed, chapters 17 and 18 of Revelation have drawn together much that these two prophets said on this subject and have put them into an eschatological context i.e. that "Babylon the great" is yet to be destroyed. This then raises the two questions of:

- What is the identity of Babylon the great in Revelation?
- How can a future Babylon become as described in Revelation before its destruction?

Chapter 36

Identifying Babylon the Great

Over the centuries there have been many proposals concerning the identity of Babylon the great. These have been that the term "Babylon the great" as a mystery is a code name for either the city of Rome (the Roman Empire), or Mecca, or New York City (as representative of America). Further proposals are that the term "Babylon" as a mystery is symbolic of the Roman Catholic Church, or of all the churches of Christendom, or of all false religion, or even of the whole of society organized in alienation from God and in opposition to Him. Furthermore, this term is also viewed by some as being a religious system in Revelation 17, but a literal commercial city in Revelation 18.

Most of these views have proponents who each present very good cases for their respective positions. Nevertheless, all of these identifications fail for the reasons presented below.

ROME AND OTHER CITIES

This view usually takes the statements about Babylon the great in both Revelation 17 and 18 as applying to the first century city of Rome. Indeed, this view applies the term "Babylon" as being a secret symbol or code term for ancient Rome and was because the early Christians supposedly feared persecution from the Roman authorities if they presented Rome in a negative light. This view is based on several suppositions:

1. On the assumption that the Apostle Peter used the term "Babylon" as a code word for Rome (1 Pet. 5:13). However, this view fails because the Apostle Peter sent greetings from a Christian community in the literal city of Babylon and not Rome. This is evident because he opens his first letter saying, "to the exiles of the Dispersion throughout Pontus, Galatia, Cappadocia, Asia, and Bithynia" and closes it with "Your sister assembly here in Babylon...sends you greetings" So because the first locations are not coded but literal then there is no reason for Babylon to be seen as a code term for Rome. The natural reading must refer to the literal Babylon still existing in Peter's day.

2. By the fact that "seven hills (mountains)" are mentioned in Revelation 17:9 and Rome is claimed to be built upon seven hills. The connection is made because 17:3 mentions seven heads on the

Antichrist Beast to which verse 9 adds that the "seven heads *are* seven mountains...and they *are* seven kings" in the sense of representing or symbolizing the reality of seven kings and, indeed, mountains are often symbolic of kingdoms (Jer. 51:25; Dan. 2:35; Zech. 4:7). So the seven hills are only a symbol rather than a geographical reality i.e. they do not relate to topography at all and therefore do not relate to Rome; and in any case these seven heads are associated with the Beast i.e. the Antichrist, rather than with the Woman as Babylon.

3. As shown in the previous chapter, the angel who is presenting the Revelation to John draws upon passages from Isaiah and Jeremiah concerning Babylon. However, in Revelation 18 he further draws on passages from Ezekiel concerning Tyre. From this fact, some commentators assume that the angel has formed a composite of Babylon and Tyre to make this a pattern for first century Rome. However, there is no mention of Tyre in the Book of Revelation and therefore no need to see the references as anything other than concerning literal Babylon.

4. From the statement in Revelation 17:9 that the "seven heads *are* seven mountains...and they *are* seven kings," some who propose Rome as being "Babylon" have listed seven Roman emperors as being "the seven kings." However, this has also been very problematic because three emperors must arbitrarily be left off the list (Galba, Otho, Vitellius) in the attempt to make this fit John's chronology, even though these were all bona fide emperors. Once again this does not fit biblically because these seven heads are associated with the Beast, rather than with the Woman as Babylon.

A further factor concerning why this view fails is the relatively late appearance of Rome as a notable empire, and yet "the woman/prostitute" is described as being "the mother of prostitutes and of earthly disgusting things" (Rev. 17:5). This indicates that she is the ancient archetype, source, and origin of metaphorical prostitution going right back through history. So, what we find in the Hebrew Scriptures is great emphasis on the empires of Egypt, Assyria, Babylon, Medo/Persia, and Greece, but with no mention of Rome. This is because these empires were noteworthy long before Rome as an empire existed and so making it impossible for her to be "the mother of prostitutes."

183

For this last reason other cities such as Mecca, as the centre of Islam, or New York, as the leading city in America, also should not be interpreted as being Babylon the great as if that city were a code term for these more recent cities. Such interpretations are simply speculative and have no basis at all.

The reality is that although there are many symbols in biblical apocalyptic writings, no prophet or Christian ever disguised their subject with codes for fear of any authorities.

ROMAN CATHOLICISM AND OTHER CHURCHES

This view also takes the statements about Babylon the great in both Revelation chapters 17 and 18 as applying to exactly the same entity, but this time applying to the Roman Catholic Church in Protestant thinking.

This allegorical view was first proposed by Martin Luther at the beginning of the Protestant Reformation and was later adopted by John Calvin. Luther had generally moved away from any allegorical interpretations of the Bible as used by the Roman Catholic Church, but then, in poor exegesis, he used it in interpreting who the "great prostitute" was along with viewing the pope as the Antichrist.

Nevertheless, this view fails because there are many features in Revelation 17 and 18 which cannot apply to the Roman Catholic Church or to its Popes. Indeed, because Babylon the great—"the mother of prostitutes" is the source and origin of this figurative prostitution going right back through history, the facts about the Catholic Church do not fit for her to be claimed as being Babylon the great. For instance, Catholicism only came into existence in the second century A.D. long after John wrote Revelation, and so she cannot be held responsible for all "the earthly disgusting things" that have occurred before she came into existence. Furthermore, the Roman Catholic Church has not prostituted herself with all 'the kings of the earth [who] committed sexual immorality with [Babylon]." In fact, many lands remain untouched by this church's influence.

All of these factors also apply to all the rest of the churches of Christendom. Clearly, Babylon the great in Revelation 17 must be something that began long before the Roman Catholic or other churches came into existence.

ALL OF SOCIETY ORGANIZED IN OPPOSITION TO GOD

This is also an allegorical view and similarly takes the statements about Babylon the great in both Revelation 17 and 18 as applying to exactly the same entity. It is applied to the world's entire political, commercial, social, and religious systems and so does not apply to any physical location, but denotes systems which promote the ungodly practices originating in Babylon and which had then spread throughout the world. However, while this global interpretation catches the thought of the real global influence of Babylon (Rev. 17:5, 15, 18; 18:24), it fails to be the correct understanding for the following reasons:

1. The political entities of the Antichrist Beast and the ten kings of the world cause the destruction of Babylon the great in 17:16-18.
2. The kings, merchants, and ship's captains mourn her demise as described in Revelation 18,
3. Babylon is a deceiver of nations (Rev. 14:8; 17:2; 18:2); therefore she cannot actually be those nations.
4. A literal city is spoken of in Revelation 17 and 18 located by the Euphrates River (9:14; 16:12) which ran through ancient Babylon.

These several factors clearly show that Babylon the great cannot be the global political, commercial, social, and religious world in its entirety and as in opposition to God.

Reasons Offered for a Mystery Babylon in Revelation 17, But a Literal City in Revelation 18

Because some translations (mostly older and a few modern ones) of Revelation 17:5 speak of "Mystery, Babylon the Great," many commentators propose that it must be understood as significantly symbolic and as referring to a religious system in Rev. 17, but in 18 it is understood as quite literally referring to a rebuilt highly commercial city of Babylon. Although this turns out to be a faulty view, the reasons given for it are:

1. Revelation 17:5 speaks of "Mystery, Babylon the Great" and therefore she is different to the "city" of chapter 18 and must be interpreted allegorically in contrast to the literal city in Chapter 18.
2. Revelation 18 begins with the statement that, "after these things I saw another angel" i.e. a different angel comes from heaven to deliver a different message to that which concerns Babylon with a secret meaning in Rev. 17.

3. The context of Revelation 18 with its many references to the kings, merchants, and commerce shows that, at this time, Babylon is in a political, economic, and commercial character, rather than in her religious role (18:11-19) in 17.

4. The city in Rev.18 is not destroyed by the ten horns (kings) as is Babylon with a secret meaning in 17:16, but directly by God. It is shown to be suddenly destroyed by God *"in one day"* (18:8), (cp. 16:19-21), whereas Babylon which has a secret meaning is left naked and her flesh eaten (17:16) so that it is a process.

5. There is a different response to the destruction of the city in Rev.18 than in Rev.17 because in 17:16 the ten horns/kings destroy the religious Babylon, but in 18:9-10 they lament the destruction of the city.

6. This event comes late in the great tribulation, just prior to the second coming of Christ, in contrast to the destruction of the prostitute in Rev.17 which seems to precede the great Tribulation and paves the way for the worship of the beast (13:8).

However, not all of the above points turn out to be factual and there are other legitimate ways to explain these points as follows:

Reasons for Babylon to Be the Same City in Both Chapters 17 and 18 of Revelation

1) It is only in older translations and a few modern ones (GW, WEB, N.T. Wright) that the rendering "Mystery, Babylon the Great" is given. For the most part modern renderings are, for example: "a name having been written upon her forehead, a mystery: "Babylon the Great" (DLNT). This shows that it is the name and her relationship with the beast which she rides on that is a mystery or has a hidden meaning and which is later revealed to John (17:7b) and so Babylon here does not need to be interpreted allegorically.

2) The statement in 18:1 that, *"After these things I saw another angel"..."* does not indicate a chronological fulfilment. Regarding six of the ten occurrences of the phrase *"after these things"* and followed by a verb of perception (*"I saw..."* or *"I heard..."*) it is simply the order in which John sees the visions (4:14; 7:1; 7:9; 15:5; 18:1; 19:1), rather than indicative of the chronological fulfilment.

However, the other four times of "after these things" without a verb of perception, do indicate the chronological fulfilment (1:19; 4:18; 9:12; 20:3).

3) There is no indication in Revelation 17 that Babylon is a religious system, but rather we are told in 17:18 that, *"the **woman** [the prostitute] which you saw symbolizes **the great city** that has dominion over the kings of the earth."* However, there is a religious aspect in 18:23 which speaks of Babylon's "occultism/sorcery." This is the very reverse of the above reasoning about Babylon. So the natural reading informs us that the reference here is to a literal city. Then in Rev.18 we are shown that this city is a significantly commercial one to the point of materialistic idolatry also viewed as occultism. So there is no significant differentiation between the two descriptions of the one city.

4) There are not different destroyers of Babylon. While 18:8 shows that Babylon is destroyed by God, 17:17 also shows such destruction to be moved by God because, "God put it into their *[the ten horns/kings]* deepest thoughts to carry out His purpose." Also the suddenness of the destruction by fire "in a single day" (18:8), or "in a single hour (18:10, 17, 19) can also be seen to harmonize with the statement in 17:16 that "the ten horns which you saw and the beast will...make her desolate and naked. They will devour her flesh and burn her up with fire." There is no real reason to imagine that this will be a long process. The fact that in chapter 18 there is a switch from "in a single day" (18:8), to "in a single hour (18:10, 17, 19) shows that these terms are not being used with exactitude.

5) George Eldon Ladd states that, "The kings of the earth [in 18:9-10] are to be distinguished from the ten kings who joined with the beast to war against the Lamb (17:12-14)." However, because the "kings of the earth" are also shown to wage war against Jesus (19:19) there must be a certain connection. So perhaps these ten kings are included within the larger body of "the kings of the earth" at a later time. Perhaps they have certain regrets for having involved themselves in the destruction of Babylon, but nevertheless "war" against Jesus. So the different response to the destruction of the city in 18 than in 17 does not mean that there are two Babylons—one symbolic and one literal.

187

6) The first mention of Babylon the great in 14:8 does not narrow down the time frame for Babylon's fall and neither does it speak of Babylon as being in two different forms. The second mention of Babylon in 16:19 also does not speak of Babylon as being in two different forms, but it does narrow the time frame to being when the seventh bowl is poured out i.e. in the time of the pouring out God's wrath in "the day of the Lord" (Isa. 13:6-11; 13:1; 14:1-3; Jer. 50:1-6). Therefore, one cannot say that the fall and destruction apply to two different Babylons, one occurring before the great tribulation and the other occurring late in the great tribulation.

Further Factors Showing That Babylon Is a Single City in Revelation 17, 18, and 19

There are many factors that are the same in these three chapters concerning Babylon the great, as seen in the following comparison:

- She is called "the notorious prostitute" (17:1; 19:2)
- She is named "Babylon the great" (17:5; 18:2)
- She is described as a city (17:18; 18:10, 16, 18, 19, 21)
- She is shown to be a great city—a powerful city (17:18; 18:10)
- She has a cup of wine is in her hand (17:4b; 18:6)
- She is drunk in sexual immorality with kings (17:2; 18:3)
- She persecutes God's people (17:6; 18:20, 24, 19:2)
- She is fabulously wealthy (17:4; 18:3, 7, 12-14)
- She is clothed in purple and scarlet, gold ornaments, precious stones, and pearls (17:4a; 18:16)
- She is covered in blasphemous names because of her occult practices (17:5; 18:23)
- She has global influence (17:1-2, 15, 18; 18:3, 9, 11; 19:2)
- God is the source of her destruction (17:17, 19; 18:8)
- She is destroyed by fire (17:16; 18:8, 18)

All of this shows that there is a considerable degree of unity between Chapters 17, 18, and 19 of Revelation and therefore indicating that the same entity is being spoken about, namely, a city. So in Revelation 17 Babylon, must therefore be understood literally, otherwise we should have the anomaly of a figure representing a figure. So, there is no such thing as "Mystic Babylon." Indeed, all further details in Revelation 18 beyond what is said in Revelation 17 simply indicate additional information that shows a resumption and expansion of what is said in Revelation 17 on the wickedness and punishment of the single city of Babylon on the Euphrates River.

She is shown to be sitting (1) "beside the waters" in Rev. 17:1 (peoples and nations etc.), (2) on the Beast (the Antichrist) in 17:3, and (3) on the seven mountains in 17:9 (seven kings). This simply shows the different aspects of her influence and control over the Antichrist, his supporting kings, and the peoples and nations.

A Fulfilment of the Prophecies by Isaiah and Jeremiah

When all these factors from Revelation are combined with the yet to be fulfilled prophecies concerning Babylon in Isaiah 13, 14, and 47 and Jeremiah 50-51, we can see that we have here a description of a still future destruction of the literal city of Babylon—a city that must first of all be fully restored and as economically vibrant.

Those who argue against Revelation 17 as referring to a literal city and yet acknowledging that the prophecies have yet to be fulfilled must answer the question: why did Jeremiah instruct Seraiah to make such a pronouncement (Jer. 51:59, 61) at the *specific geographical location of literal Babylon* if the fulfilment is to be found elsewhere? Clearly, it was not to be fulfilled at a different city (e.g., Rome, New York or Mecca) or in the destruction of a religious system, such as Roman Catholicism or all of apostate Christendom? It must therefore point to a fulfilment upon the literal city of Babylon, however difficult that idea may seem to us at the present time.

Zechariah's Prophecy on the Future City of Babylon

Some scholars and many Christians argue against the rebuilding of a literal city of Babylon. However, if that view is taken then what other way is there for the prophecies to be fulfilled? We have seen that there was never a complete fulfilment of them upon ancient Babylon with its incredible hanging gardens, and that Revelation 17, 18, and 19 are speaking about the same entity, namely, a literal city of Babylon. We have also seen many reasons for not taking "Babylon" as referring to any other city or system. So, there is no other way except to expect that a literal city of Babylon will be developed and expanded to become a commercial super city in the future, even though that may seem to be very far off into the future.

Added to this is the natural interpretation of Zechariah 5:5-11 which Zechariah wrote in 520 B.C. and which demands a restored and rebuilt Babylon. The passage states:

❖ "Then the angel who talked with me came forward, and said to me, "Lift up now your eyes, and see what is this that is appearing. I said, "What is it?" He said, "This is the **ephah** basket that is appearing." He said moreover, "This is their appearance [or "iniquity" Lit. "eye"] in all the land (and behold, a talent of lead was lifted up); and this is **a woman** sitting in the middle of the ephah basket." He said, "This is **Wickedness**"; and he threw her down into the middle of the ephah basket; and he threw the weight of lead on its mouth. Then I lifted up my eyes, and saw, and behold, there were two women, and the wind was in their wings. Now they had wings like the wings of a stork, and they lifted up the ephah basket between earth and the sky. Then to the angel who talked with me, "Where are these carrying the ephah basket?" He said to me, "To build her a house in the land of **Shinar** ["Babylonia" in several versions]. When it is prepared, she will be set there in her own place" *(WEB)*.

An ephah was the largest dry measure used by the Jews, and so was a perfect symbol of commerce. The **ephah** basket "represents their *[Jewish]* iniquity throughout all the land (MEV)." Yet, this woman called Wickedness" is flown away in the ephah basket from Jerusalem to "Babylonia so that a house may be built for the ephah basket to be placed in." It seems to be very likely that that this woman, in being "Wickedness," is the same as the woman in Revelation 17—"the mother of...the disgusting things of the earth." So this scenario in Zechariah is showing that "Wickedness" will finally be taken back to the city where mankind's first rebellion took place, namely, Babel the city of Nimrod. This fits well with the biblical picture of the final Antichrist and the godless of Judaism being removed from Jerusalem and taken to a thriving city of Babylon.

The Revelation goes further in providing information which helps Christians to understand the relationship between Babylon the great and the Antichrist.

§

Chapter 37

The Great Prostitute's Control
of the Beast

Revelation 17:1-6... The beginning of Vision Three

TEXT

Then one of the seven angels who had the seven bowls came and spoke with me, saying, "Come, I will show you the judgment of the notorious prostitute who is enthroned beside abundant waters. **2**The kings of the earth committed sexual immorality with her, and those living on the earth became drunk from the wine of her sexual immorality." **3**So he carried me away, in a prophetic trance, to a desolate wasteland. There I saw a woman seated on a scarlet-coloured ferocious beast that was covered with blasphemous names and had seven heads and ten horns. **4**This woman was clothed in purple and scarlet. She glittered with gold ornaments, precious stones, and pearls. In her hand she had a golden cup filled with the disgusting things and impurities of her sexual immorality. **5**On her forehead was written a name having a mysterious meaning: "Babylon the great, the mother of prostitutes and of earthly disgusting things." **6**Then I saw the woman drinking herself drunk with the blood of God's people, that is, with the blood of Jesus' witnesses. I was completely stunned when I saw her.

TRANSLATION POINT

17:6: This verse should be rendered "drunk with the blood of <u>God's people</u>, **that is**, with the blood of <u>Jesus' witnesses</u>" because it is epexegetical and therefore is not speaking of two bodies of people.

Overview

The statements made in Revelation 17 concerning Babylon the great are an extension of and an elaboration upon all that is said about the pouring out of the seven drink-offering bowls described in Revelation 16. This connection is made because it involves, "one of the seven angels who had the seven bowls [who] came and spoke with [John]" (17:1) concerning Babylon the great. In particular please note that 14:8 gives the first mention in Revelation of Babylon the great and shows her fall. Then in 16:19 we are informed that, "God remembered to give Babylon the great the cup of wine, namely, His fury and retribution." This is shown to occur during the pouring out of the seventh bowl.

There are four major sins that Babylon is primarily guilty of. These are: idolatry, metaphorical sexual immorality, materialistic gain producing luxury, and persecution of God's people.

Comment on Babylon's Control of the Antichrist

17:1: "**Then one of the seven angels who had the seven bowls came and spoke with me, saying, 'Come, I will show you the judgment of the notorious prostitute who is enthroned beside abundant waters.'**" The image of a prostitute is also used in the Hebrew Scriptures of other cities such as Tyre, where her trading was viewed as "the price of prostitution" (Isa. 23:16-17). Nineveh also "sells nations by her harlotries" (Nah. 3:4). However, there is never any hint that these cities are not meant to be understood literally. Furthermore, such prostitute imagery in terms of Babylon's sexual immorality is also used in 18:3 and 9. This again links the two chapters as referring to the same city. Indeed, the judgment upon the city of Babylon begins here, rather than only in the recapitulated sequence of events in chapter 18, as some believe.

The imagery of abundant waters (Rev. 17:1, 15) is reminiscent of the Euphrates and the canals of Babylon (Ps. 137:1; Jer. 51:13), but is later shown in verse 15 to be figurative in referring to "peoples and multitudes and nations and languages " who she influences or controls.

17:2: "**The kings of the earth committed sexual immorality with her and those living on the earth became drunk from the wine of her sexual immorality.**" These are not the same as the ten kings who destroy Babylon, although those ten kings seem to become part of the "kings of the earth" by the time of the events in 19:19.

Because of the descriptions of Babylon's wealth and luxurious living, the prostitution and sexual immorality described here refer to her political alliances with her client kingdoms in terms of commercial activity. Indeed, she has enticed these kings and merchants into the worship of trade in material goods as shown in Revelation 18.

This drunkenness is an allusion to Isaiah 28:7 (LXX) which says, "These have trespassed through wine; they have erred through strong drink; the priest and the prophet are mad through strong drink, they are swallowed up by reason of wine, they have staggered through drunkenness; they have erred: this is their vision." Indeed, this suggests the victimization by Babylon of "the earth dwellers" i.e. Antichrist's followers.

17:3: "**So he carried me away, in a prophetic trance, to a desolate wasteland. There I saw a woman seated on a scarlet-coloured ferocious beast that was covered with blasphemous names and had seven heads and**

ten horns." With these words of, "so he carried me away, in a prophetic trance, to a wilderness" we begin the third of John's visions which extend to 21:8. So taking into account that the Antichrist will arise from an Islamic country, it is likely that Babylon the great, which is described as a notorious commercial prostitute, will be an Islamic city as it currently is as within Iraq. Although the main focus of the descriptions is not religious as such it is certainly possible that a single repressive faith, such as Islam, could gain ascendancy and bring a forced unity by military might and enforced trade. If this is the case then Sharia Law would apply.

The fact that "the woman is seated on" the Antichrist beast probably refers to the scope of her influence and control over the Beast, and similarly with her being "enthroned beside many waters" (vs.1). This control of the Antichrist lasts only until he and the ten confederated kingdoms destroy the city by making "her desolate and naked [and] will devour her flesh and burn her up with fire" (17:16) during the pouring out of the seventh bowl (16:17, 19). Therefore, this riding of the Beast by the Woman would seem to occur only during the first half of Daniel's 70th "seven."

The heads of the beast come first in time then the uncrowned horns. Daniel's fourth Beast arrives with one head and ten horns and the eleventh horn grows from among them **after** the Beast has left the sea (Dan. 7:8) and is therefore not from the Mediterranean as are the ten horns. Indeed, it is scarlet after its slaughtering of God's people.

17:4: "**This woman was clothed in purple and scarlet. She glittered with gold ornaments, precious stones, and pearls. In her hand she had a golden cup filled with the disgusting things and impurities of her sexual immorality**." The purple of these clothes indicates Babylon's status as having a certain level of royalty, but scarlet indicates her sinfulness (Isa. 1:18).

Such a golden cup (Jer. 51:7), like a communion cup of demons (1Cor.10:19-21), looks inviting and holds the promise of good things. However, inside it is full of disgusting idolatry with reference to her commercial prostitution brought about by her political alliances.

17:5: "**On her forehead was written a name having a mysterious meaning: "Babylon the great, the mother of prostitutes and of earthly disgusting things**." As the mother of prostitutes Babylon is the original and archetypal city going back to ancient Babel in her depravity and idolatry

193

regarding her wealth. She is fabulously wealthy just as was Nebuchadnezzar's Babylon. However, she has led others into doing the same sinful things in the worship of material things rather than God. Her daughter prostitutes are those "cities of the nations" which are to be destroyed when the seventh bowl is poured out (Rev. 16:19) because they also worship the same material wealth.

17:6: "**Then I saw the woman drinking herself drunk with the blood of God's people, that is, with the blood of Jesus' witnesses. I was completely stunned when I saw her.**" Being "drunk with the blood of..." means having revelled in the murder of persons. In this case it is the murder of those who are loyal to Messiah.

§

Chapter 38

Identifying the Beast's Heads
Revelation 17:7-11

TEXT

⁷"Why are you so astounded?" asked the angel. "I will explain the secret meaning of the woman to you, and of the beast that carries her—the one with the seven heads and ten horns. ⁸The beast you saw was, and is not, but is about to come up from the abyss and is headed for destruction. Those who live on the earth whose names haven't been written in the scroll of life since the foundation of the world will be amazed when they see the beast that was, and is not, but will be present again.

⁹All of this requires an insightful mind. The seven heads are seven mountains that the woman sits on. They are also seven kings: ¹⁰five have fallen; one is, and the other has not yet come, but when he does come, he must remain for only a short time. ¹¹The ferocious beast that was, and is not, is himself an eighth king, and yet is one of the seven and is headed for destruction.

Comment on the Seven Heads

17:7: "**Why are you so astounded?" asked the angel. I will explain the secret meaning of the woman to you, and of the beast that carries her—the one with the seven heads and ten horns.**" John is evidently perplexed to see Israel's old enemy described in such luxury rather than seeing her judgment (17:1). So the angel realizes that John needs an explanation.

The involvement of the beast with Babylon shows that the secret meaning concerns the single subject of the relationship between the Woman and the Beast. The angel has chosen to deal with the salient features of the vision summarized in verse 7 in two complexes in reverse order i.e. dealing with the Beast first.

17:8a: "**The beast you saw <u>was</u>, and <u>is not</u>, but is <u>about to come up from the abyss</u> and is headed for destruction.**" This statement means: the Beast "who lived" and "who no longer lives [i.e., 'is dead'] and "will live again." In Revelation 13:3 one of the beast's "heads appeared to have been fatally wounded." So at this point the Beast "is not," i.e. he is momentarily dead at a point during the first half of the 70th "seven," but "then his fatal wound was healed," at which point he will have "come up from the abyss" alive i.e. no longer restrained, and as fully satanic (2 Thess. 2:9, 10). He "will make war on" God's people during the great tribulation, "and defeat them and kill them" (11:7). His rulership is for 3½ years "and then he goes off into destruction." (Dan. 7:11).

195

17:8b: "Those who live on the earth whose names haven't been written in the scroll of life since the foundation of the world will be amazed when they see the beast that was, and is not, but will be present again." In Rev.13:8 the Greek word order shows that the rendering should be: "the Lamb who was slaughtered from the foundation of the world" so that the phrase "the foundation of the world" is not a reference to the earth-dwellers, but rather to Messiah. However, here it is different because this is a reference to the earth-dwellers as never having had their names written in the scroll of life. In fact, in Rev. 3:5 we learn that even a Christian may have his or her name removed from the scroll of life and so showing that the concept of once saved always saved is not the biblical picture of Christian salvation.

The statement that "the beast that was, and is not, but will be present again" is the third reference to his ascending from the abyss (please see 11:7 and 13:1) and refers to the final Antichrist's appearance before he is destroyed by Messiah Jesus (2 Thess. 2:8-9).

17:9: "All of this requires an insightful mind. The seven heads are seven mountains that the woman sits on. They are also seven kings." These seven mountains are seven kingdoms and the kings are representative of them just as with Nebuchadnezzar being the golden head representing the Babylonian kingdom (Dan. 2:38, 39).

17:10-11: "Five have fallen; one is, and the other has not yet come, but when he does come, he must remain for only a short time. The ferocious beast that was, and is not, is himself an eighth king, and yet is one of the seven and is headed for destruction."'" The traditional Historicist view is that, rather than representing kings of empires, these are all actual empires that have had control of Israel:

1. The Egyptian Empire
2. The Assyrian Empire
3. The Babylonian Empire
4. The Medo-Persian Empire
5. The Greek Empire, including the Seleucids in the Middle-East.
6. The Roman Empire (Eastern half fell in AD 1453)
7. A revived Roman Empire based on the European Community.

However, today's traditional understanding of the seventh empire cannot be exactly correct because there is nothing about the European Community that fits the biblical picture. In reality, there are many more

196

than ten "crowns" or countries in the E.U.. Also in #7 a revived Roman Empire must be discounted as the final worldly empire because the Beast as an eighth king is "one of the seven" (Rev. 17:11) and can only come from the area of the ancient Seleucid Empire (Dan. 8:9; Rev 2:13; 13:2). Furthermore, in Historicist and Preterist terms it is difficult to account for their version of the seventh empire as being short lived. In fact, none of this scheme fully represents the historical reality because it fails to take into account the long-lived Ottoman Empire (1299-1920) and the fairly long-lived British Empire (1700s to 1960s) both of which had control of Israel for some time. Yet in 17:9 we are told that these are seven **kings** and 17:11 shows that there will be an eighth king (not kingdom). This fact alone shows that the first seven are also kings of empires rather than simply their empires. Indeed, Keil shows that there are some eleven discrepancies with the Historicist approach to this passage. So because these are kings in Rev. 17:10 we find the exact biblical pattern of, *"one is, and the other has not yet come, but when he does come, he must remain for only a short time"* in Daniel 11 which shows the "**five have fallen**" as being four Persian Kings along with Alexander the Great (Dan. 11:1-5) as the fifth king. Sir Robert Anderson understands these four Medo-Persian monarchs to have been:

- Darius II Nothus (Neh. 12:2)   423-404. B.C.E
- Artaxerxes II Mnemon   404-359.
- Artaxerxes III Ochus   359-338
- Darius III Codomannus   338-3
- Alexander invades Persia in 334. Dies in 323. B.C.E

So after noting that, from a revelatory perspective, these five, as recorded in Daniel, are possibly the "five have fallen" of Rev.17:10 we must now analyse where in Daniel we will find the "one is" and "the other has not yet come, but when he does come he must remain for only a short time."

Firstly, Daniel 10:14 shows that this prophecy concerns the future "in the days to come (Heb. *acharit-hayamim*)." Although this phrase does not necessarily refer to "the end of the age," it does show events that will precede the appearance of Antichrist, as well as showing that there is a break from the ancient past in verse 5 with mention of the first King of the South. This, therefore, shows that the Kings of the North from Daniel 11:6ff are still to appear.

197

NOTE: Please see the book *Prophecies Related to the Return of Jesus* page176 to note the arbitrary and unnecessary complexities of the Historicist and Preterist interpretation of Daniel 11.

Secondly, in Daniel 11, by following the antecedents of 'he', 'him', and 'his' in the vision, it becomes evident that the passage speaks of only three Kings of the North in total.

Thirdly, Daniel 11:4 notes the breaking up of Alexander's kingdom as being "parcelled out toward the four points of the compass" i.e. divided into four parts under his four generals and later consolidated into two kingdoms—Ptolemaic and Seleucid. So the ancient southern Ptolemaic kingdom forms the basis for the future King of the South in verse 5 and the northern Seleucid kingdom forms the basis for the future King of the North in verse 6. So the pattern of the Kings of the North is as follows:

- The first "king of the North" is in 11:6-9 and includes his sons (or (son) in 11:10-19. It is this King of the North that is the "**one is**"— the *sixth king* in Rev.17:10. He appears, not during John's lifetime, but as in prophecy in the distant future and so cannot presently be identified.

- The second "king of the North" is the one described in Daniel 11:20 as a replacement for the previous King of the North. This king of the North sends out a tax collector. However, "after a few days [this king of the North] will be destroyed." He is also one that will appear in the future as, "**the other has not yet come**...he must remain for only a short time" noted in Rev. 17:10. He is the *seventh king* in Rev.17:10 and so also cannot presently be identified.

- The third and last "King of the North is the "despicable person" *[the Antichrist]* in 11:21-45. While Daniel 11 does not differentiate between his non-satanic and his satanic forms, Rev.17:11. shows "the beast" as the *eighth king* and coming out of the abyss (11:7; 17:8) in his Satanic form by this time (2 Thess.2:9-10).

This eighth king as "the despicable person" of Daniel 11:21-45 is the Antichrist and as "the little horn," he comes from one of the Greek four horns. Then Daniel 8:9 shows that he "grew exceedingly great toward the south (Egypt), toward the east (Persia), and toward the beautiful land (Israel)." So the north must refer to Turkey (ancient Asia Minor)/Syria/Babylon and this interpretation is clinched by the fact that in 167 B.C Antiochus Epiphanes of the Seleucid Empire became a type of the little horn.

So in being "one of the seven" this eighth king first appears during the first half of the 70th "seven" in his non-satanic form as one of those seven kings. But which one is he? It seems likely that he is the future sixth king of Rev.17:10 i.e. the first King of the North in Daniel 11:6 and with his sons (son) in 11:10. This means that the seventh king (the second of Daniel 11:20—the one with a short reign) reigns during Antichrist's absence when he remains dead (Rev.13:3) and before his coming out of the abyss in his satanic form (11:7) at the beginning of the second half of the 70th "seven."

So within Daniel 11 we have found all seven kings that are mentioned in Rev.17:10 and the eighth of 17:11. These are: the four Persian kings, Alexander the great as being #5, the first King of the North as being #6, the second King of the North as being #7, and the third King of the North as being #8. This is also a more biblical approach than simply constructing a list of empires through history as is traditionally set out.

Chapter 39

The Ten Horns and Antichrist Destroy Babylon the Great
Revelation 17:12-18

TEXT

¹²The ten horns that you saw are ten kings who have not yet received a kingdom, but will receive authority as kings with the beast for a single hour. ¹³These have a single purpose: to give their power and authority to the beast. ¹⁴They will make war with the Lamb, but the Lamb will conquer them, because he is Lord of lords and King of kings. Those with him are called and chosen and faithful."

¹⁵"The waters you saw where the prostitute resides," he continued. "These symbolize nations, populations, races, and languages. ¹⁶The ten horns which you saw and the beast will hate the prostitute and make her desolate and naked. They will devour her flesh and burn her up with fire. ¹⁷In fact, God put it into their deepest thoughts to carry out His purpose, even to carry out their single purpose —even to give their royal power to the beast—until God's words will have been accomplished. ¹⁸And the woman that you saw symbolizes the great city that has dominion over the kings of the earth."

Comment on the Ten Horns and the Destruction of Babylon

17:12-13: "**The ten horns that you saw are ten kings who have not yet received a kingdom, but will receive authority as kings with the beast for a single hour. These have a single purpose: to give their power and authority to the beast.**" The first mention of these as horns is in Daniel 7:7, 24 concerning the fourth beast and its ten horns. As shown earlier these are not ten European nations as part of the European Union. In fact, they only become kings when Antichrist appears in his satanic form. They are ten contemporary kings who are under Antichrist's authority for the 42 months, metaphorically "a single hour" i.e. a short period compared to the ages of Satan's kingdom. Furthermore, they are not the same as "the kings of the earth," but probably join forces with them by the time of the events in 19:19.

Biblically, these "horns" could be the ten kings of an Arab (likely Islamic) confederacy described in Psalm 83:2-9. These are: Edom, Ishmael, Moab, Hagarenes, Gebal, Ammon, Amalek, Philistia, Tyre, and Assyria. Could this involve the current Arab league? Alternatively, the prophets note an attack on Babylon by the Medes (Isa. 13:17 and Jer. 51:11, 28).

200

17:14: "[They] will make war with the Lamb, but the Lamb will conquer them, because he is Lord of lords and King of kings. Those with him are called and chosen and faithful." This is proleptic of the final conflict which occurs in 19:17-21. These kings were shown as existing and already gathered for war at the time of the pouring out of the sixth bowl (16:12-16) even though the reality does not occur until later.

While it is not explicitly said that the "called and chosen and faithful" battle alongside Messiah it is certainly implied that they are with him as the Christian messianic army of 144,000 (7:1-9; 14:1-5). Certainly, Jesus wins this war because he is God's representative having been granted one of God's own titles as, "Lord of lords and King of kings (also see 19:16)."

17:15: "The waters that you saw, where the prostitute resides," he continued. "These symbolize nations, populations, races, and languages." This is an interjection into the passage. It focuses on Satan's domain as the waters or sea in symbolism as the turbulent part of mankind. Isaiah 17:12 speaks of "the uproar of many peoples who roar like the roaring of the seas." Such "waters" would also include the rivers and springs of water as fresh waters, but nevertheless turbulent compared to the solidity of the earth.

17:16: "The ten horns which you saw and the beast will hate the prostitute and make her desolate and naked. They will devour her flesh and burn her up with fire." Again we note the possible identity of the ten horns as an Arab (likely Islamic) confederacy described in Psalm 83:2-9. However, the order of events here is not significant because these passages are proleptic of future events. So it is clear that the prostitute Babylon is destroyed before the Lamb defeats the ten (horns) kings (vs. 14).

The Beast described here is pictorial of Antichrist's kingdom with him as its head. This is based on Daniel's fourth beast which comes out of the Mediterranean (Dan. 7:7). These are also the feet and toes of iron/clay of the image in Daniel 2 that are the end-time development from the iron legs of the Islamic Empire. It is also shown in its composite form in Revelation 13:1-3.

As God's plan (verse 17), the desolating of Babylon refers to the depopulating of her and the devouring of her flesh which indicates that she deserves no burial, but is metaphorically eaten up by wild dogs (2 Kings 9:10, Rev. 2:20-23). The destruction of Babylon through plagues, famine, and fire (18:8) by this confederacy takes place in "one hour/one day" i.e. over a short period of time, but long enough for her to suffer pestilence, famine, and fire so that she is "devoured" and burned up. This burning was well described by Jeremiah when he said, "[Babylon's] dwelling places are set on fire, her bars are broken ... The wall of Babylon...will be set aflame with fire" *(Jer. 51:30, 58)*.

This attack upon Babylon by the ten horns produces a civil war as foretold in Ezekiel 38:21 and Zechariah 14:12, 13. Here we learn that everyone's hand will be against his neighbour and "every man's sword will be against his brother." However, the total destruction of Babylon appears to be by means of an earthquake and therefore by God as is shown when the seventh bowl is poured out:

❖ "The great city was split into three parts, and the cities of the nations collapsed. God remembered to give Babylon the great the cup of wine, namely, His fury and retribution." *(Rev. 16:19)*.

17:17: "**In fact, God put it into their deepest thoughts to carry out His purpose, even to carry out their single purpose—even to give their royal power to the beast—until God's words will have been accomplished.**" This shows that these kings and Antichrist do not naturally wish to destroy Babylon, but that it will be through divine intervention that this miracle of their forming such a single purpose occurs. In other words, God uses these ten horns (kings) to destroy Babylon.

17:18: "**And the woman that you saw symbolizes the great city that has dominion over the kings of the earth.**" This passage shows that Babylon the great is a literal city in Revelation 17 just as much as in chapter 18 with its world dominating religion of worship of Antichrist's image based on commercialism. The city becomes the greatest commercial centre and is linked with "Wickedness" in the ephah (Jewish symbolism for commercialism) described in Zechariah 5. This city is a future rebuilt Babylon on the banks of the Euphrates. It is "wickedness" in its final form as the end-times idolatrous political and commercial city that is to be destroyed by God using human agency.

§

Chapter 40

Why Babylon Is to Be Punished
Revelation 18:1-8

After these things I saw another angel, possessing exceptional authority. He was coming down out of the sky, and the earth was illuminated by his splendour. **2**He shouted out with a powerful voice:

"Fallen, fallen, is Babylon the great! She has become a habitat for demons, a hiding place for every unclean spirit, a cage for every unclean bird, a haunt for every unclean and detested beast. **3**Furthermore, all the nations have been ruined because they drank of the wine that is her unrestrained passion for immorality. And the kings of the earth have committed sexual immorality with her and the merchants of the earth have grown wealthy from the abundance of her luxury."

4Then I heard another voice from heaven saying,

"Come out of her, my people, so that you won't participate in her sins, and so that you won't receive some of her plagues. **5**Her sins have piled up all the way to heaven, and God has remembered her crimes. **6**Treat her the same way she has treated others; pay her back double corresponding to her deeds. Mix her a double portion in the cup she mixed. **7**As much as she glorified herself and lived in luxury, to this extent give her severe pain and grief because she said to herself, 'I sit as queen! I am no widow! I will never experience mourning!' **8**For this reason, the plagues will come upon her in a single day: death-dealing disease, mourning, and famine. She will be burned up with fire, because the LORD God who judges her is powerful!"

Overview

This new angel now expands the previous scenario into a complete picture. He follows the same theme given in Revelation 17, but with greater detail concerning Babylon's punishment for all of her economic idolatry, immorality and oppression, but now also showing the reaction of all those who dealt with her as the great commercial city. The angel accomplishes this by referring to the unfulfilled prophecies against Babylon as found in Isaiah 13-14 and Jeremiah 50-51. He also draws upon certain phrases of prophecy in Ezekiel 26-28 concerning the destruction of Tyre.

Revelation 18 can be broken down into five major parts. These are:

- The announcement of the fall of Babylon (1-3)
- The command for believers to flee from Babylon (4-8)
- The laments of the kings, merchants, and seafarers (9-19)
- The call for Christians to rejoice (20)
- The destruction and desolation of Babylon (21-24)

Comment on Why Babylon Is Punished

18:1: "**After these things I saw another angel, possessing exceptional authority. He was coming down out of the sky, and the earth was illuminated by his splendour.**" Although this introduces a new textual unit as with 4:1; 7:1, 9; 15:5; and 19:1 it is not a new vision. This angel is so blindingly glorious, but is nevertheless certain to be outshone by Messiah Jesus when he returns.

18:2: "**He shouted out with a powerful voice: 'Fallen, fallen, is Babylon the great! She has become a habitat for demons, a hiding place for every unclean spirit, a cage for every unclean bird, a haunt for every unclean and detested beast.'**" The exclamation that "Babylon the great has fallen" was said earlier in 14:8. However, this exclamation is originally found in Isaiah 21:9 and Jeremiah 51:8. Also Isaiah 13:21 points out that Babylon will become a habitat for demons and the description that "desert creatures will live there with jackals, and daughters of ostriches will inhabit her...she will not be inhabited again forever, and she will not be dwelt in for all generations" comes from Jeremiah 50:39.

The reference to unclean birds and detested beasts concerns all that is demonic i.e. the unclean spirits.

18:3: "**Furthermore, all the nations have been ruined because they drank of the wine that is her unrestrained passion for immorality. And the kings of the earth have committed sexual immorality with her and the merchants of the earth have grown wealthy from the abundance of her luxury.**" This cup containing Babylon's "unrestrained passion for immorality" is clearly a cup full of sin. So this is the first reason given for her coming devastation. She is a totally negative influence on the nations, including her deluding of them by her occultism (vs. 23).

These "kings of the earth" are not specifically the ten Kings allied with Antichrist who are shown to be the instruments of Babylon's destruction, but rather they are those who had benefited from their immoral relationship with her. However, those ten may well join with the "kings of the earth" in the lament over her destruction because of regretting it, in spite of the fact that God used them to bring about that destruction.

18:4: "**Then I heard another voice from heaven saying, Come out of her, my people, so that you won't participate in her sins, and so that you won't receive some of her plagues.**" This other voice is likely to be that of Jesus. This command was first said by Jeremiah (Jer. 51:45). Indeed, along with Matthew 24:22 and Revelation 7:14-15, this suggests that not all Christians will be martyrs during the great tribulation. Certainly, true Christians and some of the Jews living in Babylon would distance themselves morally and perhaps socially from her because of her seductive influences. However, as with the original call by Jeremiah this also means escaping from Babylon and getting as far away as possible.

18:5: "**Her sins have piled up all the way to heaven, and God has remembered her crimes.**" Future Babylon's sins and crimes concern her self-glorification, her promoting of a narcissistic culture with idolatrous revelling in her materialistic luxury which has become the new religion and the new "god," as well as her oppression and murder of people, including God's people. In fact, Jeremiah had previously shown that, "clear to the heavens her judgement has reached..." *(Jer. 51:9)* and so indicating the magnitude of her sins.

The background allusion of her sins being "piled up" is possibly a reference to the piling up of bricks in building the Tower of Babel, but it may also be a reference to Nebuchadnezzar's great boasting about his rebuilding of the city into something glorious, but idolatrous.

18:6: "**Treat her the same way she has treated others; pay her back double corresponding to her deeds. Mix her a double portion in the cup she mixed.**" Similarly, Jeremiah 50:15 says, "For this is the vengeance of Yahweh. Take revenge on her. As she has done to others, so do to her" *(LEB).* In both of these texts in Revelation and Jeremiah this is the language of revenge. However, a theological argument that this cannot refer to Christians as taking revenge is because they are to be forgiving of those who persecute them (Rom. 12:14, 17), to love their enemies, and not to retaliate (Matt. 5:39, 43). So one would imagine that this taking of revenge is likely to refer to the action of God Himself (Rom. 12:19) when He uses the ten horns to bring about her destruction, so that

He will repay all those who have persecuted God's people.

Indeed, the punishment of "a double portion" is based on the principle of *lex talionis* meaning "proportional retribution in kind" e.g. "an eye for an eye" (Ex. 21:23). So Babylon will simply get all that she deserves!

18:7: **"As much as she glorified herself and lived in luxury, to this extent give her severe pain and grief because she said to herself, 'I sit as queen! I am no widow! I will never experience mourning!'"** Babylon is a prostitute, but in her heart she sees herself as royalty. This boast is drawn from Isaiah 47:7-9 and is one of Babylon's sins (vs. 5) leading her to deny God and to dispense with Him. This leads her on to seduce the nations into the same misguided thinking. They think that their security comes from their materialism—their faith is in their economic system—this is their new religion!

18:8: **"For this reason, the plagues will come upon her in a single day: death-dealing disease, mourning, and famine. She will be burned up with fire, because the LORD God who judges her is powerful!"** This statement is a repeat of what is said in 17:16 when, as motivated by God, the ten horns (kings) and Antichrist "will devour her flesh and burn her up with fire." However, this gives a picture of a prolonged siege leading to famine, yet the term "in one hour" as meaning 'in a moment' (also "in a single day" (Isa. 47:9)) means 'in a very short time' i.e. "suddenly Babylon has fallen, so that she is broken..." *(Jer. 51:8).* So either this "moment" leading to famine must still take time or it must happen miraculously fast.

§

Chapter 41

Lamenting Babylon's Destruction
Revelation 18:9-19

TEXT

⁹Then the kings of the earth who have committed sexually immoral acts with her and lived in luxury with her will cry and mourn over her when they are looking at the smoke from the burning of her. ¹⁰They will stand at a distance, in fear of her severe pain. They will be saying,

> "What calamity, what calamity for Babylon! O great city, you powerful city! In a single hour your punishment has come."

¹¹Then the merchants of the earth will cry and mourn over her, because no one buys their merchandise anymore—¹²merchandise of gold, silver, precious stones and pearls; of fine linen, purple cloth, silk, and scarlet cloth; of all kinds of citron wood products, and all kinds of objects made of ivory, expensive wood, bronze, iron and marble; ¹³of cinnamon, Indian amomum spice, incense, myrrh and frankincense; of wine and olive oil; of fine flour and wheat; of cattle and sheep; horses and wagons; and of slaves—yes, human lives.

¹⁴"The ripe fruit you craved has left you, and all your luxurious and glamorous things have gone from you—you won't ever find them again!"

¹⁵The merchants who sold these things, and who became rich from her, will stand at a distance in fear of her severe pain. They will cry and mourn, ¹⁶saying,

> "What calamity, what calamity, O great city—clothed in fine linen, purple and scarlet clothing, and adorned with gold, precious stones, and pearls—¹⁷because in a single hour such fabulous wealth has been laid waste!"

And every ship's captain, everyone sailing the routes, sailors, and all who make their living from the sea, stood at a distance. ¹⁸As they watched the smoke from the burning up of her, they began shouting out, "What can compare with the great city?" ¹⁹And they threw dust on their heads and shouted out while crying and mourning,

> "What calamity, what calamity, O great city, in which all those who had ships on the sea became rich from her wealth, because in a single hour she has been laid waste!"

Comment on Lamenting Babylon's Destruction

18:9: **"Then the kings of the earth who have committed sexually immoral acts with her and lived in luxury with her will cry and mourn over her** when they are looking at the smoke from the burning of her." These kings are not the same as the "ten kings" who destroy Babylon (17:12-14), although they may include them at this point in the events. These "kings of the earth" are those who had been seduced by Babylon. These kings are the political rulers of the day who had benefitted from this immoral relationship. They have not been so openly devoted to the satanic purposes of the ferocious beast as were the ten kings, but were deceived by her glamour. They now realize just how deceived they have been and that security did not lie with her. Instead, "Her dwelling places are set on fire, her bars are broken ... The wall of Babylon...will be set aflame with fire" *(Jer. 51:30, 58).* The background information for this event is also found in Isaiah 13, 14, 47, 48 and Jeremiah 50:51 which all apply in *"the day of Yahweh"* (Isa. 13:6, 9) and when there will be the miraculous darkening of the sun, moon and stars (13:10, 13). So these political leaders now see Babylon as a failed system and that it is with God that true power and security lie.

"The smoke from the burning of her" likely goes on forever as shown in Isaiah 34:9-10 and as the background to Revelation 14:10-11 in symbolizing the permanent evidence of Babylon's eternal destruction.

18:10: "They will stand at a distance, in fear of her severe pain. They will be saying, "What calamity, what calamity for Babylon! O great city, you powerful city! In a single hour your punishment has come." These political leaders are shocked at the sudden and unexpected destruction of Babylon. They lament the loss of their 'gravy train,' and fear that the judgment on Babylon could also be brought down on them because of their involvement in her sins and crimes. However, at this point it is imperative that these kings, like Nebuchadnezzar, change their arrogant ways and acknowledge God's sovereignty (Dan. 3:28-29; 4:2-3; Ps. 2).

18:11-13: "Then the merchants of the earth will cry and mourn over her, because no one buys their merchandise anymore—[12]merchandise of gold, silver, precious stones and pearls; of fine linen, purple cloth, silk, and scarlet cloth; of all kinds of citron wood products, and all kinds of objects made of ivory, expensive wood, bronze, iron and marble; [13]of cinnamon, Indian amomum spice, incense, myrrh and frankincense; of wine and olive oil; of fine flour and wheat; of cattle and sheep; horses and wagons; and of slaves—yes, human lives." The list of items traded in is found in the dirge over Tyre in Ezekiel 27:5-24. This list in Revelation can be classified as: precious metals and stones, fine clothing materials, expensive items for decoration, fragrances, foodstuffs, domestic animals, and slaves. All of this reflects the opulence of Babylon in its ostentatious materialism and its willingness to trade in "human lives," and so treating them as an item of merchandise.

18:14: "**The ripe fruit you craved has left you, and all your luxurious and glamorous things have gone from you—you won't ever find them again!**" The "ripe fruit" here is a metaphor for all of the luxurious goods listed in verses 12 and 13. Although we all need certain things in our modern world for normal functioning and good quality lasts longer, yet it is pertinent at this point to ask ourselves just how materialistic are we today? Do we have or crave an abundance of the above listed or other things? Do we even seek these things as some kind of status symbol? If we put too much emphasis on such luxury and glamour we are eventually going to be very disappointed as all these things disappear from us in the end times. This all shows the folly of any love for material things and is here shown as being immoral in God's eyes (vs. 3). Indeed, Jesus tells us to seek "treasures in heaven" rather than "treasures on earth" *(Matt. 6:19-20)* because, "you who are rich will have trouble. You have already had your good times" *(Luke 6:24 WE)*. In fact, for Babylon's luxuries, she "won't ever find them again" just as James said of Christians who fall into the trap of materialism:

❖ "Your wealth has rotted, and your clothes have become moth-eaten. Your gold and silver have corroded, and their corrosion will be evidence against you; and like a fire it will consume your flesh. You have piled up treasure in the last days...⁵You have lived off the land in self-indulgence and luxury" *(James 5:2-3, 5)*.

18:15-17a: "**The merchants who sold these things, and who became rich from her, will stand at a distance in fear of her severe pain. They will cry and mourn, ¹⁶saying, "What calamity, what calamity, O great city— clothed in fine linen, purple and scarlet clothing, and adorned with gold, precious stones, and pearls—¹⁷because in a single hour such fabulous wealth has been laid waste!**" These merchants, primarily from exporting lands, selfishly mourn because of their loss of trade. It means their economic ruin. As with the political leaders these merchants also lament the loss of their easily gained wealth and fear that the judgment on Babylon could also be brought down on them because of their involvement with her in her sins and crimes.

18:17b-18: "And every ship's captain, everyone sailing the routes, sailors, and all who make their living from the sea, stood at a distance. ¹⁸As they watched the smoke from the burning up of her, they began shouting out, "What can compare with the great city?"" These sea-farers as a third category of mourners over Babylon's demise were the means to transport goods to Babylon and exports from her to many other lands. These are not those small businesses which are mainly pushed into bankruptcy by these shipping magnates. Yet, these major transporters of goods will no longer be needed and so will lose their significant incomes. No wonder they lament Babylon's destruction!

18:19: "And they threw dust on their heads and shouted out while crying and mourning, "What calamity, what calamity, O great city, in which all those who had ships on the sea became rich from her wealth, because in a single hour she has been laid waste!" The act of throwing dust on one's head was an act of showing one's mourning or sorrow (Josh. 7:6). Although the grief of these seafarers is intense it is a matter of selfish mourning over Babylon's destruction.

§

Chapter 42

Rejoicing and Praising God for Destroying Babylon
Revelation 18:20-19:5

TEXT - 18:20-24

²⁰Rejoice over her, O heaven and you holy ones, apostles and prophets, because God has executed the same judgment against her that she executed against you! ²¹Then a certain powerful angel picked up a boulder like a huge millstone and threw it into the sea, saying:

> "In this way, Babylon the great city will be thrown down with force, and will never be seen again! ²²Never again will the sound of harpists, singers, flute players, and trumpeters be heard in you; never again will a craftsman of any trade be found in you; never again will the sound of a millstone be heard in you. ²³Never again will the light from a lamp shine in you! The voices of bridegrooms and brides will never be heard in you again. Your merchants were the commercial magnates of the world; all the nations were deluded by the spell you cast over them! ²⁴The blood of prophets and holy ones has been found in her, along with the blood of all those who had been slaughtered on the earth."

Comment on Rejoicing over the Destruction of Babylon

18:20: "**Rejoice over her, O heaven and you holy ones, apostles and prophets, because God has executed the same judgment against her that she executed against you!**" This is now the time for God's people to rejoice. This rejoicing is not out of selfishness, but it is time for them to be vindicated and for God's justice to be seen to have been executed and for His righteousness to be vindicated. The fact that the twelve apostles and prophets (both OT and NT) rejoice at this time shows that the first resurrection has already taken place.

This judgment against Babylon is a restatement of Babylon's destruction when the ten horns and Antichrist turn against her as described in 17:16. This is not a second destruction as if there are two Babylons, but is a showing of how this destruction takes place and its effects upon her admirers.

18:21: "**Then a certain powerful angel picked up a boulder like a huge millstone and threw it into the sea, saying: "In this way, Babylon the great city will be thrown down with force, and will never be seen again!**" Similarly, Jeremiah had been told: "...when you finish reading aloud this scroll, you must tie a stone on it, and you must throw it into the middle of the Euphrates. And you must say, 'this is how Babylon will sink down and never rise up" *(Jer. 51:63).* The fact that Jeremiah says that Babylon will "never rise up" and Revelation says she "will never be seen again" shows that this is all prophecy of future events and that it was not fulfilled in ancient times, but will be fulfilled when Jesus returns.

The angel's casting into the sea of Babylon like a millstone is a prophetic acted parable, and the simile of the huge millstone is apt because actual millstones often were so heavy that a donkey was required to turn them around on their pivotal point. Such were not the same as the small hand mills used by women for grinding grain.

18:22: "Never again will the sound of harpists, singers, flute players, and trumpeters be heard in you; never again will a craftsman of any trade be found in you; never again will the sound of a millstone be heard in you." This builds on Isaiah's bleak picture for Babylon in 24:8, "The mirth of tambourines ceases. The sound of those who rejoice ends. The joy of the harp ceases" *(WEB).* Furthermore, the removal of the craftsmen means that all business dies leading to the abandoning of the city itself and therefore, the complete failure of the Babylonian economic system. Also with no millstones in operation there would be no grain i.e., no food.

18:23: "Never again will the light from a lamp shine in you! The voices of bridegrooms and brides will never be heard in you again. Your merchants were the commercial magnates of the world; all the nations were deluded by the spell you cast over them!" Indeed, the lights that light up the homes of the inhabitants of Babylon will simply go out permanently and so indicating that there is now a complete lack of people and life in the city. Even the most joyful of events of weddings will never again happen in Babylon. But when all this is happening, God's people will experience the joy of becoming Messiah's bride.

These merchants here are those of Babylon herself and, in being "the commercial magnates of the world," their arrogance and self-exaltation is implied. So the spell here is really a metaphorical reference to Babylon's demonic deluding of the nations, that is, her charm in seducing them into the worship of all things material and so ignoring the honouring of God. This will be done with "the wine that is her unrestrained passion for immorality" (vs. 3) for the security she imagines can be found in crass materialism and luxury. Indeed, as the mother of prostitutes Babylon will influence all the cities of the world into this kind of mind set.

18:24: "**The blood of prophets and holy ones has been found in her, along with the blood of all those who had been slaughtered on the earth**." This last of the mentioned major sins shows that Babylon is charged with murder as originally stated by Jeremiah that, "not only was Babylon the cause for the slain ones of Israel to fall but also at Babylon the slain ones of all the earth have fallen" *(Jer. 51:49).* There are two groups noted here. They are: "prophets and holy ones" as martyrs and "all those who had been slaughtered on the earth." This latter class refers hyperbolically to the unbelievers who have died at Babylon's hand, rather than to everyone who has ever been murdered.

⅄

TEXT – 19:1-5

"After these things I heard what seemed to be the loud voice of a vast assembled crowd in heaven, saying,

> "*Praise Yah!* Victory and glory and power belong to our God! ²His judgments are true and just. Indeed, He has passed judgment on the notorious prostitute who corrupted the earth with her sexual immorality, and has avenged His servants' blood which was on her hands!"

³Then a second time the assembled crowd shouted, "*Praise Yah!* The smoke rises from her forever and ever."

⁴The twenty-four elders and the four living creatures fell to the ground and knelt in worship before God who was seated on the throne. "Amen!" they were saying, "*Praise Yah!*" ⁵Then a voice came from the throne, saying:

> "Praise our God all you His servants, and all you who revere Him, both the lowly and the prominent!"

Comment on the Praising of God for Destroying Babylon

19:1: "**After these things I heard what seemed to be the loud voice of a vast assembled crowd in heaven saying '*Praise Yah!* Victory and glory and power belong to our God!**'" This crowd is most likely a reference to a combination of angelic beings and God's people (please see comment on Revelation 3:10). These Christians are described here as "in heaven." Certainly, many times in the book of Revelation the word "the heaven" (Gk. *ouranios*) is a literal reference to the sky (earth's atmosphere). So too, with Revelation 19:1 as presented in the UVNT which reads: *"After that I seemed to hear the sound of a great multitude of people in the sky saying..."* This matches the description of Christians as being "caught up... in the clouds to meet the Lord in the air" (1 Thess. 4:17) and being "caught up in a cloud" (Rev. 11:12) to meet Jesus and his angels (Matt.

24:31, 2 Thess.1:7). This is also true of the two witnesses of 11:12 who "went up into heaven in a cloud" i.e. *"they passed up into the sky* (Gk. *ouranos*) *in a cloud while their enemies looked on."* In fact, both the passages in 11:12 and 19:1 match with the details of the rapture given by Paul in 1 Thessalonians 4:16, 17.

This is the first of four occurrences of the shortened form of God's name, the others occurring in verses 3, 4, and 6. The full name of "Yahweh" occurs some 6,800 times in the Hebrew Scriptures, and is therefore very important for Christians. Nevertheless, Jesus taught his followers to refer to God as "Father" in their prayers, and Paul shows the closeness of that relationship when we use "Abba, Father" (Rom. 8:15; Gal. 4:6), a term which Jesus himself used (Mark 14:36).

God's victory here, through Messiah Jesus, means the removal of all that might try to frustrate God's purpose. So the removal of "Babylon the great" makes way for the coming of God's Kingdom and is the answer to the prayers of all of God's people.

19:2: "His judgments are true and just. Indeed, He has passed judgment on the notorious prostitute who corrupted the earth with her sexual immorality, and has avenged His servants' blood which was on her hands!" This is a repeat of Babylon's description as "the notorious prostitute" (17:1, 19:2) who persecutes God's people (17:6, 18:20, 24, 19:2) and has global influence (17:1-2, 15, 18; 18:3, 9, 11, 19:2). So everyone is now able to see God's justice in action. Especially is this meaningful for Christians.

19:3: "Then a second time the assembled crowd shouted, *"Praise Yah!* The smoke rises from her forever and ever." This is a poetic metaphor. It is drawn from Isaiah 34:10 as part of the prophecy about Edom's destruction and shows the normal devastation as a result of war (Isa. 34:6-15). It is the same hyperbole as in Rev.19:3 where lasting destruction forever is portrayed. The destruction of Babylon will be the first great act of the Kingdom of God.

19:4: "The twenty-four elders and the four living creatures fell to the ground and knelt in worship before God who was seated on the throne. "Amen!" they were saying, *"Praise Yah!"'* These are not Christians, but angelic beings. This is proven by the five pieces of biblical evidence given in *4:4:.* So these twenty-four elders are angelic beings who demonstrate their adoration of God just as in Revelation 5:14.

214

The four living creatures seem to combine the features of the *seraphim* (Isa. 6:2) and the *cherubim* (Ezek 1:5-14), although giving mostly the features of the cherubim.

It is likely that both the twenty-four elders and the four living creatures are God's divine council (Dan 7:9).

19:5: "**Then a voice came from the throne, saying: "Praise our God all you His servants, and all you who revere Him, both the lowly and the prominent!**" This cannot be God's voice because it admonishes others "to praise God." So, here it is possible that it is the voice of Jesus, but more likely the voice of one of the four living creatures or one of the twenty four elders in giving praise to God.

§

Chapter 43

The Wedding of the Lamb and His Bride
Revelation 19:6-10

TEXT

⁶Then I heard what was like the sound of a vast assembled crowd, like the sound of a torrent of waters, and like the sound of loud thunderclaps. They were shouting:

"*Praise Yah!* Because the LORD our God, the All-Powerful, has begun to reign! ⁷Let us keep celebrating and exulting and giving Him glory, because the wedding day of the Lamb has come, and his bride has prepared herself. ⁸She was allowed to be dressed in fine linen, bright and clean, because the fine linen is the deeds of God's people—deeds having God's approval."

⁹"Write this," he said to me, "Blessed are those who are invited to the wedding banquet of the Lamb!" He also said to me, "These are the exact and true words of God." ¹⁰So I knelt at his feet in worship of him, but he said, "Don't do that! I am only a fellow servant of you and of your brothers and sisters who hold to the testimony of Jesus. You must worship God!" (For the testimony of Jesus is the spirit of prophecy).

Comment on the Lamb's Wedding

19:6: "**Then I heard what was like the sound** (lit. "voice") **of a vast assembled crowd, like the sound of a torrent of waters, and like the sound of loud thunderclaps. They were shouting:** "*Praise Yah!* **Because the LORD our God, the All-Powerful, has begun to reign!**" As with 19:1 this description is also likely to be a combination of angelic beings and God's people. This sound is, "...like the roar of waters" as with the 144,000 in 14:2. These ones bear witness to God's triumph which leads to the wedding of the Lamb. Here we have the last of the four occurrences of the phrase "praise Yah" using the shortened form of God's personal name.

19:7: "**Let us keep celebrating and exulting and giving Him glory, because the wedding day of the Lamb has come and his bride has prepared herself.**" This wedding motif is used to represent Jesus' reuniting with his disciples at his return—it will be an eschatological spiritual marriage.

The term "bride" or "wife" really means "fiancée" (Matt.1:20) in modern-day terms. This is because an engaged woman in biblical times was viewed as being "a betrothed wife." In fact, Paul uses the metaphor of a "wife" to show Jesus' very close relationship with his body of followers (Eph. 5:25ff, 32).

216

This wedding motif shows that a reuniting of Jesus and his people is about to take place after he returns, most likely to Mount Sinai (please see *Prophecies Related to the Return of Jesus*, Chapter 52—The Preparation for the Kingdom and the Messianic March).

In Jesus' illustrative story or parable of the wedding feast (Matt. 22:1-14) the bride is not mentioned, but only the guests, and so showing the flexible nature of parabolic language.

However, this wedding cannot be for only the end-time survivors of the great tribulation. Indeed, the writer to the Hebrews stated that, "apart from us they will not be made perfect" (Heb. 11:40), hence the conjoining of the faithful over the centuries by means of the first resurrection and all being caught up together to meet Jesus as he returns. Once they have descended the wedding celebration begins.

19:8: "**She was allowed to be dressed in fine linen** (Gk. *byssinos*), **bright and clean, because the fine linen is the deeds of God's people—deeds having God's approval.**" The dressing of the bride in such pure clothes is a divine gift to her because she has proven herself faithful and worthy, having performed "deeds having God's approval." These pure clothes are in stark contrast to the gaudy clothes and the pretentious way of dressing by the notorious prostitute. The clothes of Christ's bride are clean because they have been washed and "made...white in the blood of the Lamb (7:14).

19:9: "'**Write this,**' he said to me, '**Blessed are those invited to the wedding banquet of the Lamb!**' **These are the exact and true words of God.**" This wedding banquet occurs as the beginning of the Kingdom era. If, at the return of Jesus, his descent with his entourage of Christians to Mount Sinai is the correct scenario (please see *Prophecies Related to the Return of Jesus*, chapter 52—The Preparation for the Kingdom and the Messianic March), then this metaphorical wedding and feast will occur at that time on or near Mount Sinai in Arabia (Gal. 4:25).

The parable of the marriage feast in Matthew 22 contains many details to show that it takes place on earth. Also in Matthew 26:29 Jesus stated that he will drink of the vine on "that day...with you in my father's kingdom" as well as saying: "Let me tell you, many will come from the east and from the west and recline at the banqueting table with Abraham, Isaac, and Jacob in the Kingdom of Heaven" *(Matt. 8:11),* and so showing that this banquet will be on earth.

19:10: "So I knelt at his feet in worship of him, but he said, "Don't do that! I am only a fellow servant of you and of your brothers and sisters who hold to the testimony of Jesus. You must worship God!" (For the testimony of Jesus is the spirit of prophecy)." John falls into this pattern of worship a second time in Revelation 22:8-9 and is once more warned by the angel about who should be worshipped. This is a similar situation to the time when the Apostle Peter rebuked Cornelius for falling down at his feet (Acts 10:25) in an act of worship. In the case of John falling at the angel's feet there is the same issue because angels are simply equal to humans and not superior to them. There was, therefore, the need for this angel to rebuke John for worshipping him.

A further point is that there may have been a tendency for some Christians to venerate angels even as Paul showed in Colossians 2:18. So some scholars feel that this is recorded in Revelation as a polemically motivated attempt to counter this practice of angel worship within Christianity.

There seem to be two opposing views of what "the testimony of Jesus" might mean. The first is that it means that the testimony that Jesus gave is the very heart or essence of prophecy. The second is that it means the testimony about Jesus. I take the former as the most likely view.

§

Chapter 44

The Defeat of the Antichrist by Jesus
Revelation 19:11-16

TEXT

11Then I saw the sky opening up. There was a white horse, and the one mounted on it was called "Faithful" and "True." With justice he judges and wages war. **12**His eyes are like a raging fire, and there are many diadem-crowns (Gk *diadema*) on his head. He has a name inscribed that no one knows except himself. **13**He is clothed with a robe that had been dipped in blood, and his name is called "The Revelation of God." **14**Heaven's armies kept following him on white horses. They are dressed in the finest of pure white linen. **15**A sharp sword extended from his mouth, so that he can strike the nations with it. He will rule them with an iron sceptre, and he will trample the winepress of the fury of the retribution of God, the All-Powerful. **16**He has a name written on his robe and on his thigh: "King of kings and Lord of lords."

Overview

All earlier passages which show Jesus as the conquering warrior (6:16; 11:15; 14:14; 17:14) are proleptic (in which a future event is pre-figured), and so anticipating Jesus' return—his *parousia*. However, it is only in the literary description of 19:11-21 that his return as a conquering warrior becomes a reality. So this chapter shows Jesus as confronting and defeating the Antichrist and his armies.

Here there are several qualities of Jesus that are displayed: He is faithful and true, displays justice, has penetrating eyes, has a name that only he knows, and is "the Revelation of God." Also there are certain specific actions of Jesus that are focused upon: He holds the sword of judgment, shepherds with an iron rod, treads the winepress of God's wrath, and demonstrates his kingship.

Comment on Jesus' Defeat of the Antichrist

19:11: "**Then I saw the sky opening up. There was a white horse, and the one mounted on it was called "Faithful" and "True." With justice he judges and wages war**." The sky has been split open to reveal Messiah Jesus mounted as a warrior. The white horse imagery is drawn from Roman triumphalism i.e. Jesus is a victor, but it is a symbol of decisive and final victory. However, this does not show Jesus as charging into battle but mounted and simply controlling the battle.

The words "Faithful" and "True" are virtually synonymous and so emphasize Jesus' reliability and trustworthiness. Therefore, we can know that when Jesus makes war it will be a just war based on God's righteous standards—a discriminatory war with the spirit of wisdom and justice (Isa. 11:4). This war is the only actual holy war, ever, and follows the rule of *lex talionis* meaning "the law of retribution" which is shown throughout Revelation.

19:12: "His eyes are like a raging fire, and there are many diadem-crowns on his head. He has a name inscribed that no one knows except himself." This shows Jesus' penetrating all-searching gaze so that nothing is hidden from him (2:18) and that he can give "fiery" judgments to the incorrigibly wicked.

The *diadema* is a crown worn by a ruler in contrast to the wreath-like *stephanos* for a victor. As pretenders to the throne the Dragon (12:3), and the beast (13:1) also wear a *diadema*, but it is mentioned nowhere else in the New Testament.

Here Jesus is shown to have a secret name, the meaning of which, no mortal human mind can grasp. Perhaps this is, "the name that is above every name" mentioned in Philippians 2:9 because Jesus is shown as the returning exalted Messiah and every knee must bow to him. At that future time this name will reveal more of the true nature of Messiah in a way that our current finite ability cannot grasp.

19:13: "He is clothed with a robe that had been dipped in blood, and his name is called "The Revelation of God." Some have proposed that this "blood" refers to Jesus' sacrifice. However, it is more likely that this refers to his warrior role and so is the blood from the destruction of his enemies as described in Isaiah 63:2-3 and as part of the events during the Messianic march northward toward Jerusalem.

Regarding Jesus' name as being "The Revelation of God" commonly rendered "the Word of God," this is not a reference to John 1:1 as if to indicate that John 1:1 concerns Jesus, rather than simply concerning the impersonal "word of God" and so to make it appear that Jesus pre-existed. Indeed, the Revelation from Chapter 4 forward presents an entirely future scenario. So Jesus' title "the Revelation (Gk *logos*) of God" in 19:13 applies particularly to the future. Indeed, he is never given that title at any time prior to or after his baptism or even after his resurrection. It is only here in Rev.19 at this one time of his return that he is given this title.

So, because the prologue of John speaks of God's impersonal word it is <u>incorrect to read back</u> the future scenario of Jesus in 19:13 into the pre-creation scenario of God's *logos* or revelation/message in John 1:1.

In fact, the reason for Jesus being given the title "the Revelation of God" is that this "word/revelation/message" specifically concerns the destruction of Antichrist and all his hordes and establishes the basis for God's Kingdom.

19:14: **"Heaven's armies kept following him on white horses. They are dressed in the finest of pure white linen."** The term "heaven's armies" should not be rendered as in the KJV etc. - "armies which are <u>in</u> heaven." This is because the Greek is in the genitive showing possession, whereby God is Himself called "Heaven" as in other places in the New Testament (Matt. 5.10; 6:20; Mark 11:30; Luke 10:20; John 3:27) and so showing that these are "armies belonging to Heaven" i.e. armies belonging to God.

Because of the context of this passage such armies are likely to be composed of the angels who accompany Jesus at his return to earth (2 Thess.1:7) as well as the entire body of Christians (Rev. 17:14) who have been "caught up" to meet Jesus in earth's atmosphere (1 Thess. 4:17). These Christians (symbolic number of 144,000 in Rev.7 and 14) are also end-time spiritual warriors. Both angels and Christians account for the use of the plural term "armies." These Christians are "arrayed in white linen" as are the holy ones/great multitude and shows that they are part of the army in a victory marching order.

19:15: **"A sharp sword extended from his mouth, so that he can strike the nations with it. He will rule them with an iron sceptre, and he will trample the winepress of the fury of the retribution of God, the All-Powerful."'** Clearly, this is not a literal sword (Heb. 4:12), but the power of Jesus' words (Isa. 11:1; 2 Thess. 2:8) and is a symbol of "the sword of the spirit" (Eph. 6:17; Heb. 4:12) as a sword of judgment; and so whatever Jesus speaks simply happens, as when God spoke, and it was done in Genesis 1:3 etc. Jesus uses this symbolic sword to destroy the wicked nations (Rev.19:15). It is also described as "the breath of his mouth" with which he destroys the Antichrist (2 Thess. 2:8). This was prophesied by Isaiah when he wrote, "Yahweh called me from the womb; from the body of my mother he made my name known. And he made <u>my mouth like a sharp sword</u>" (Isa 49:1-2). Indeed, it appears that

221

this is the only weapon shown to be used against the Antichrist and his armies. Nevertheless it is totally destructive.

Such an iron sceptre has the same force as "the sharp sword." Indeed the idea of Messiah as ruling the nations with an iron sceptre was first stated in Psalm 2:9. So this passage reflects both the promise to faithful Christians that they, too, will rule the nations with an iron sceptre (2:27). It also reflects the grape harvest in 14:19-20 where the winepress is shown as a symbol of the destruction of the incorrigibly wicked.

19:16: **"He has a name written on his robe and on his thigh: "King of kings and Lord of lords**." Such a title was given to Nebuchadnezzar (Dan; 2:37). However, this is primarily a title for God (1 Tim. 6:15), and yet as with Pharaoh's conferring of the complete rulership of Egypt upon Joseph (Gen.41:38-45), so too, God confers rulership of the world and this corresponding title upon Jesus to give him sovereign authority (17:14).

§

Chapter 45

The Great Supper of God
Revelation 19:17-21

TEXT

17Then I saw one particular angel standing in the sun, and he shouted out in a loud voice to all the birds flying in mid-air, "Come and gather together for the great supper of God, **18**so that you may eat the flesh of kings, the flesh of commanders, the flesh of powerful people, the flesh of horses and their riders, and the flesh of everyone, both free and bond-servant, and lowly and prominent!" **19**Then I saw the ferocious beast and the kings of the earth and their armies assembled to wage war with the one mounted on the horse and with his army. **20**But the beast was captured, and along with him the false prophet who had performed the signs on his authority, by which he deceived those who had received the brand-mark of the beast and those who had worshipped his image. Both of them were thrown alive into the lake of fire that burns with sulphur. **21**The rest were killed by the sword that extended out of the mouth of the one mounted on the horse, and all the birds gorged themselves on their flesh.

Comment on the Great Supper of God

19:17: "**Then I saw one particular angel standing in the sun, and he shouted out in a loud voice to all the birds flying in mid-air, 'Come and gather together for the great supper of God.'**" The rendering here could also be "standing <u>on</u> the sun." In Jewish tradition there was a belief that there was an angel in charge of the sun. Either way this shows this angel as reflecting the radiance of God and of Jesus.

At the same time that the Antichrist and his forces gather for battle, these figurative carrion "birds" gather for the aftermath of the certain slaughter of those forces. This "supper of God" is an allusion to Ezekiel 39:17 as part of the prophecy against Gog—another term for the Antichrist. Indeed, this banquet for "the birds" is a parody on the Messianic banquet, but comes not long after it and indicates, in picture language, that these evil forces are not worthy of a burial. The effect is the same as when Jezebel was eaten up by the dogs (2 Kings 9:36-37) so that she is shown to be not worthy of a burial. So, too, "the great supper of God" is the ultimate degradation for these evil forces.

19:18: "**So that you may eat the flesh of kings, the flesh of commanders, the flesh of powerful people, the flesh of horses and their riders, and the flesh of everyone, both free and bond-servant, and lowly and prominent!**" This picture gives the same effect as the symbol of the winepress, the

223

lake of fire, and other pictures of the destruction of the wicked.

Clearly, this destruction is not of absolutely all of mankind, but of all who were followers and worshippers of the Antichrist and significantly his armies. These ones had taken the brand-mark of the Antichrist and so gave their total allegiance to him.

19:19: **"Then I saw the ferocious beast and the kings of the earth and their armies assembled to wage war with the one mounted on the horse and with his army."** After all of the earlier anticipatory statements made about the absolute and certain victory by Jesus over the forces of evil, it is only in these last verses of chapter 19 that we see the description of the actual defeat of those evil forces. This is the final battle described in Zechariah 12:4-9; and 14:3-7; Ezekiel 38:17-23; and Joel 3:1-18.

The "kings of the earth" are not exactly the same as "the ten kings (horns)" in Revelation 17. However, these ten kings likely will be incorporated into the larger body of "the kings of the earth" ruling the nations. These "kings of the earth" are shown to wage war against Jesus here and the ten kings are shown to wage war against him in 17:14. Perhaps the ten kings will have certain regrets for having involved themselves in the destruction of Babylon. Nevertheless they "war" against Jesus.

Although Jesus has "his army" of angels and Christians, it seems that the Christians are just onlookers as Jesus himself produces the slaughter of these evil forces by means of "the sword of his mouth," that is "by the sword that extended out of the mouth of the one *[Jesus]* mounted on the horse" (vs. 21).

19:20: **"But the beast was captured, and along with him the false prophet who had performed the signs on his authority, by which he deceived those who had received the brand-mark of the beast and those who had worshipped his image. Both of them were thrown alive into the lake of fire that burns with sulphur."** In these passages there is no description of the actual battle because it seems to be over instantly and the main focus is upon what next happens to the defeated Antichrist and his forces.

In Revelation this is the first mention of the lake of fire. It is another description of Jesus' term of Gehenna i.e. "the fire of the age to come that has been prepared for the devil and his angels" (Matt. 25:41). This lake of fire, into which the Antichrist beast and the false prophet (the beast from the land in 13:11-17) are now thrown, does not produce eternal torture even though they are thrown "alive" into it. However, we must remember that this lake is only a symbol of the complete destruction of these evil characters. (Please see my book *Delusions and Truths Concerning the Future Life*).

19:21: "**The rest were killed by the sword that extended out of the mouth of the one mounted on the horse, and all the birds gorged themselves on their flesh**." Again this pictures total annihilation because Jesus destroys these ones with the word of his mouth. Again there is emphasis on the fact that these armies are not worthy of a burial because they are eaten up by the carrion birds.

§

Chapter 46

Satan Will Be Shackled for a Thousand years
Revelation 20:1-3

TEXT

Then I saw an angel descending from heaven. In his hand was the key to the abyss, and a huge chain. ²He seized the Dragon—the ancient Serpent, who is the Devil and the Satan—and bound him for a thousand years. ³He threw him into the abyss, then locked and sealed it over him so that he couldn't deceive the nations anymore, until the one thousand years were completed. After these things he must be released for a short period of time.

Comment on the Restraining of Satan

20:1: **"Then I saw an angel descending from heaven. In his hand was the key to the abyss, and a huge chain."** As in *9:1b* the abyss (Gk *abyssos*) is that of "an exceedingly deep" and vast place of restraint often with reference to the sea. It is so deep that only God can bring someone back from it. The term is further defined as "a prison" in Revelation 20:7. However, it is not a literal place but is figurative of an infinite void of absolute restraint. It is also the place from which Antichrist will emerge (11:7; 17:8) and where Satan will be imprisoned for the one thousand years (20:1-3).

So the "key" and the "shaft" to the abyss are also symbolic and simply show the angel's control over imprisonment by such total restraint or release from it. The chain is a symbol of holding Satan in complete darkness (2 Pet. 2:4), so that he is unable to affect anyone or anything.

20:2: **"He seized the Dragon—the ancient Serpent, who is the Devil and the Satan—and bound him for a thousand years."** Amazingly this angel has enough power to seize Satan. However, as with Michael's throwing of Satan out of heaven (12:9) this would be with God's power.

As with 12:9, this set of descriptive terms or aliases show that "the Serpent" in the Garden of Eden was not a literal snake, but that this term is descriptive in showing the deceptive character of this evil being. Also the presumption is that the demons will also be thrown into this same abyss at the same time. This is confirmed when they said to Jesus *"have you come here to torment us before the time"* (Matt. 8:29). What would be the point of locking Satan away if his agents are free to cause havoc during this glorious period of human freedom.

226

This is the first mention of the one thousand years in all the Scriptures. It must be a quite literal period i.e. a real period of time as a partial manifestation of the Kingdom. This is so for the following reasons:

- A time element is contained in the terms "this age" i.e. "the present age" and "that age" i.e. "the age to come" *(Luke 20:34, 35; Matt. 12:32; Mark 10:30).*

- Both the first resurrection of Revelation 20:4 and the "coming to life of the rest of the dead' in verse 5 are proven to be literal resurrections with the 1,000 years between them and so a literal period of time is involved.

- Satan is cast into the lake of fire at the final battle which is after the one thousand years. Yet the beast and the false prophet were already there, having been thrown alive into the lake a thousand years earlier. If the one thousand years is figurative then when could these events happen?

- There are situations described in Revelation which cannot exist simultaneously, such as:

  ❖ "...the great dragon [Satan] was thrown down, who deceives the whole world" *(Rev.12:9).*
  ❖ "an angel...threw him [Satan] into the abyss...so that he would deceive the nations no longer" *(Rev. 20:3).*
     Both situations cannot exist simultaneously.

  ....

  ❖ "...the devil has come down to you...knowing that he has only a short time ... he persecuted the woman" *(Rev. 12:12, 13).*
  ❖ "...an angel ... laid hold of the dragon [Satan], and bound him for a thousand years" *(Rev. 20:1-2).*
  Satan cannot be simultaneously active on earth and yet be bound at the same time.

  ....

  ❖ "...the beast...and with him the false prophet...were thrown alive into the Lake of fire" *(Rev. 19:20).* This occurs at the battle for Jerusalem when Christ returns.

  ❖ "When the thousand years were completed the devil ... was thrown into the lake of fire and sulphur where the beast and the false prophet were" *(Rev. 20: 7, 10).*

227

Furthermore, the earliest church fathers, such as Justin Martyr and Irenaeus taught that the Revelation spoke of a literal one thousand years.

20:3: "**He threw him into the abyss, then locked and sealed it over him so that he couldn't deceive the nations anymore, until the one thousand years were completed. After these things he must be released for a short period of time.**" Clearly, this is symbolic language to show the complete blocking of Satan's deceptive activities throughout the thousand year period of the transitional Kingdom. The fact that he is later released after the one thousand year period shows this binding to be different from the binding of Satan by Jesus in his earthly ministry (Matt. 12:28-29).

§

Chapter 47

The Thousand Year Gap between Resurrections
Revelation 20:4-6

TEXT

4Then I saw thrones and those who sat on them; and authority to govern in justice was committed to them, even those people who had been beheaded because of their testimony about Jesus and for proclaiming God's message, and those who had refused to worship the beast or his image, and who had refused to receive his brand-mark on their forehead or hand. They came to life and reigned with the Messiah for a thousand years. **5**(The rest of the dead didn't come to life until the thousand years were completed.) This is the first resurrection. **6**Blessed and holy is everyone who has a share in the first resurrection! Over such ones the second death has no authority, but they will be priests of God and of the Messiah, and they will reign with him for a thousand years.

Comment on the Two Resurrections

20:4a: "**Then I saw thrones and those who sat on them; and authority to govern in justice was committed to them, even those people who had been beheaded because of their testimony about Jesus and for proclaiming God's message, and those who had refused to worship the beast or his image, and who had refused to receive his brand-mark on their forehead or hand.**" The mention of thrones is probably an allusion to Daniel 7:9-10. However, this is not merely authority to judge, because the Greek word *krino* can have the broader meaning of "to rule" as with the judges of Israel. In fact, Christians will share Messiah's throne in rulership (3:21) and the apostles will sit on twelve thrones (Matt. 19:28, 1 Cor. 6:2).

The grammar here indicates two groups. However, it seems clear from the biblical pattern that the martyrs (6:9) are within the main group because all Christians will be raised together and rule together (see verse 6; 3:21; 1 Thess. 4:17; and Heb. 11:30).

20:4b: "**They came to life and reigned with the Messiah for a thousand years.**" The idea that this refers to a spiritual resurrection cannot be proven. So these ones "came to life" because of being physically resurrected as was the case with all resurrections. This is because each one conquered, as in the seven communities and based on the law of former reference. Indeed, all who come forth in the first resurrection will reign with Jesus (20:4, 6).

229

20:5: "(**The rest of the dead didn't come to life until the thousand years were completed.) This is the first resurrection.**" When the phrase "the rest of the dead" is placed in parenthesis, as in David Aune's rendering and that of others, (Mounce, Moffatt, CJB, GNT, LEB, NET, NIV, NRSV, NLT), then the passage becomes clear so that a second resurrection after the thousand years becomes evident, even though only implied. Furthermore, the term "first resurrection" also makes the second fully evident. Certainly, both Daniel and Jesus referred to two resurrections (Dan. 12:2; John 5:28-29). This second resurrection after the thousand year period is to mortal life for all the rest of unbelieving mankind who have ever lived and died. It brings them to a point in time whereby they must stand before the great white throne (20:12-13) to be judged.

These scenes concerning the resurrection of "the rest of the dead" (Rev. 20:5) refer to a general resurrection. So this second resurrection is in fulfilment of Daniel 12:1, 2 at a point shortly after the one thousand years are completed. It seems that there are two groups of people presented here, the first of which are 'the important and the unimportant' i.e. the righteous converts to Jesus during the Millennium as well as all those who through the ages never had been presented with the truth concerning the Kingdom and Messiah. Then the second group is of the dead who are given up by the sea (a personification of evil) and Death and Hades. The sea and Death and Hades are virtually synonymous terms for the unrighteous dead.

The fact that only the first group are described as *standing before the throne* indicates that God looks upon them favourably. Furthermore, because "the scroll of life" was opened there is an indication that their names may already be written in it. If so, then it will be by their response to Christ's kingdom (Matt. 13:18, 23) that Jesus "will never blot [their] name out of the book of life" (Rev. 3:5).

20:6: "**Blessed and holy is everyone who has a share in the first resurrection! Over such ones the second death has no authority, but they will be priests of God and of the Messiah, and they will reign with him for a thousand years.**" The first resurrection occurs when Messiah returns (1 Cor. 15:22-23). It is first in both time and importance.

The second death is mentioned four times in Revelation. The 'first death' is the death that is common to all mortal humans and which they currently experience in time. The "second death" is a final death—a death forever from which there will be no resurrection. It is symbolized in Revelation by "the lake of fire" as well as several other symbols, but does not involve eternal torment, but a cessation of all life. Indeed, faithful Christians will not experience the second death because they will have been granted immortality (1 Cor. 15:42-57).

In being priests of God and of the Messiah, the likely reference is Exodus 19:6 as originally promised to Israel if they remained faithful and obedient. This statement parallels Revelation 1:6 and 5:10 but please note Paul's sarcasm to those "super apostles" in the Corinthian Christian community who had decided that they were already reigning (1 Cor. 4:7-8). Nevertheless, faithful and humble Christians will have this privilege to be priests to the mortal population during the one thousand years.

Chapter 48

The Satan Inspired Rebellion Is Destroyed
Revelation 20:7-10

TEXT

⁷When the thousand years are completed, the Satan will be released from his prison. ⁸He will go out to deceive the nations at the four corners of the earth, Gog and Magog, and to assemble them together for the battle. Their number is as the sand of the sea. ⁹They went up on the broad plain of the earth, and surrounded the encampment of God's people, namely, the beloved city. But fire came down out of the sky and consumed them. ¹⁰And the Devil who deceived them was thrown into the lake of fire and sulphur where the ferocious beast and the false prophet had been thrown. There they will be inflicted with severe pain day and night forever and ever.

Comment on the Satan Inspired Rebellion

20:7: "**When the thousand years are completed, the Satan will be released from his prison.**" Grammatically this releasing can be construed as a passive of divine activity and therefore can be understood to mean, 'God will release Satan from his prison.' Such releasing of Satan as an evil being seems strange, but is, in fact, part of God's plan to reveal further evil among humans and then to eradicate it.

20:8: "**He will go out to deceive the nations at the four corners of the earth, Gog and Magog, and to assemble them together for the battle. Their number is as the sand of the sea.**" This releasing and with further human rebellion against God makes it evident that the one thousand years is that of only a transitional kingdom. However, the everlasting Kingdom will come into operation after these very last attempts at deception by Satan and the fiery destruction of those final rebels.

The term "Gog and Magog" is a symbol of the godless masses of deceived nations hostile to God. This is because the term "Gog and Magog" is in apposition to the term "the nations." In fact, there is a general relationship between this passage and Ezekiel 36-40 perhaps indicating that one is a type of the other. However in Ezekiel 38 and 39 the individual person called Gog is provably the Antichrist (please see Chapters 42 and 43 of my book: *Prophecies Related to the Return of Jesus*). In contrast to this, at the end of the one thousand year period, the term Gog and Magog represents entire rebellious nations which are deceived into hostility toward God.

This event shows that humans are not sinful just because of their circumstances or because of any inadequate social conditions as in today's world. During the Millennium they will have lived in the most wonderful and peaceful conditions, and yet many who were born during the Millennium still get led into rebellion against God and so showing that the problem lies in human hearts. (Rom. 1:20).

20:9: "**They went up on the broad plain of the earth, and surrounded the encampment of God's people, namely, the beloved city. But fire came down out of the sky and consumed them.**" This beloved city is Jerusalem as being the capital of the Kingdom. However, this beloved city must be symbolic because not all of God's people would fit into Jerusalem. So perhaps it symbolizes all of the cities where God's people are throughout the earth (Luke 19:17-19).

This is the second of three stages of the eradication of evil, the first having been the destruction of Antichrist and his worshippers at the beginning of the one thousand year period. Similar to the punitive miracle twice performed by Elijah (2 kings 1:9-12), this fire brings about the destruction of these rebels. They are "consumed" and so cease to exist and are therefore not "alive in torment forever" because such would imply that they had been granted immortality—a privilege granted only to faithful Christians.

20:10: "**And the Devil who deceived them was thrown into the lake of fire and sulphur where the ferocious beast and the false prophet had been thrown. There they will be inflicted with severe pain day and night forever and ever.**" This continues the second stage of the eradication of evil and does not concern wicked mankind in general who were destroyed in the attack upon God's people. Also please note that the beast and the false prophet are thrown "alive" into the lake of fire (19:20). This is symbolical of their sudden and irreversible destruction. It is similar to the severe pain of destruction of Babylon the great (18:7-8) as being destroyed "in one day...burned up by fire." The smoke from this goes on forever as shown in Isaiah 34:9-10 as the background to Revelation 14:10-11 in symbolizing the permanent evidence of their eternal destruction, but not literal eternal torment. Wonderfully, at this point in time Satan the Devil and his demons cease to exist (Matt. 25:41).

§

Chapter 49

The White Throne Judgment
Revelation 20:11-15

TEXT
¹¹Then I saw a magnificent white throne and someone seated on it. The earth and the sky fled away from his presence, and there was no place for them. ¹²And I saw the dead, the prominent and the lowly, standing in front of the throne. Scrolls were opened, and another scroll was opened—the scroll of life. And the dead were judged on the basis of what was written in the scrolls, according to their deeds. ¹³And the Sea gave up the dead who were in it; and Death and Hades gave up the dead who were in them; and each person was judged according to their deeds. ¹⁴Then Death and Hades were thrown into the lake of fire. This symbolizes the second death—the lake of fire. ¹⁵And if anyone's name wasn't found written in the scroll of life, that person was thrown into the lake of fire.

Comment on the White Throne Judgment

20:11a: "**Then I saw a magnificent white throne and someone seated on it.**" The question here is: who is the "someone" seated on this throne—is it God or Jesus? Although God is seen as sitting on His throne throughout Revelation as a parallel to Daniel 7:9-10, this "someone" here is likely to be Jesus because he is God's primary representative and appointed judge. Indeed, "[God] has given all judgment to the Son" (John 5:2). Also in 22:1 we find that it is "the throne of God and of the Lamb." In fact, in all of Revelation it is the Son (the Lamb) who acts in opening the seven seals, treading the winepress, etc.

Absolutely just judgments will come from Jesus because his throne is white for purity and holiness. Also, because Jesus will have returned to the earth at the beginning of the Millennium, it will be in Jerusalem that this judging will take place.

20:11b: "**The earth and the sky fled away from his presence, and there was no place for them.**" This poetic imagery is in terms of a personification as showing the "the earth (or land) and the sky" fleeing as an animal might flee in fear. So this simply indicates that the one thousand years of the interim Kingdom have come to an end and have transitioned to the everlasting Kingdom. The old earth and sky society will have perished in the sense that: "they shall be *changed*" (Ps.102:26; Heb.1:10). Therefore, they have vanished (Isa. 51:6), faded away so that society is renewed once again i.e. "a new heavens and a new earth"

(21:1) because now the everlasting Kingdom has arrived so that there will be no more decay (Rom 8:19-21).

20:12a: "And I saw the dead, the prominent and the lowly, standing in front of the throne." "The dead" are the same as "the rest of the dead" in 20:5. Here the second resurrection is implied so that the judgment may take place. Indeed, this judgment is one which will decide the final destiny of all of the rest of humanity i.e. all of those had been unbelievers throughout time, but now are raised for this judgment.

20:12b: "Scrolls were opened, and another scroll was opened—the scroll of life. And the dead were judged on the basis of what was written in the scrolls, according to their deeds." "The scroll of the perfect life" is, of course, the scroll which contains all the names of the faithful of all ages, but also has spaces for others as seen in 20:15.

These first mentioned metaphorical scrolls that are opened contain a record of all of the personal behaviour of the individual unbelievers of both their good deeds and their bad deeds, and all of this judgment "according to their deeds" concerns their deeds prior to resurrection and since that event. Certainly, this will not be any kind of capricious judgment, but a judgment that is completely just (Rom. 2:5-6).

In contrast to Satan's being granted a specific time of release there is no time scale stated concerning how long the white throne judgment will last. So, based on God's love and justice one would imagine that resurrected individuals would be granted whatever amount of time God would deem as necessary for them to repent and to accept Him and all of His arrangements, including the Kingdom. This may explain why Revelation 22:1-2 speaks of:

❖ "...a river of life-giving water ... On each bank of the river are life-giving trees, producing twelve kinds of fruit, yielding their crops of fruit—one each month. The leaves of the trees are for the **healing of the nations**."

20:13: "And the Sea gave up the dead who were in it; and Death and Hades gave up the dead who were in them; and each person was judged according to their deeds." Hades is the common grave of mankind where all aspects and functions of humans are literally dead; and so death and Hades are part of the same thing, namely, the cessation of life. So here Death and Hades are combined and personified as acting to throw o~

235

dead as a metaphorical way to indicate the resurrection of the unbelievers for judgment. The Sea, as the most turbulent of mankind (Isa. 57:20) is also personified to show the resurrection of the most troublesome of people. All of this shows the all encompassing nature of this resurrection of every unbeliever who has ever lived and died. In fact, Jesus had stated the same, as recorded in John's Gospel, when he said:

❖ "...a time is coming when **all who are in the memorial tombs** will hear his voice. They will come out—the ones who have practiced what is good, to the resurrection of perfect life, and the ones who have practiced what is bad, to the resurrection of judgment.

(John 5:28-29).

All such "who have practiced what is bad" will be raised as mortal because they have yet to be judged and so their final destiny is not known at this point in time. So, all these will stand before "the magnificent white throne" to be judged according to all of their personal behaviour.

20:14: "**Then Death and Hades were thrown into the lake of fire. This symbolizes the second death—the lake of fire.**" This also shows that the lake of fire is a symbol and so making it evident that if death and the grave have been destroyed then there will be no more death of humans. By his sacrificial death Jesus has broken the power of death (2Tim. 1:10), but by this point after the Millennium "death is no more" (Rev. 22:4). This implies that there will be no mortality on earth for humans and so further implying that some who were judged favourably (vs. 15) would be granted immortality.

20:15: "**And if anyone's name wasn't found written in the scroll of life, that person was thrown into the lake of fire.**" This implies that most are found in the scroll of life. The force of this is that it is the minority who are not written in this scroll.

This is the third and final stage in the eradication of evil.

§

Chapter 50

The Beginning of
a New Heavens and a New Earth
Revelation 21:1-8

TEXT

Then I saw a new heavens and a new earth. The first heavens and the first earth had passed away, and there was no longer any sea. **2**And I saw the holy city, the New Jerusalem, descending out of the sky from God, prepared like a bride adorned for her husband. **3**And I heard a loud voice from the throne saying, "See! God's place of residence is in the midst of mankind. He will live among them, and they will be His people, and God Himself will be with them. **4**He will wipe away every tear from their eyes. There will be no more death; neither will there be mourning nor crying nor pain, because the first order of things has passed away."

5The One sitting on the throne said, "See! I am making everything new!" Then he said to me, "Write, because this message is trustworthy and true." **6**Then he said to me, "It is finished! I am the Alpha and the Omega, the beginning and the end. To anyone who is thirsty I will freely give water from the spring of the life-giving water. **7**Those who conquer will inherit these things. I will be their God and they will be my children. **8**But as for the cowards and the faithless, the sexual perverts and the murderers, the peddlers of immoral sex and occultists, the idolaters and every sort of deceiver—their destiny will be the lake that burns with fire and sulphur, which means the second death."

Overview

This is the beginning of a rather difficult section in regard to the timing of the fulfilment of the things stated. This is because, if, as most scholars do, one takes this passage as following sequentially as a direct continuation from Revelation 20, and so to assume that it speaks of time after the Millennium, then it would seem to give a description of the continuing existence of "the cowards and the faithless, the sexual perverts and the murderers, the peddlers of immoral sex and occultists, the idolaters and every sort of deceiver" (verse 8) in the full manifestation of the kingdom of God of supposedly total perfection. This would indeed be rather contradictory. Furthermore, verse 27 states that, "nothing ritually impure, that is, anyone who does perverted things, or deceives with lies will ever enter into [Jerusalem]." This seems to imply the existence of such bad people at that post-millennial time and would be completely inappropriate for this full manifestation of God's kingdom.

Nevertheless, most leading commentators do take this passage as being post-millennial. One reason is that verse 4 speaks of the time of "no more death" and therefore it appears that all humans would have immortality which is not the case during the Millennium when mortals do still die (Isa. 65:20).

It seems that the answer to these issues concerns the second resurrection of people of "the nations" i.e. non-Christians of whom some are given a favourable judgment at the time of the Great White Throne judgment so that they will not be thrown into the lake of fire.

So when Revelation 22:2 states that, "the leaves of the [life-giving] trees are for the healing of the nations" it seems to apply to these resurrected non-Christians who are given a favourable judgment and will experience "no more death" (vs 4); whereas when verse 15 notes that, "Outside are the dogs and the occultists and the sexually immoral and the murderers and the idolaters, and everyone who loves and practices deception!" the reference is being made to those given an unfavourable judgment when standing before the Great White Throne. These ones are later thrown into the lake of fire i.e. they are destroyed.

Comment on the Everlasting Kingdom

21:1: "**Then I saw a new** (Gk *kaine*) **heavens and a new earth. The first heavens and the first earth had passed away. And there was no longer any sea.**" The Greek word *kaine* means new in quality or fresh, rather than new in time (Gk *neos*).

This "new heavens and a new earth" is a further stage in God's plan for humankind i.e. the next phase after the Millennium. In fact, the term "new heavens and a new earth" refers to human society, and this definition can be seen from the description of the world in Noah's day i.e. the wicked society of people who were destroyed, but it did not apply to planet Earth (2 Pet. 3:6-13). So the first heavens and earth of today will pass away because society will be purged of its wicked followers and worshippers of Antichrist and his false prophet. Also Satan will be locked away at that time, as stated in 20:2-3. However, the result of this renewed society does also mean that the literal planet Earth is to be fully renovated during this first phase of God's Kingdom, rather than being an entirely new planet. Then after the Millennium a further new heavens begins at which point Satan is finally destroyed in the lake of fire.

Throughout the entire Bible God's purpose has always been for human life to be on the earth, rather than in heaven because there is no destiny for humans to be in heaven (Please see my book *Delusions and Truths Concerning the Future Life*). In fact, this "heaven-bound' concept is simply a pagan concept originating in ancient Egypt and then idealized by the Greek philosopher Plato whose possible sojourn in Egypt for thirteen years and tutorage by an Egyptian Horite priest led him to the false idea of an immortal soul which separates from the body at death.

The phrase "no longer any sea" does not literally mean that there will be no physical sea. In ancient times the term "sea" was seen as the realm of darkness, primeval chaos, and treachery and was often applied to people because, "the wicked are like the storm-tossed sea, for it cannot be still, and its waters churn up mire and muck" (Isa. 57:20). So here, in 21:1b we have a statement showing that there will never again be any wicked people in control of earth's affairs.

21:2: "**And I saw the holy city, the New Jerusalem, descending out of the sky from God, prepared like a bride adorned for her husband.**" This is the old literal Jerusalem made new i.e. renewed and therefore concerns the future city of Jerusalem with particular focus on its people. Its beauty is shown in the phrase "prepared like a bride." In fact, the use of a simile here of "like a bride" later becomes a metaphor in 21:9 and so with no change in meaning i.e. it still describes the city. However, because the word "city" can simply mean all inhabitants or citizens of a place, the New Jerusalem refers to all of God's people, both human and angelic. Furthermore, God and Jesus are also shown to be there. It is "the City of Truth" (Zech. 8:3) and is the same as the "heavenly Jerusalem" described in the letter to the Hebrews, where the writer states that Christians right now:

- ❖ "...have approached Mount Zion and the city of the living God, the heavenly Jerusalem. You have come to innumerable angels in festal gathering; and to the community of the firstborn ones who are registered in heaven. You have come to God, the judge of all, and to the spiritual lives of the rightly approved people who have been brought to completeness, and to Jesus, the mediator."

(Heb. 12:22-24).

The "New Jerusalem" is also described as the Lamb's wife coming down out of heaven and so is figurative of God's provision of the everlasting government and as having the glory of God. Indeed, all of this shows that the New Jerusalem comes from God—it does not literally descend from heaven, but comes in the same way Jesus first came from

God (Please see my book *God, Jesus, and the Holy Spirit*). However, the literal Jerusalem will be the capital of God's kingdom.

21:3: "And I heard a loud voice from the throne saying, "See! God's place of residence is in the midst of mankind. He will live among them, and they will be His people, and God Himself will be with them." This unidentified voice proclaims things about God, so it cannot be God's voice. However, because it comes from the throne, it is most likely the voice of Jesus.

The original place of God's residence metaphorically was the tabernacle set up in the desert area of Sinai in Arabia (Gal.4:25) and made according to God's set plan and dimensions. This was later replaced by the temple built by Solomon as the place of God's glory. Now, at this point in 21:3 in the future of salvation history, God Himself is shown to live with His people. This reflects the same promise made to Israel in Leviticus 26:11:12 and which was repeated often (Jer. 321:3; Ezek 37:27; Zech 2:11).

21:4: "He will wipe away every tear from their eyes. There will be no more death; neither will there be mourning nor crying nor pain, because the first order of things has passed away." This is verbatim the same as in 7:17 and alludes to Isaiah 25:8.

At this point in time after the Great White Throne judgment there will be no further tragedies and nothing that could cause any sorrow for God's people because even the Millennial transitional Kingdom will be gone. Indeed, in the future full manifestation of the Kingdom only true worshippers of God will exist and so everyone will live forever with no more mourning, crying, or pain.

21:5: "The One sitting on the throne said, "See! I am making everything new (Gk *kainos)!"* Then he said to me, "Write, because this message is trustworthy and true." As in verse one this is a qualitative newness and does not mean that there will be a new planet with new features. Instead it will be a renovation i.e. a "new heavens and earth" which means a new society and a new order or arrangement of things. Indeed, for that future time Romans 8:21 promises that, "even creation itself will be freed from slavery to decay, so that it will share the glorious freedom of God's children." This condition will exist only in the everlasting Kingdom.

21:6: "Then he said to me, "It is finished! I am the Alpha and the Omega, the beginning and the end. To anyone who is thirsty I will freely give

water from the spring of the life-giving water." The phrase "it is finished" is actually in the plural as if saying "they are done" and referring to all the things that John was told.

As shown earlier the title *"Alpha and Omega"* is based on the first and last letters of the Greek alphabet. They appear only in Revelation 1:8, here in 21:6, and in 22:13. In 1:8 this title clearly applies to *"the LORD God...the Almighty"* and not to Jesus. In 21:6 it clearly applies to *"He who sits on the throne"* (verse 5), namely God Himself and not to the Lamb. (Please see notes on the application of the phrase in 22:13). In fact, to the Jews the phrase *"Alpha and Omega"* simply meant "the whole extent of a thing i.e. in its entirety—a totality," or that which contains everything else. In the context of the statements in Revelation it gives complete assurance that God is "all in all" and that he has the ultimate and total power and control to bring about His complete purpose for our planet.

It is God who is the ultimate source of life-giving water although provided through Jesus according to John 7:37-38. Here thirst refers to one's thirst for spiritual things, including thirsting after God (Ps. 63:1). Only He, through Jesus, can satisfy these things. This is also an invitation to all those who are not yet Christians to drink freely of all God's provisions and so to finally gain immortality.

21:7: "**Those who conquer will inherit these things. I will be their God and they will be my children**." For those who prove their allegiance to God and Messiah Jesus in the face of all difficulties and persecution at any time, especially during the great tribulation, they have this wonderful promise of always being in God's family in a truly loving relationship. This includes inheriting all the promises given to the seven Christian communities described in Revelation 2 and 3 to "grant for them to eat of the tree of the perfect life, which is in the paradise of God;'" that they "will never be harmed by the second death.'" Indeed, Jesus "will give [them] some of the hidden manna...and "give them a white stone with a new name written on it." They will be "given authority over the nations, to rule them with an iron sceptre." Furthermore, Jesus "will give them the morning star" and they will be "clothed in white clothing." He will also, "never erase their name from the scroll of life" because he "will confess their name in the presence of [his] Father and of His angels" and will "make them...a pillar in the sanctuary of [his] God, and they won't go out of it anymore. He "will write on them the name of [his] God and the name of the city of [his] God, the New Jerusalem, which comes down out of heaven from [his] God, and [his] new name." Finally Jesus "will give permission for them to sit with [him] on [his] throne."

The words of Revelation 21:7 and 8 present a challenge to the readers of Revelation for each one to be a conqueror rather than a coward. Those who conquer by the blood of the lamb will be those who are thirsty for God and drink freely of life's water.

21:8: "But as for the cowards and the faithless, the sexual perverts and the murderers, the peddlers of immoral sex and occultists, the idolaters and every sort of deceiver—their destiny will be the lake that burns with fire and sulphur, which means the second death." This vice list speaks of categories of sinners from the second resurrection who specialize in certain vices and who refuse to repent and so are given a judgment of condemnation. So this verse repeats what was said in 20:15 as the destiny of their destruction in the lake of fire.

Once again we see that "the lake of fire" is not literal, but is a symbol for "the second death." This is the death that is permanent and is not a place for immortal individuals literally burning forever. In fact, immortality is reserved only for those who love and obey God.

§

Chapter 51

The Sanctuary-City of New Jerusalem
Revelation 21:9-27 ... The beginning of Vision Four

TEXT

⁹Then one of the seven angels who had held the seven bowls full of the seven final plagues came and spoke with me, saying, "Come, I will show you the bride, the Lamb's wife!" ¹⁰So he carried me away in a prophetic trance to a very high mountain, and he showed me the holy city, Jerusalem, descending out of the sky from God. ¹¹It is arrayed with God's glory; its radiance is like a precious jewel—like a jasper stone, clear as crystal. ¹²It has a broad and high wall with twelve gates, with twelve angels at the gates, and the names of the twelve tribes of the children of Israel are inscribed on the gates. ¹³There are three gates on the east, three gates on the north, three gates on the south, and three gates on the west. ¹⁴The city wall has twelve foundation stones, and on them are the twelve names of the twelve apostles of the Lamb.

¹⁵The one who was speaking with me had a gold measuring rod to measure the city, its gates, and its walls. ¹⁶Now the city is laid out as a square, its length the same as its width. He measured the city with the measuring rod: it is 12,000 stadia. The length, width, and height of the city are equal. ¹⁷He also measured its wall: it is 144 cubits according to human measurement, (which was what the angel used). ¹⁸The wall was constructed of jasper, and the city was pure gold, like transparent glass. ¹⁹The foundations of the city's wall are adorned with every kind of precious stone. The first foundation is jasper, the second sapphire, the third chalcedony, the fourth emerald, ²⁰the fifth onyx, the sixth carnelian, the seventh chrysolite, the eighth beryl, the ninth topaz, the tenth chrysoprase, the eleventh jacinth, and the twelfth amethyst. ²¹The twelve gates are twelve pearls; each one of the gates was made from a single pearl. The broad avenue of the city was pure gold, like transparent glass.

²²I didn't see a sanctuary in it, because the LORD God—the All-Powerful—and the Lamb are its sanctuary. ²³The city doesn't need the sun or the moon to shine on it, because God's glory illuminates it, and its lamp is the Lamb. ²⁴The nations will walk around by its light, and the kings of the earth will bring their glory into it. ²⁵On no day will its gates be closed at any time, since there will be no night there. ²⁶They will bring the glory and wealth of the nations into it. ²⁷But nothing ritually impure that is, anyone who does perverted things or deceives with lies will ever enter into it. Only those whose names are written in the Lamb's scroll of life will enter the city.

Overview

This is the fourth and last of John's visions which have been set out as: FIRST VISION 1:9 to 3:22; SECOND VISION 4:2 to 16:17; THIRD VISION 17:1 to 21:8.

243

So this FOURTH VISION 21:9 to 22:9 continues the description of the future life and gives a wonderful description of the New Jerusalem as a real city, but in terms of its people and so pictures the corporate community of God's people. It is built with the most beautiful of gem stones to show how glorious and precious "the Lamb's wife" is in God's eyes and to radiate His glory as well as the future glory of God's people. Furthermore, this passage highlights the holiness of this temple-city and those in it.

This description is modelled in part after the temple description of Ezekiel 40-48 and so showing that this is a sanctuary-city—even entirely the most holy room where God figuratively resides.

Comment on the New Jerusalem

21:9: "**Then one of the seven angels who had held the seven bowls full of seven final plagues came and spoke with me, saying, "Come, I will show you the bride, the Lamb's wife!"** The angel here is, no doubt, one of the archangels. This symbol of "the Lamb's wife" shows the close and intimate relationship the body of Christ has with Jesus, but the term "bride" indicates the newness of the marriage. It is reminiscent of Israel being treated by God as His wife.

21:10-11: "**So he carried me away in a prophetic trance to a very high mountain, and he showed me the holy city, Jerusalem, descending out of the sky from God. ¹¹It is arrayed with God's glory; its radiance is like a precious jewel—like a jasper stone, clear as crystal.**" As a contrast to Satan's taking of Jesus to a high mountain and showing him all the world's kingdoms, John is shown from a similar vantage point the real Kingdom for ruling the earth.

In "descending out of the sky from God" this city is shown to originate with God and does not literally descend through earth's atmosphere. This parallels John's earlier descriptions of Jesus' "descending from God" (John 3:13; 3:31; 6:33-58; 8:23; and 16:28) as meaning that he originates from God. Indeed, theologian Bruce Metzger in his book *Breaking the Code* (pp. 100, 101) states that: "The expression involves more than a spatial metaphor: the city comes from God...The description is architecturally preposterous, and must not be taken with flat-footed literalism."

The beauty of this literal city and its inhabitants is symbolically described so that it reflects God's glory and the glory of Jesus, along with all those who belong to him. A further contrast is the New Jerusalem as the capital city of the new world as compared with the earlier Babylon the great with all its disgusting aspects.

21:12-13: "**It has a broad and high wall with twelve gates, with twelve angels at the gates, and the names of the twelve tribes of the children of Israel are inscribed on the gates. There are three gates on the east, three gates on the north, three gates on the south, and three gates on the west.**" These features are taken directly from Ezekiel 48:31ff. Such walls, gates, and foundations indicate the total security this city has along with the angels who act as watchmen (Isa. 62:6). But why would it be necessary to have angels posted at these gates? Clearly, even after the Millennium there will be those of the second resurrection who have been condemned for their vices and who are unrepentant. These ones are not worthy of access to the city and so must be kept out of it until they are destroyed in the lake of fire. This picture also shows that if anyone wishes to be in the sanctuary-city they must be "conquerors" (22:8). Nevertheless, the prime focus here is on the fact that all who are in the sanctuary-city will feel totally secure.

21:14: "**The city wall has twelve foundation stones, and on them are the twelve names of the twelve apostles of the Lamb**." These features of the city also indicate the organizational completeness of Messiah's government, namely twelve gates having the twelve names of the twelve tribes of Israel i.e. spiritual Israel inscribed on them. These twelve tribes are not the Jewish people per se, but are the restored Israel, namely those who are redeemed by the Lamb's blood as Christians.

In having the twelve names of the apostles—the twelve foundation stones (Eph. 2:20)—it is further shown that the Kingdom government is built on the foundation of the Truth as taught by the apostles. By the use of the number twelve there is a further indicator that the 144,000 described in Revelation chapters 7 and 14 is a symbolic number for the people of God i.e. multi-national Christians.

The picture of the gates means that entrance into the New Jerusalem comes through "the twelve tribes of the children of Israel" i.e. God's people founded upon the twelve apostles.

21:15: "**The one who was speaking with me had a gold measuring rod to measure the city, its gates, and its walls**." This speaker is one of the seven angels who had poured out the bowls of God's wrath (see verse 9).

245

Similar to the measuring rod used by John in Revelation 11:1 this rod used by the angel would be about 10 feet 4 inches long (Ezek. 40:3-5). This act of measuring is a prophetic action to determine the boundaries of such a structure and its appropriation (Ezekiel 40-42) and to show the magnitude of the city. However, such measuring is not literal, but is metaphorical in symbolizing God's ownership and protection of His people.

The fact that the measuring rod is gold is appropriate for measuring a city of gold—a royal city that originates with God. So for any long-time neglected sanctuary structure the measuring or surveying of it implies that it is about to be inhabited once again.

21:16: "**Now the city is laid out as a square, its length the same as its width. He measured the city with the measuring rod: it is 12,000 stadia. The length, width, and height of the city are equal.**" This is the Most Holy place as the corporate community of God's people. The allusion here is to Zechariah 2:2 where a man (an angel vs. 3) replies to Zechariah that he will "measure Jerusalem to see how wide it is and how long it is." However, this foursquare or cubical structure is reminiscent of the most holy compartment of God's sanctuary (20 cubits square) and so this city also has an ideal or perfect symmetry as well as showing the vastness of the city. In fact, 12,000 stadia was the length, in John's day, of the Roman Empire from Spain to the Euphrates River and so indicating that this city is large enough to accommodate all of God's people.

A Greek *stadion* (stadium) was not an exactly fixed measurement, but varied between 607 and 631 feet (190 to 210 metres). So this dimension of 12,000 stadia is equal to between 1,416 and 1,566 miles and must be a symbolic or hyperbolic measurement and so showing the city's greatness and impregnability. If the measurements were literal then such a structure would go right into outer space with the possibility of affecting the balance of the earth.

Also please note that the numbers twelve and one thousand are often used in Revelation and elsewhere as symbolic numbers and so further indicating that these are symbolic measurements of the glorious future Jerusalem. So these measurements further indicate the organizational completeness of Messiah's government.

21:17: "**He also measured its wall: it is 144 cubits according to human measurement, (which was what the angel used).**" 144 cubits is about 200 feet and is most probably the thickness of this wall and not its height.

This is because in its counterpart temple Ezekiel's man measured only the thickness of the wall (Ezek. 41:5, 9, 12). If this measurement concerned the wall's height it would appear ridiculously small compared to the rest of the gigantic structure. Once again this is a symbolic measurement in harmony with the other dimensions. Also a twelve by twelve measurement strongly hints that this city is being described symbolically as the people of God inhabiting Jerusalem.

21:18: "**The wall was constructed of jasper, and the city was pure gold, like transparent glass.**" This verse echoes God's statement in Isaiah 54:11-12 that God would rebuild Jerusalem of such semi-precious stones, but which refers to the restoration and transformation of "the daughter of Zion."

The description of the wall as constructed of jasper is because this jewel was used as a symbol for God in 4.3. This wall is not simply inlaid with jasper, but is actually made of it as one of the most brilliant of jewels. Similarly, the city and "the broad avenue" are not merely inlaid with gold, as was Solomon's sanctuary, but actually made of solid gold which is unlike any earthly gold because it is also transparent so that God's glory shines through it.

21:19-20: "**The foundations of the city's wall are adorned with every kind of precious stone. The first foundation is jasper, the second sapphire, the third chalcedony, the fourth emerald, [20]the fifth onyx, the sixth carnelian, the seventh chrysolite, the eighth beryl, the ninth topaz, the tenth chrysoprase, the eleventh jacinth, and the twelfth amethyst.**" Here the unusual term "adorned" is reminiscent of Isaiah's words in 61:10 which describe the returning Jewish exiles as a bride adorned with jewels.

These twelve foundation stones show that the twelve apostles are the foundation of God's people because they have taught *the truth*. Also, although these are different stones to those in the breastplate of judgment of the high priest of Israel (Ex. 28:16-20; 39:9-13), the arrangement here has that in mind to show the priestly nature of the community of God's people.

Indeed, this is a further description showing the beauty of the city as radiating the glory of God, the Lamb, and God's people.

21:21: "**The twelve gates are twelve pearls; each one of the gates was made from a single pearl. The broad avenue of the city was pure gold, like transparent glass.**" The idea of twelve gates is taken from Ezekiel 48:30-

35 and shows the plentiful access for those of the second resurrection who have been given a favourable judgment. They are shown as having been healed and then granted access to join with those of God's people who were already granted immortality at the beginning of the Millennium.

In being the most valuable of all jewels in the ancient world, pearls were precious beyond price (Matt. 13:45-46). So in total this temple-city, as symbolizing God's people, shows them to be precious beyond compare.

21:22: "**I didn't see a sanctuary in it, because the LORD God—the All-Powerful—and the Lamb are its sanctuary.**" Evidently, John expected to see a sanctuary building in the city and was surprised that there wasn't one. In fact, although Ezekiel's building is described in terms of a temple sanctuary where God resides (Ezek. 48:35) it is really a description of this future sanctuary-city in Revelation which is described in terms of the most holy compartment. Here, the focus is on the sacrifice which God made of His Son and has nothing to do with animal sacrifices. Therefore, God and the Lamb are the sanctuary (Gk *naos*) and are shown to be in their greatest unity. In fact, Jesus was shown to be this sanctuary by his words in John's gospel when he said, "Destroy this sanctuary and in three days I will raise it up" *(John 2:19).* Therefore no physical temple is needed just as Jeremiah prophesied:

❖ And it will be when you have multiplied and become fruitful in the land in those days," declares Yahweh, "they will no longer say, 'The ark of the covenant of Yahweh.' And it will not come to mind, nor will they remember it, nor will they miss it, nor will it be made again. At that time they will call Jerusalem 'The Throne of Yahweh,' and all the nations will be gathered to it, to the name of Yahweh, to Jerusalem, and they will no longer go after the stubbornness of their evil heart" (Jer. 3:16-17).

21:23: "**The city doesn't need the sun or the moon to shine on it, because God's glory illuminates it and its lamp is the Lamb.**" This situation was prophesied by Isaiah in saying, "The sun shall no longer be your light by day, and for bright light the moon shall not give you light, but Yahweh will be your everlasting light, and your God your glory" (Isa. 60:19). Indeed, the New Jerusalem is really more than simply a place—it is a community of God's people; and is filled with enlightened people who have the truth concerning all things because of the light of truth that comes from God and the Lamb. This thought is restated in 22:5.

The phrase, "its lamp is the Lamb" is a possible allusion to Psalm 132:17 where Yahweh says, "I have prepared a lamp for my anointed one," in which "Lamb" has been substituted for "anointed one" i.e. the lamp of the Messiah.

21:24: **"The nations will walk around by its light, and the kings of the earth will bring their glory into it."** The nations are all those who are deemed worthy of life after the Great White Throne judgment. In fact, the phrase "the kings of the earth," occurs eight times in Revelation and they are now seen here as not hostile toward God in contrast to previous references to them (except in 1:5). So these are clearly the nations and some of the kings of the earth who had repented at the Great White Throne judgment and then became united with God's people.

The term "light" is used in the Hebrew Scriptures as a metaphor for "the law of Yahweh" or "Torah" (Ps 119:105; Prov. 6:23).

21:25: **"On no day will its gates be closed at any time, since there will be no night there."** In his commentary on Revelation Grant Osborne points out that this is probably idiomatic for "the gates will never be shut day by day" because gates are never normally shut during the day. So this means that the gates are permanently open. Also "no night there" is a reference to the fact that the darkness of sin and its effects have now gone forever for those in the city.

21:26: **"They will bring the glory and wealth of the nations into it."** "They" refers to the previously mentioned "kings of the earth." So by bringing their glory and wealth to God they are shown to now worship Him.

21:27a: **"But nothing ritually impure, that is, anyone who does perverted things, or deceives with lies will ever enter into it. Only those whose names are written in the Lamb's scroll of life will enter the city."** Entering the city is a metaphor for salvation as well as for entering into the Kingdom to live on a renewed earth. This statement certainly highlights the moral purity and sacredness of all who inhabit God's Kingdom and that the repentant "nations" and the repentant "kings of the earth" (vs. 24) are also now becoming morally pure. It is impossible that anything i.e. anyone impure could enter the city because God Himself is there.

This is the last mention of the scroll of life in the Book of Revelation. However, back in 20:15 the noting of it there concerns the results of the White Throne judgment some short time after the Millennium is completed. It is at this point that the scroll of life will contain all who are now God's people and follow the Lamb, having fully gained salvation.

§

Chapter 52

Life in the Post-Millennial Kingdom
Revelation 22:1-5

TEXT

Then he showed me a river of life-giving water, sparkling like crystal, flowing out from the throne of God and of the Lamb ²and down the middle of the city's broad avenue. On each bank of the river are life-giving trees, producing twelve kinds of fruit, yielding their crops of fruit—one each month. The leaves of the trees are for the healing of the nations. ³No longer will there be any "curse of war." The throne of God and the Lamb will be in the city. His servants will devotedly serve Him, ⁴and they will see His face and His name will be on their foreheads. ⁵There will be no more night, and they will not need lamplight or sunlight, because the LORD God will shine light on them. And they will reign forever and ever.

TRANSLATION POINTS

22:2: As shown by Aune, Osborne, Lohmeyer et al, the rendering in the plural of "trees" is because it is a collective singular and so is properly a reference to trees which line each bank of the river, rather than a single tree.

22:3: As Aune shows, the phrase "curse of war" (Gk *katathema*) is the more accurate rendering, rather than the phrase "accursed thing" or "accursed person." This is because the meaning of the Greek term is shaped by the allusion to Zechariah 14:11 with its reference to the things and people to be "devoted to destruction" as a result of holy war. It, therefore, does not refer to general curses, but to the "curse of war."

Overview

After the beautiful description of the New Jerusalem as the future capital of God's Kingdom, this section of Revelation describes what life will be like for the immortal Christians, as well as for the favourably judged mortal population after the second resurrection as worthy to live in the post-Millennial Kingdom. Much of John's description here is similar to Ezekiel's description of the future temple in Ezekiel 47:1-12 with its river which rapidly increases in depth and volume.

Comment on Life in the Post-Millennial Kingdom

22:1-2a: "**Then he showed me a river of life-giving water, sparkling like crystal, flowing out from the throne of God and of the Lamb and down**

251

the middle of the city's broad avenue." This speaker is still one of the seven angels who poured out the bowls of God's retribution (see verses 9 and 15).

The "New Jerusalem" incorporates various features of the Garden of Eden, including its river. Indeed, God is the source of this river with its "life-giving water," which shows that he is the true source of perfect life as given through Messiah Jesus. The river symbolizes the wonderful spiritual life of God's people who have been totally cleansed of all sin.

22:2b: "On each bank of the river are life-giving trees, producing twelve kinds of fruit, yielding their crops of fruit—one each month. The leaves of the trees are for the healing (Gk *therapeia*) **of the nations."** After speaking of the "life-giving waters" John is now presented with a second metaphor concerning immortality, namely, "life-giving trees." The "healing" here is not simply healing of any illnesses suffered by these righteous mortals who have experienced the second resurrection, but because the leaves are from the "life-giving trees" this healing will actually grant them everlasting life—immortality.

After the Great White Throne judgment and therefore after the Millennium there will be those of the second resurrection who are not "thrown into the lake of fire" (20:15). So it is at this point that such ones from "the nations" will be healed and this appears to be a process which goes on for some time in the ultimate Kingdom. Certainly such healing leaves are not needed by those who have already been made immortal at the beginning of the Millennium.

Because God's cleansing spirit works through Jesus and his bride, these "life-giving trees" may picture the glorified Christians who each act as an immortality-giving tree because they have already saturated themselves with the water of life.

22:3-4: "No longer will there be any "curse of war." The throne of God and the Lamb will be in the city. His servants will devotedly serve Him, ⁴and they will see His face and His name will be on their foreheads." As shown regarding the translation here the world will now be free from the "curse of war" because God's Kingdom rule is fully established (Isa. 2:4).

The throne here symbolizes the sovereign rule of God as judge of the world and protector of His people. This applies also to the Lamb as God's appointed King of Earth. The phrase "seeing His face" is a term used for a true understanding of who God is and therefore having a right relationship with Him (Job.33:26) in a greater way than ever before. It is also a term for being granted an audience with Him in direct and personal conversation (Gen. 43:3, 5; Ex. 10:28, 29), so that there is enjoyment of a relationship of absolute trust and openness with Him and with Jesus (1 Cor. 13:12; 1 John 3:2). Indeed, the preciousness of this relationship is seen in the statement that, "His name will be on their foreheads." This was promised back in 3:12 and so showing God's ownership of them and His complete protection of them.

22:5: **"There will be no more night, and they will not need lamplight or sunlight, because the LORD God will shine light on them. And they will reign forever and ever."** "No more night" is a repeat of what was said in 21:25 and is a fitting metaphor for salvation because all people are now God's people and are completely free from the effects of sin and never again to be in spiritual darkness. In every way they have the light of truth from the LORD God (Isa. 60:19). So the phrase "no more night" is not to be taken in a literalistic way as if there will never again be a literal night-time.

God's holy people will reign with Jesus as promised in 3:21 with authority over the nations (2:26-27) for the one thousand year period (20:4). However, this promise is here extended into the everlasting Kingdom of perfection so that they will "reign forever and ever."

Chapter 53

Keep Ready Because the Time Is Near
Revelation 22:6-21

TEXT

6"These words," he said to me, "are trustworthy and true. The LORD, the God of the spirits of the prophets, has sent His angel to show His bond-servants what must speedily take place."

7"Pay attention: I am coming quickly! Blessed is the one who obeys the prophetic message in this scroll."

8I, John, am the one who heard and saw these things. And when I heard and saw them, I knelt in worship at the feet of the angel who was showing me these things. **9**But he said to me, "Be careful! Don't do that! I am a fellow servant with you and your brothers and sisters the prophets as those who are obeying the words of this scroll. Kneel in worship before God!"

10"Don't seal up the words of the prophecy contained in this scroll," he said to me "because the time is near. **11**Let those who are unjust continue to be unjust, and the morally depraved continue to be depraved. Let those who follow God's ways continue to follow God's ways, and let those who are holy continue to be holy."

12"Pay attention: I am coming quickly, and my reward is with me, to repay everyone as their activities deserve. **13**I am the Alpha and the Omega, the first and the last, the beginning and the end!

14 Blessed are those who wash their robes, so that they will have access to the tree of life and so that they may enter the city through its gates. **15**Outside are the dogs and the occultists and the sexually immoral and the murderers and the idolaters, and everyone who loves and practices deception!

16"I, Jesus, have sent my angel to testify to all of you about these things for the benefit of the communities of believers. I am the root-shoot, that is, the descendant of David, the bright morning star!"

17The spirit and the bride say, "Come!" And let anyone who hears say: "Come!" And let anyone who is thirsty come; let anyone who wishes take the water of life freely.

18I solemnly testify to everyone hearing the words of the prophecy in this scroll: if anyone adds to them, God will add to that person the plagues that are written in this scroll. **19**And if anyone takes away any part of the message of this scroll of prophecy, God will take away that person's share in the tree of life, and in the holy city, which are described in this scroll.

20The one testifying to these things says, "Yes, I am coming quickly!" Amen! Come, Lord Jesus!

21The gracious favour of the Lord Jesus be with all the holy ones. Amen.

TRANSLATION POINTS

22:7: "I am coming quickly!" Please see *1:1b:* on "speedily take place."

22:16: "I am the root-shoot (Gk *riza*), that is, the descendant of David" Although the word *riza* can mean "root" it also means "that which grows from a root" according to *Bauer's Greek-English Lexicon*, hence the rendering "root-shoot" here. According to David Aune in the *Word Biblical Commentary* this is a hendiadys giving a single thought and so is also epexegetical and therefore is not speaking of two separate facets of Jesus, but that "root-shoot" singularly means "descendent."

Overview

This passage is really the epilogue to the whole of the Book of Revelation. Although some would place the beginning of the epilogue as verse 10, there are strong reasons to understand it as beginning with verse 6.

The purpose of this epilogue is to affirm the authority that is behind this work, namely God, but given through Jesus. It also includes a number of exhortations with emphasis on the sovereignty of God, the return of Messiah Jesus, the necessity for unbelievers to follow Jesus, and for believers to persevere and to strengthen their relationship with God and with Jesus.

Comment on the Time as Being Near

22:6: ""These words," he said to me, "are trustworthy and true. The LORD, the God of the spirits of the prophets, has sent His angel to show His bond-servants what must speedily take place."" This speaker is still the same 'bowl-pouring' angel as from Revelation 21:9 and 15 onward. He is showing that we can have complete confidence in all of these divine visions in the Revelation, so that it guarantees the truth of all that has been written here.

The angel that has been sent to reveal all these things is most likely the interpreting angel of 1:1 who received the message from Jesus who had first received it from God Himself. So clearly, the moment it is God's appointed time to make all these things happen it will be concluded decisively and in a short time i.e. speedily.

The phrase "the spirits of the prophets" is the same as is said by Paul in 1 Corinthians 14:32 and refers to the natural mental faculties and motivations of the Prophets whose utterances are controlled by God.

255

22:7: "Pay attention: I am coming quickly! Blessed is the one who obeys the prophetic message in this scroll." These may be God's or Jesus' words as "coming quickly." If they are God's words then the way He will be "coming quickly" will be through His Son, Jesus, at the *parousia* whereby at that arrival everything will move ahead quickly.

Certainly, it is imperative that Christians "obey" what is stated in the Revelation. This means works of faith (Jas. 2:18, 20). Nevertheless, those who promote the "once saved always saved" doctrine say that all one needs is faith and therefore, no "works" are required. However, Revelation 22:7 shows that obedience to this message is required (Please see my book *How God Works in Human Affairs* for the many biblical reasons that the "once saved always saved" doctrine is false to the Bible).

22:8: "I, John, am the one who heard and saw these things. And when I heard and saw them, I knelt in worship (Gk *proskyneo*) at the feet of the angel who was showing me these things." When John says that he "heard and saw" he is referring to the two prime ways that he has received his visions as a confirmation of the veracity of the Revelation. Sadly this produces his reaction of worshipping the angel. Indeed, this is the second time John has done this, the first time being in Revelation 19:10. Wrongly, John has been drawn into the common angel worship which was prevalent in his day and he makes this mistake twice. This false worship was condemned by the Apostle Paul in Colossians 2:18.

22:9: "But he said to me, "Be careful! Don't do that! I am a fellow servant with you and your brothers and sisters the prophets as those who are obeying the words of this scroll. Kneel in worship (Gk *proskyneo*) before God!" Evidently, John's brothers and sisters are the prophets; and yet there are not two groups here, but only the Christians who are obedient to this message. This is shown logically and by a variant text which omits the Greek word *kai* meaning "and" or "even."

The Greek word *proskyneo* varies in strength of meaning according to the circumstances of who it applies to. So when individuals approach Jesus in seeing him as "teacher" they simply kneel "in honour" of him i.e. respectfully. But when they recognize him as the Messiah they kneel before him "in profound reverence." However, when the word is used of God it is a reference to "worship" of Him.

22:10: "Don't seal up the words of the prophecy contained in this scroll," he said to me "because the time is near (Gk *eggus*)." These are likely to

256

be the words of the interpreting angel. Indeed, for the command in the previous verse to be carried out by those "obeying the words of this scroll" it must remain unsealed.

The phrase "the time is near," which has the thought of "imminence," is the common Jewish way to keep God's people focused and alert. It was also used by God's prophets in ancient times to bring God's promises to the fore of their minds e.g. "...for the day of Yahweh is coming—**it is indeed near**. [2] A day of darkness and gloom..." *(Joel 2:1b, 2 LEB)*. Yet most of these types of prophecies were not going to be fulfilled until long after their pronouncement, and in some cases hundreds of years after they were written. For the prophets the future was always viewed as imminent—they blended the near and distant perspectives so that their readers would take their message very seriously. Here, John does the same and so gives the reader a sense of tangibility. Unfortunately, Preterists sometimes misuse this phrase to say that all prophecy was fulfilled in the 70 C.E. destruction of Jerusalem. However, this is to misunderstand the angel's meaning.

22:11 "Let those who are unjust continue to be unjust, and the morally depraved continue to be depraved. Let those who follow God's ways continue to follow God's ways, and let those who are holy continue to be holy." This verse alludes to Daniel 12:9-10 and seems to be a rhetorical command to both the rebellious/apostate Christians and the righteous Christians to consider their behaviour because "the time is near." So when that time comes swiftly, there will be no time for any further change of mind and actions.

22:12: "Pay attention: I am coming quickly, and my reward is with me, to repay everyone as their activities deserve. Jesus' earlier warning that, "the Son of Man is going to come...then he will reward each person according to what they have done" (Matt. 16:27) and also the warning in Rev. 2:23 are both based on the last thought in Proverbs 24:12 which gives the warning of, "won't he pay back people for what they do."

22:13: "I am the Alpha and the Omega, the first and the last, the beginning and the end!" The similar title of *"the first and the last"* in Isaiah 44:6 and 48:12 is applied to Yahweh. The title *"Alpha and Omega"* uses the first and last letters of the Greek alphabet and appears only in Revelation 1:8, 21:6 and 22:13. In 1:8 it clearly applies to *"the LORD God...the Almighty"* and not to Jesus in that verse. Additionally, in 21:6 it clearly applies to *"He who sits on the throne,"* i.e. God (verse 5) and so not to the Lamb.

Along with the phrase *"the first and the last"* the Jews understood this term simply to mean "the whole extent of a thing i.e. in its entirety—a totality," or that which contains everything else. In the context of the statements in Revelation it gives complete assurance that God is "all in all" and that He has the total power and control to bring about His complete purpose for the world.

However, at first glance the phrase, *"I am the Alpha and the Omega"* in 22:13 appears to be the words of Jesus because of the earlier phrase "I am coming quickly" (22:7, 12) and so this is presented as such in the many red-letter Bibles. Nevertheless, there are two possible answers to this issue:

1. The phrase does apply to Jesus because divine titles have been conferred upon him. He is indeed "the first and the last" because he is "the one who pioneered the faith and brought it to completion." (Heb.12:2). This is similar to the fact that Jesus has been granted God's title of "King of kings and Lord of lords" in Revelation 17:14. Nevertheless, no such titles ever mean that Jesus is the Lord God Almighty, but rather that he is "the Lord Messiah" as God's primary representative and is "the first and the last" who, in contrast to God, died (1:17). If this is the case then the phrase "I am coming quickly" refers to Jesus as going into action.

2. Because 22:6 says, "And *he* said to me..." with a reference to "God's angel" there is a connection back to one of the seven angels (21:9) as the speaker. There appears to be no change of speaker after 22:6 until Jesus begins to speak in 22:16. Therefore, all the words in 22:7, 12 and 13 may be those of God's <u>angel who evidently is speaking as His representative,</u> as if God Himself i.e. the Father were speaking. So then it appears to be the Father who is "the Alpha and Omega" in 22:13 just as also in Revelation 1:8 and 21:6. If this is the case then the phrase "I am coming quickly" refers to God going into action through Jesus.

Although this is difficult, I see the second explanation as rather weak and so I favour the first explanation and application.

22:14: "**Blessed are those who wash their robes, so that they will have access to the tree of life and so that they may enter the city through its gates.**" The ongoing washing of their robes is a metaphor for moral and spiritual cleansing and serves to show that those who do this will be victors (2:7). Clearly these ones from the second resurrection have done this after their judgment at the Great White Throne and thereby allowing them access to the life-giving trees, thereby gaining immortality.

22:15: "**Outside are the dogs and the occultists and the sexually immoral and the murderers and the idolaters, and everyone who loves and practices deception!**" "Outside" of the city parallels that of Jesus' dying "outside the camp" (Heb. 13:12-13) and means exclusion because of being treated as a blasphemer (Lev. 24:14, 23). So it shows that the ones described here have cut themselves off from God by their vices, having done so when standing before the Great White Throne. Later these ones are thrown into the lake of fire (20:15) and so do not exist in the future.

Once again we note that "the city" is a symbol for the future realization of the corporate community of God's people.

The term "dogs" is used differently under different circumstances. Sometimes it referred to Gentiles (Matt. 15:26), sometimes to the Judaizers (Phil. 3:2-3), and sometimes to male prostitutes (Deut. 23:18) —all depending on the context. So here it is most likely used in its broadest sense to encompass all of these unclean categories and can be summed up as referring to those who resist God's will and involve themselves in whatever is against His will.

22:16: "**I, Jesus, have sent my angel to testify to all of you about these things for the benefit of the communities of believers. I am the root-shoot, that is, the descendant of David, the bright morning star!**" The "you" here is plural and shows that the entire message of Revelation is sent to all the Christian communities including those of the future from the time of John's writing.

The term "my angel" is probably a collective singular referring to all the angelic messengers mentioned in the Revelation. Clearly Jesus has his own angels. However, this does not mean that he was an archangel prior to his conception in Mary's womb (Heb. 1:5, 13). Instead he is "the Son of man"—an immortal human being—and has now been granted his own body of angels.

Because the sentence "I am the root-shoot, that is, the descendant of David" is the figurative language of hendiadys, this focuses on Jesus' descent through the line of David and is absolutely not saying that David is a descendent of Jesus, but rather that Jesus is the prime descendent of David and therefore in the kingly line and that he is the Messiah.

In being called "the bright morning star" Jesus is shown to fulfil the description of Messiah in Numbers 24:17 of "a star shall come forth from Jacob." as the one who will destroy God's enemies.

22:17: "**The spirit and the bride say, 'Come!' And let anyone who hears say: 'Come!' And let anyone who is thirsty come; let anyone who wishes take the water of life freely.**" The spirit here is the spirit of God and of Jesus (Phil 1:19; Gal. 4:61; John 2:1). The bride is the body of his loyal followers, the Lamb's wife (21:9-10). The appeal to "come!" is primarily for all those readers who have not yet made a decision to follow Messiah Jesus. Indeed, contrary to Calvinist teachings everyone can make genuine choices in their lives and so here anyone can make a genuine choice to follow Jesus (John 1:17) and so showing that we are all responsible for our relationship with God and with Jesus.

In being thirsty for God one would be desirous of the water of life which is a wonderful free gift as also shown in 21:6 where Jesus says, "To anyone who is thirsty I will freely give water from the spring of the life-giving water." This admonition not only calls unbelievers to come to Messiah, but also calls wavering believers to a closer walk with him in their perseverance as noted in the failures of some of the believing communities in Revelation chapters 2 and 3. So the taking of the water of life results in everlasting life because one is now an immortal human.

22:18: "**I solemnly testify to everyone hearing the words of the prophecy in this scroll: if anyone adds to them, God will add to that person the plagues that are written in this scroll.**" The speaker here is Jesus as the prime recipient of the Revelation. Once again we see that it is an apocalyptic prophecy (see 1:3).

The admonition here and in verse 19 of not adding to or subtracting from this prophecy is based upon Deuteronomy 4:2. This does not mean that commentators won't interpret certain details differently from one another, but rather that no one should misuse the Revelation to restructure the Christian faith and so turning it into a different gospel as has been done by Gentile Christians of the second and third centuries onward (Gal. 1:8-9).

22:19: "And if anyone takes away any part of the message of this scroll of prophecy, God will take away that person's share in the tree of life, and in the holy city, which are described in this scroll." Similar to the "adding to" the scroll, so too, the removal of any part of the message brings God's severe displeasure because these actions are tantamount to apostasy. In fact, this warning is so severe that the punishment is the punishment of the plagues described here including the loss of one's future life by being thrown into the lake of fire—the second death.

22:20: "The one testifying to these things says, "Yes, I am coming quickly! Amen! Come, Lord Jesus!"" Although God is the ultimate source of this prophecy, it is Jesus who shows that it is true and that it concerns his second coming, which when it occurs will bring a part of God's purpose to completion quickly.

The request for Jesus to come soon is the natural response of all Christians and showing their strong desire for Jesus' soon return.

22:21: "The gracious favour of the Lord Jesus be with all the holy ones. Amen." This benediction is much the same as those used by the Apostle Paul and the writer to the Hebrews and therefore, indicates that the Revelation is in the form of a letter. It calls for the readers to obey its message, to follow the solutions offered here to their issues. Furthermore, it encourages them to continue in their faithfulness.

§

Appendix A

Why Various Main Views of the 144,000 Fail

These are the views noted in Chapter 14 under the heading: Different Views on Identifying the 144,000 (Rev. 7) on page 72.

View 1

This view presents a literal number of 144,000 of the entire age-long multi-ethnic Christian *"Israel of God"* (spiritual Israel) from the **first century** onward.

VIEW 1 FAILS BECAUSE OF THE DEFINITE FACTORS THAT:

- The 144,000 appear only in the end-time as above.

- The sealing of the 144,000 shows that they belong to God and concerns their protection during the pouring out of God's wrath, rather than their being sealed with holy spirit.

- The 144,000 are only part of *"the sons of Israel/the Israel of God,"* in contradiction of the view that the 144,000 are the entire spiritual Israel from the first century onward.

- All 144,000 positions would have been filled by the second century and so leaving no positions for Christians to be filled in the end-times. Even in the first and second centuries there were already 100's of thousands of Christians. B. Reike gives one of the conservative estimates that there were about 40,000 Christians in A.D.67, with a total of 320,000 at about the turn of the first century just after Revelation was written.

- There could not be literally only 144,000 Christians for all time, because the number will be greater than the numbers of national Israel which has always amounted to far more than 144,000: *"...for the children [Christians] of the desolate woman are more numerous than those [the Israelites] of her who has the husband" (Gal. 4:27).*

*THE STRONGLY CONNECTED FACTORS INDICATING THE **FAILURE** OF VIEW 1*

- The number 144,000 is symbolic to indicate completeness so that not one of the redeemed is missing. There is an inconsistency in this scheme by the mixing of a literal number with a symbolic "twelve tribes."

- If the *"great multitude"* were not the same as the 144,000 they would not be *"sealed,"* thereby leaving them unprotected during the time of

God's wrath. This would make no sense in view of the fact that Paul said that Christians would not be victims of God's wrath (2 Thess. 5:9, Rom. 5:9).

* The 144,000 have many of the same characteristics and experiences as the *"great multitude."* One strong connection is that they are both associated with the new song (5:9, 15:3) that only the 144,000 can sing (14:3). This seems to strongly indicate that the 144,000 and the *"great multitude"* are one and the same group.

* Because John hears the number but sees a *"great multitude which no one could count,"* as well as several other factors, it is logical to understand that the 144,000 and the *"great multitude"* are the same group of Christians, but from different perspectives, one military, and the other as priests.

* The presentation of the *"great multitude"* is as a body of priests serving in God's sanctuary. This is the Greek term *naos* showing that these ones serve in the holy compartment, and so they are not a secondary class of Christians.

♣

View 2

This view presents a symbolic number of 144,000 of the entire age-long multi-ethnic Christian *"Israel of God"* (spiritual Israel) from the **first century** onward.

VIEW 2 FAILS BECAUSE OF THE DEFINITE FACTORS THAT:

* The 144,000 appear only in the end-time. They appear on the scene just prior to the time of God's wrath and so do not picture all Christians from the first century onward.

* The sealing of the 144,000 shows that they belong to God and concerns their protection during the pouring out of God's wrath, rather than their being sealed with holy spirit.

* The 144,000 are only part of *"the sons of Israel/the Israel of God,"* in contradiction of the view that the 144,000 are the entire spiritual Israel from the first century onward.

♣

View 3

This view presents a literal number of 144,000 of an unconverted remnant of ethnic Israelites in the **end-time** who become Christians by the time of the situation described in Revelation 14.

VIEW 3 <u>FAILS</u> BECAUSE OF THE DEFINITE FACTOR THAT:

- They are already Christians because they are *"the servants of our God"* (7:3). So this cannot be a non-Christian group separate from Christians because only believers are *"the servants of our God."*

*THE STRONGLY CONNECTED FACTORS INDICATING THE **FAILURE** OF VIEW 3*

- *The sons of Israel"* (7:4) are, in New Testament terms, *"the Israel of God"*—Christians. Notwithstanding the statements in Romans 11, the New Testament emphasis is on *"spiritual Israel"* (Rom 2:28-29, 9:8; Phil 3:3; Gal. 3:29, 6:16) rather than on *"Israel according to the flesh"* (1 Cor.10:18).

- The irregular and peculiar listing of the tribes indicates that the 144,000 are of the multi-ethnic Christian *"Israel of God."*

- The number 144,000 is symbolic to indicate completeness so that not one of the redeemed is missing.

- The role of the 144,000 is as a Messianic i.e. Christian army organized in military marching order and led by Jesus— *"the lion of the tribe of Judah"* (5:5, 7:5), thereby excluding anyone unconverted.

- It would make no sense if the *"great multitude"* of Christians were left as not "sealed," thereby leaving them unprotected during the time of God's wrath, and yet unbelieving Jews were sealed during this time (2 Thess. 5:9, Rom. 5:9).

- The 144,000 have many of the same characteristics and experiences as the *"great multitude"* i.e. both are associated with the new song (5:9, 15:3) that only the 144,000 can sing (14:3). This seems to strongly indicate that the 144,000 and the *"great multitude"* are one and the same group, rather than unbelieving Jews.

- Because John hears the number, but sees a *"great multitude which no one could count."* As well as several other factors, it is logical to understand that the 144,000 and the *"great multitude"* are the same group of Christians, but from different perspectives, one military, and the other as priests.

♣

View 4

This view presents a literal number of 144,000 Jewish Christians who form the Messianic army of the Lion of Judah in the **end-time**. They have been separated out from among *"the great multitude"* of Christians.

264

VIEW 4 FAILS BECAUSE OF THE DEFINITE FACTORS THAT:

- The two descriptions of the 144,000 in Revelation 7 and 14 are evidently of the same group of people. So because they are *"redeemed from mankind"* i.e. multi-ethnic Christians in 14:4, then they are the same in Revelation 7, rather than Jewish Christians only.

- The 144,000 is a group that is taken from *"the sons of Israel"* and not from the *"great multitude."*

- The *"great multitude"* is comprised of Jewish as well as Gentile Christians and therefore not completely distinct from the 144,000 in terms of ethnicity.

THE STRONGLY CONNECTED FACTORS INDICATING THE FAILURE OF VIEW 4

- The irregular and peculiar listing of the tribes indicates that the 144,000 are of the <u>multi-ethnic</u> Christian *"Israel of God"* and not limited to Jewish Christians.

- The number 144,000 is symbolic to indicate completeness so that not one of the redeemed is missing.

- If the *"great multitude"* were not the same as the 144,000 they would not be *"sealed,"* and so unprotected during the time of God's wrath. It would make no sense that only Jewish Christians would be so protected in view of the fact that Paul said that Christians would not be victims of God's wrath (2 Thess. 5:9, Rom. 5:9).

- The 144,000 have many of the same characteristics and experiences as the *"great multitude."* One strong connection is that they are both associated with the new song (5:9, 15:3) that only the 144,000 can sing (14:3). This seems to strongly indicate that the 144,000 and the *"great multitude"* are one and the same group, rather than the 144,000 being only Jewish Christians.

- Because John hears the number but sees a *"great multitude which no one could count,"* as well as several other factors, it is logical to understand that the 144,000 and the *"great multitude"* are the same group of Christians, but from different perspectives, one military, and the other as priests. In their role as the 144,000 they are a Messianic army organized in military marching order and led by Jesus— *"the lion of the tribe of Judah"* (5:5, 7:5) and in their the role as the *"great multitude"* they are a body of Christian priests.

——— ❑ ———

Appendix B

Why the Variations on the View of 144,000 As Christians Fail

The following concern the three variations on view #5. All three of these views correctly present the 144,000 as a symbolic number of spiritual Israel i.e. Christians. These variations are described on pages 73 and 84-86. However, these variations fail for the following reasons:

View 6: These Christians are **selected from the** *"great multitude"* **for special work** and protected so that, in the end-time, they all survive the great tribulation.

VIEW 6 FAILS BECAUSE OF THE DEFINITE FACTOR THAT:

- The 144,000 is a group that is taken from *"the sons of Israel"* mentioned in 7:4 and not from the *"great multitude."*

THE STRONGLY CONNECTED FACTORS INDICATING THE FAILURE OF VIEW 6

- If the *"great multitude"* were not the same as the 144,000 they would not be *"sealed,"* thereby leaving them unprotected during the time of God's wrath. It makes no sense that 144,000 elite Christians would be protected as *"sealed"* against God's wrath while other Christians i.e. *"the great multitude"* are excluded from this specific protection, especially in view of the fact that Paul said that Christians would not be victims of God's wrath (2 Thess. 5:9, Rom. 5:9).

- The 144,000 have many of the same characteristics and experiences as the *"great multitude."* One strong connection is that they are both associated with the new song (5:9, 15:3) that only the 144,000 can sing (14:3). This seems to strongly indicate that the 144,000 and the *"great multitude"* are one and the same group.

- Because John hears the number but sees a *"great multitude which no one could count,"* as well as several other factors, it is logical to understand that the 144,000 and the *"great multitude"* are the same group of Christians, but from different perspectives, one military, and the other as priests.

♣

View 7: These Christians are **the true church selected from the professing church** (i.e. nominal and carnal) i.e. from the *"great multitude"* in the end-time.

266

VIEW 7 FAILS BECAUSE OF THE DEFINITE FACTORS THAT:

The 144,000 is a group that is taken from *"the sons of Israel"* and not from the proposed professed Christians pictured by the *"great multitude"*

* Biblically the *"great multitude"* is a body of true Christians as shown by their being dressed in white robes; whereas the professing (nominal and carnal) church would never be classified that way because as Jesus said: "On that day many will say to me, 'Lord, Lord, did we not prophesy in your name, and in your name cast out demons, and in your name do many mighty works?' And then will I declare to them, 'I never knew you; go away from me, you who practice lawlessness.'" *(Matt. 7:22-23).*

THE STRONGLY CONNECTED FACTORS INDICATING THE FAILURE OF VIEW 7

* If the *"great multitude"* were not the same as the 144,000 they would not be *"sealed,"* thereby leaving them unprotected during the time of God's wrath. This would make no sense in view of the fact that Paul said that true Christians would not be victims of God's wrath (2 Thess. 5:9, Rom. 5:9). Yet, nominal Christians may not be afforded such protection.

* The 144,000 have many of the same characteristics and experiences as the *"great multitude."* One strong connection is that they are both associated with the new song (5:9, 15:3) that only the 144,000 can sing (14:3). This seems to strongly indicate that the 144,000 and the *"great multitude"* are one and the same group.

* Because John hears the number but sees a *"great multitude which no one could count,"* as well as several other factors, it is logical to understand that the 144,000 and the *"great multitude"* are the same group of Christians, but from different perspectives, one military, and the other priestly.

♣

View 8: These Rev. 7 Christians are living in **Judea** in the end-time.

THE DEFINITE FACTOR INDICATING THE FAILURE OF VIEW 8

* The problem here is in limiting the 144,000 to Judea at this early stage just before God's wrath begins. In fact, the 144,000 in Revelation 7 exist throughout the earth at this point of time, but later arrive at literal Mount Zion in Judea (Rev. 14).

——— ❑ ———

Appendix C

Why the "Great Multitude" Are
Not Literally in Heaven

Those of the *"great multitude"* are depicted as *"standing before the throne and before the Lamb,... And all the angels were standing around the throne and around the elders and the four living creatures."* Those of the *"great multitude"* are also depicted as serving God *"day and night in his temple* (Gk *naos*)." So do these descriptions mean that Christians will actually be in heaven as is taught by the majority of churches?

If we reference other parts of the New Testament we will see that the *"great multitude"* are *"standing before the throne and before the Lamb"*- in heaven in a spiritual but not literal sense. There is no requirement that individuals literally be in heaven to stand before God's throne just as the Israelites did not need to go to heaven when told to *"come near before Yahweh"* (Ex.16:9). With reference to the expression *"to behold my [God's] face"* in Isaiah 1:12 the *Encyclopedia of Bible Difficulties* p. 43 says: "it is quite possible that by Isaiah's time this had become an idiomatic expression for coming to the temple for worship and prayer."

So while currently on earth and in their mortal state Christians are viewed as **spiritually in heaven** with Christ until he returns as shown by Paul in Ephesians 1:3, 20; and 2:6. In fact, my book *Delusions and Truths Concerning the Future Life* demonstrates that the destiny of Christians is never heaven but that of a renewed earth with them having been granted glorified immortal bodies. Furthermore, the *Expositors Bible Commentary* notes that: *"standing before the throne and in front of the Lamb"* signifies their position of acceptance and honour as God's true servants," p. 486.

———— ❑ ————

268

Appendix D

During the Last Trumpet

The trumpet blasts of Revelation occur over a period of time in harmony with the rendering, "...during (Gk *en*) the last trumpet" (1 Cor. 15:52) as rendered in *Rotherham's Emphasized Bible.* Also *Young's Literal Translation* renders it as "in the last trumpet." The Greek word **en** with the dative noun with reference to time means "within" or "during" according to *Liddell and Scott's Greek Dictionary* and *Bauer's Greek-English Lexicon.* Also see p. 193 of Lang's book *The Revelation of Jesus Christ.* Furthermore, Revelation 10:7 says "in the <u>days</u> of the sounding of the seventh angel."

——— ❑ ———

Appendix E

Why Antichrist's Kingdom Is Not World-Wide

The argument that Antichrist's kingdom will be world-wide is based on several verses in the Revelation Chapter 13. These state that:

❖ "He *[The Beast-the Antichrist]* was given authority over every tribe, nation, language, and race. And everyone living on the earth will worship him—everyone whose name hasn't been written in the scroll of life of the Lamb..." (13:7b-8).

❖ "He *[The second Beast-the false prophet]* also forces everyone—lowly and prominent, rich and poor, free and bond-servant—to be given a mark on their right hand or on their forehead, [17]so that no one can buy or sell things unless he has the mark, that is, the beast's name or the number of his name" (13:16-17).

However, terms such as "every," "everyone," and "no one" are not always universal, but must be understood in their context. For instance, in the prophecies of Daniel 2:38, 2:39, and 7:23-24 it would be out of touch with reality to treat such terms in a universal way, so that Nebuchadnezzar did not rule all men in the entire world, nor did the Greek empire rule over the entire earth, but within certain bounds. In these cases Daniel was simply using the figure of speech called synecdoche—a figure of speech in which a part is used for the whole or the whole for a part. Indeed the same figure of speech applies to John's writings in the Book of Revelation.

In fact, Antichrist's Kingdom is shown by Daniel to occupy the same geographical areas as the ancient kingdoms of Babylon, Medo-Persia Greece/Seleucid Greece, and to their fullest extent (Dan. 2:31-35). Furthermore, in the same time frame Antichrist meets with fierce opposition from the King of the south and from nations in the north and the east, according to Daniel 11:44-45 and so showing that those countries will not be under his immediate control.

FURTHER EVIDENCE FOR THE GEOGRAPHICAL LIMITS TO ANTICHRIST'S KINGDOM

▪ In Daniel 11:41 it states that Antichrist will enter into the "Beautiful Land" of Israel, but Edom, Moab, and Ammon (Jordan) will be rescued from him. So it seems that Antichrist is limited in his ability to conquer even the lands of the Middle-East. So what chance does he have of conquering the major nations of the rest of the world?

- It is evident that the seven trumpet judgments of Revelation 8 through 11 are poured out upon a geographically limited kingdom, Later the fifth bowl plague is poured out only on the "throne of the ferocious beast" (16:10). Once again this shows that Antichrist's Kingdom is not world-wide.

So this kingdom of the Beast appears to occupy the area from the Euphrates River (9:14) right up to where the Apostle John sees the symbolic mountain falling into the eastern Mediterranean. However, none of this will detract from the fact that Antichrist also has his worshippers as existing world-wide and that his influence over everyone is world-wide, with the major exception of loyal Christians.

——— ❑ ———

Appendix F

Conditions That Will Exist During
the Millennium

The following Scriptures show details of what life will be like under the rulership of Messiah Jesus during his one thousand year rule of the earth. They also show various factors about his rulership:

GOD'S RULE IS ESTABLISHED
* ❖ "…in the last days" *(the days of Messiah in a Millennial setting as shown by verse 2)* "the mountain of the house of Yahweh will be established as the chief of the mountains" *(Isa. 2:2).*

This is also shown by the parallel account in Micah:
* ❖ "…in the last days … Each of them will sit under his vine and under his fig tree, with no one to make them afraid" *(Mic. 4:1-4).*

THE KINGDOM IS EVERLASTING
* ❖ "…he will reign over the house of Jacob *forever*, and his kingdom will have no end" *(Luke 1:33).*
* ❖ "…an everlasting dominion, which shall *not pass away*, and his kingdom one that shall not be destroyed"*(Dan. 7:14b).*
* ❖ "But the holy ones of the Most High will receive the kingdom, and they will take possession of the kingdom forever, forever and ever"
(Dan. 7:18),

THE WICKED ARE REMOVED
* ❖ "…the wicked will be no more" *(Ps. 37:10).*
This does not refer to people who are imperfect and are not yet Christians, but rather it refers to the incorrigibly wicked who totally resist God and oppose the setting up of God's kingdom.

PROSPERITY
* ❖ "…abundance of grain" *(Ps. 72:16)* and
* ❖ "…a lavish banquet for all the peoples" *(Isa. 25:6).*

PEACE AND RIGHTEOUSNESS
* ❖ "…the righteous will flourish, and abundance of peace" *(Ps. 72: 7).*
* ❖ 'wolf/lamb; leopard/young goat; calf/young lion; cow/bear; a little boy will lead them' *(Isa. 11:6-9).*

PARADISE ON EARTH
* ❖ "And God planted a *paradeison* (garden) eastward in Eden"
(Gen. 2:8).

The Septuagint translates garden as *paradeisos*. (See also Genesis 2:9; 2:10; 2:15 and 3:2). There are only three references to the word "paradise" in the New Testament. These are:

❖ "...remember me when you come into your kingdom!" He *[Jesus]* said to him, "truly I say to you today, you will be with me in <u>paradise</u>"" *(Luke 23:42, 43).*

❖ "To him who overcomes, I will grant to eat of the tree of life in the <u>paradise</u> of God" *(Rev. 2:7).*

❖ "...a man was caught up to the third heaven ... was caught up into <u>paradise</u>" *(2 Cor. 12:2, 4).*

This is the third heavens and earth that Peter described in 2 Peter 3:5, 7 and 13 as *"new heavens and a new earth."* Therefore, this is not a reference to a separate paradise in heaven. There is only an earthly paradise where Jesus will be along with the resurrected criminal and where faithful ones may eat of the tree of life.

THERE WILL BE MORTAL NATIONS IN THE MILLENNIUM

❖ "...no longer the voice of weeping ... no longer an infant who lives but a few days, or an old man who does not live out his days *(natural death of mortals at very old ages still occurs in this quasi Millennial paradise);* for the youth will die at the age of a hundred and the one who does not reach the age of a hundred will be thought of as accursed. They will build houses...plant vineyards ... for as the lifetime of a tree so will be the days of my people"

(Isa. 65:19-25).

❖ "On that day, <u>Israel</u> will be *the* third with Egypt and Assyria, a blessing in the midst of the earth, whom Yahweh of hosts blessed, saying, "May <u>Egypt my people</u> be blessed, and Assyria, the work of my hands, and my inheritance, Israel"" *(Isa. 19:24, 25 LEB).*

❖ "Thus says Yahweh: "...for my salvation *is* close to coming, and my justice to being revealed ... [6]And the *foreigners who* join themselves to Yahweh to serve him and to love the name of Yahweh... [7]I will bring them to *my holy mountain;* I will make them merry in my house of prayer *[the Millennial temple Ezek 40-44].* Their burnt offerings and their sacrifices *[in commemoration of Messiah's redemption] will be accepted* on my altar, for my house shall be called a house of prayer for all peoples"

(Isa. 56:1, 6-7 LEB).

273

❖ "After this, all <u>the survivors</u> *of all the nations* which have attacked Jerusalem will come up year after year *to worship the king,* Yahweh Sabaoth" *(Zech. 14:16 NJB).*

Such survivors cannot be Christians because the possibility is presented that some of them refuse to *"go up to Jerusalem to worship the King"* and will receive *"the punishment to all the nations that do not go up to keep the Feast of Booths" (Zech. 14:17-19 NJB).*

REPENTING NON-CHRISTIAN GENTILES AT ARMAGEDDON

❖ "The nations will see and be ashamed because of all their might. [17]... They will come trembling from their strongholds to Yahweh our God. Let them fear and be afraid of you" *(Mic. 7:16, 17 LEB).*

Generally, the terms *nations* and *tribes of the earth* are not used to refer to Christians although they are *"purchased...from every tribe and tongue and people and nation."*

❖ "Immediately after the tribulation of those days the sun will be darkened...the stars will fall from heaven, and the powers of the heavens will be shaken. Then will appear in heaven the sign of the Son of Man, and then *all the tribes of the earth* <u>will mourn</u>..."

(Matt. 24:30).

❖ "Behold he is coming with the clouds, and every eye will see him, even those who pierced him, and *all the tribes of the earth* <u>will wail on account of him</u>" *(Rev. 1:7).*

❖ "And so I will exalt myself, and I will show myself holy, and I will make myself known before the eyes of many *nations,* <u>and they will know that I am</u> Yahweh" *(Ezek. 38:23 LEB).*

This is after the Armageddon scenario of verses 16ff. So if these nations are only from then on to *"know that I am the LORD"* then they cannot be Christians prior to the Millennium.

THE RESTORATION OF A REMNANT OF ISRAEL

❖ "And I will pour out on the house of David and the inhabitants of Jerusalem a spirit of grace and pleas for mercy, so that when they look on me, on him whom they have pierced, they <u>shall mourn for him</u>...*On that day* the mourning in Jerusalem will be as great as the mourning for Hadad-rimmon in the plain of Megiddo"

(Zech. 12:10, 11).

274

❖ "Afterward the children of Israel shall return and seek Yahweh their God, and David their king, and they <u>shall come in fear to Yahweh</u> and to his goodness *in the latter days" (Hos. 3:5).*

❖ "...these bones are the whole house of Israel ... I will place you in your own land" *(Ezek. 37:11, 14).*

❖ "Jacob shall <u>return</u> and have full ease ... I will make a full end of all the nations among which I scattered you, but of you I will not make a full end" *(Jer. 30:10, 11).*

❖ "In that day Yahweh will extend his hand yet *a second time* to recover <u>the remnant</u> that remains of his people" *(Isa. 11:11). The first time was from ancient Babylon.*

❖ "I will restore the fortunes of my people Israel, and they shall rebuild the ruined cities ... I will plant them on their land and they shall never again be uprooted out of the land that I have given them" *(Amos 9:14, 15).*

This is not to imply that all Jews will accept Christ Jesus; yet the Scriptures direct our attention to an end-time Jewish remnant that will turn to him.

Does 2 Thessalonians 1:6-10 Prove That All Survivors into the Millennium Must Be Christians?

❖ "...since indeed God considers it just to repay with affliction those who afflict you ... when the Lord Jesus is revealed from heaven with his mighty angels in flaming fire, dealing out *retribution* to those who do not know (*acknowledge*) God and to those who do not obey the gospel of our Lord Jesus. They will suffer the punishment of eternal destruction away from the presence of the Lord and from the glory of his might when he comes on that day..."

This passage refers to the coming great tribulation. If these words applied to <u>all</u> unsaved men then there would be no one to live in natural mortal bodies during the Millennium for the propagation of the human race. However, just as when Genesis 6:17 spoke of the destruction of *all flesh* as evidently being in a limited sense, so too, the end-times retribution will be limited to *"those who afflict you"* (verse 6).

275

The phrase *"those who do not know God"* means that they do not acknowledge God when he sends Jesus. Also, the phrase *"those who do not obey the gospel of our Lord Jesus"* means that they directly oppose Jesus by resisting the incoming Kingdom. Many will not resist this yet will not be Christians at that time. This is shown in Zechariah 14:16: "...any who are left of all the nations that went against Jerusalem."

NOT OF THE HOUSEHOLD OF GOD

❖ "If anyone suffers as a Christian ... For it is time for the judgement to begin at the household of God; and if it begins with us, what will the outcome be for those who do not obey the gospel of God?"

(1 Pet. 4:16, 17).

Because these repenting mortals are not of "the household of God" they cannot be classified as Christians.

———— ❑ ————

Index to Main Scriptures

This index does not include the easily found passages of Revelation which are directly commented on.

Non-Canonical Writing

1 Enoch

———— ❑ ————

Printed in Great Britain
by Amazon